In Clouds of Glory

In Clouds of Glory

AMERICAN AIRMEN
WHO FLEW WITH THE BRITISH
DURING THE GREAT WAR

James J. Hudson

THE UNIVERSITY OF ARKANSAS PRESS

Fayetteville   London   1990

Designer: B. J. Zodrow
Typeface: Linotron 202 Primer
Typesetter: G & S Typesetters, Inc.
Printer: Braun-Brumfield Inc.
Binder: Braun-Brumfield Inc.

The paper used in this publication meets the minimum requirements
of the American National Standard for Permanence of Paper for
Printed Library Materials Z39.48-1984. ∞

Library of Congress Cataloging-in-Publication Data

Hudson, James J.
   In clouds of glory : American airmen who flew with the British
during the Great War
      p.   cm.
   Includes bibliographical references.
   ISBN 1-55728-123-8.—ISBN 1-55728-124-6 (pbk.)
   1. World War, 1914–1918—Aerial operations, British.   2. Fighter
pilots—United States—Biography.   3. Great Britain. Royal Air
Force—History—World War, 1914–1918.   I. Title.
D602.H78   1990
940.54'4941—dc20   89-37122
                                                            CIP

To
Lee Hudson Grimes
and
Zachary Keith Hudson-Muir

Contents

Illustrations

FIGURES

MAPS   *Following Page 148*

Acknowledgments

This study of American air aces who flew only with the Royal Flying Corps, Royal Naval Air Service, and the Royal Air Force during World War I could not have been written without the help of a great number of individuals. Grateful acknowledgment is made to more than a score of air combat scholars who have spent much of their time in researching the first great air war. I am especially indebted to the following persons: Dr. James J. Parks, Ola A. Sater, George H. Williams, Jack Eder, Stewart K. Taylor, Dr. Robin Higham, Dr. Sydney F. Wise, Dr. Lawrence Kinnaird, Wing Commander F. F. Lambert, Group Captain F. W. Winterbotham, Wayne R. Braby, Dave Kealy, Edward W. Lawler, Iver Penttlinen, Ira Milton Jones, Mrs. F. P. Magoun, Mrs. William L. Dougan, Dr. Michael Dougan, Dennis Connell, J. J. Smith, Dr. David Hart, Dr. James White, Charles A. Pineau, and Mrs. Camille Foster.

For endless courtesies and much valuable assistance, I thank Dr. Alan Borg, director of the Imperial War Museum in London, and his very helpful staff; P G. Murton, keeper of aviation records in the Royal Air Force Museum at Hendon, England; the Public Records Office staff in England; Air Commodore H. A. Probert, director of the Air Historial Branch in the British Ministry of Defence, and his staff; Air Commodore R. A. Mason, director of personnel management, Ministry of Defence, Royal Air Force Personnel Management Center, Gloucester, England; Dr. W. A. B. Douglas, director, Directorate of History, National Defence Department, Ottawa, Canada; Charles Worman, chief, research division, U.S. Air Force Museum, Wright-Patterson Air Force Base, Ohio; Robert J. Smith, Office of History, Headquarters Air Force Logistic Command, Wright-Patterson Air Force Base, Ohio; Duane J. Reed, chief of Special Collections Branch, U.S. Air

Force Academy; and Donald J. Barrett, librarian, Gimbel Aeronautical History Collection, U.S. Air Force Academy.

Individuals at the University of Arkansas have also been of great help. President Ray Thornton, Interim Chancellor James Halligan, Interim Vice Chancellor Milton Copeland, and Vice President Charles Oxford convinced the University of Arkansas Board of Trustees to grant me a six months research leave in England in 1984. The Graduate School staff handled much of my graduate dean's work while I was in England. University of Arkansas Chancellor Willard Gatewood gave me considerable encouragement in 1985. Chancellor Daniel Ferritor and Vice Chancellors Donald Pederson and Carol Hartley helped a great deal in providing me with an office and secretarial assistance during the last several months. Dr. Orland Maxfield of the geography department performed the cartographic work for the book. John Harrison, director of Mullins Library at the University of Arkansas, secured many books in support of my research. Mrs. Terry Garrity typed the manuscript and made helpful suggestions about its format.

My greatest debt is to my wife, Mabel Elizabeth, who accompanied me on my research trip to London, England, and encouraged me in the writing of the book and tolerated my neglect in performing many duties at home.

Finally, my thanks are extended to the U.S. Air Force for teaching me to fly and having enough confidence in me to allow me to serve as a fighter pilot in the European Theatre during World War II. In that war I learned some of the thrills, terrors, and problems of air combat. Because of that experience I developed an understanding of the pursuit pilots who fought in the first great air war.

In Clouds of Glory

Introduction

I t is now nearly three quarters of a century since young men first flew in Europe's hostile wind-swept skies to battle the enemy in the First World War. This book deals with those American aces who flew only with the British Royal Flying Corps and the Royal Naval Air Service, which, after 1 April 1918, were combined to form the Royal Air Force. Although the term "ace" was not officially recognized by the military services of the various nations in World War I, it became an accepted word used to describe a flier, who, in war, had succeeded in shooting down a certain number of enemy aircraft and observation balloons. Actually, the use of the term to designate superior fighter pilots originated with the French Air Service in the First World War. The word itself comes from the French *l'as,* meaning the highest card in a suit. The title originally signified any pilot of outstanding skill and bravery, no matter how many victories he had made. As the war progressed, the French escadrilles established the standard of five enemy aircraft destroyed in combat as a measure for acedom. This standard has been used ever since.

Even though there were a small number of individuals prior to 1914 who recognized the potential of the airplane as a weapon, the military leaders of the major powers did little to make the airplane practical and effective. At the beginning of the war, the German Air Force claimed a strength of 294 aircraft, while the French forces numbered fewer than 150 planes. The British Royal Flying Corps, according to William E. Barrett in his book *The First War Planes,* "had a total of 179 machines, of which less than half were capable of flying the English Channel." There was also a British Royal Navy air wing (the Royal Naval Air Service) that possessed some 93 planes.

In the early months of the conflict, German squadrons were made up of Taubes and standard tractor-powered two-seaters, such as the Albatros, LVG, Aviatik, and DFW (Deutsche Flugzeug Werke). In addition, the Germans had a few Euler pushers. The French had Bleriots, Henri Farmans, Maurice Farmans, Moranes, Deperdussins, Breguets, Voisins, Caudrons, and Nieuports. The English flew BEs, Moranes, Bleriots, Henri Farmans, and Avros during the early stages of the war.

At the beginning of the war these aircraft were unarmed and were used to observe enemy positions and troop movements. Observation flights, however, quickly led to aerial combat as pilots and observers shot at other pilots and observers with shotguns, pistols, and rifles. In addition, they tried dropping bricks, chains, and hand grenades on enemy aircraft. Attempts at the use of front-firing machine guns on tractor-powered planes proved disastrous at first since the pilot succeeded in shooting off his own propeller. Rear-mounted machine guns were effective against aircraft approaching from behind. In no sense could such an aircraft be considered a pursuit or fighter plane. However, in April of 1915 a French pilot, Roland Garros, took the first step in creating a true fighter plane when he equipped the propeller of his tiny Morane single-seat monoplane with triangular metal deflection plates. This innovation allowed him to fire a forward-mounted machine gun through the rapidly rotating propeller. At least some of the bullets managed to miss the propeller and hit the target ahead. With this system, Garros was able to shoot down several unsuspecting German airmen. After a brief period of success, the Frenchman had engine failure behind the German lines, and his secret was discovered.

When Anthony Fokker, the Dutch aeronautical engineer who had been selling aircraft to the Germans, was asked to install the Garros system on German planes, he declined to do so. He recognized the Garros invention as a crude makeshift and put his effort into creating a mechanism that would synchronize the propeller and the machine gun. To do this, Fokker fixed a cam on the propeller shaft and calculated the timing equation, taking into account the rate of fire and engine revolutions, so that his cam would trip the gun only when the field was clear, never when the propeller blade was in front of the gun. Within a few days Fokker had solved the problem, and in a short time German planes, including the Fokker Eindekker, were equipped with the synchronized system.

Because of the new synchronization system and the steady

improvement of the Fokker single-seaters, the Germans were able to maintain aerial superiority until 1916, when the French and the British were able to put improved planes in the air equipped with forward-firing machine guns. Indeed, the changing factors of the air war between 1914 and 1918 were largely the results of aeronautical developments, with first one side and then the other gaining a temporary advantage because of some new advanced type of plane or item of equipment. In the Royal Flying Corps, for example, the DH-2 was replaced first by the Nieuport, then by the Sopwith Camel, and finally by the SE-5 in 1917. The French also progressed from the various models of the Nieuport and ultimately to the Spad-13. The Albatros, the Pfalz, the Fokker triplane and the Fokker D-7 were in the German progress cycle. During the last few months of the war, the British equipped a few squadrons with the Sopwith Dolphin and the Sopwith Snipe, while the Germans introduced the Fokker D-8 and the Siemens-Shuckert fighters. Generally speaking, however, the SE-5 and the Camel, along with the Fokker D-7, continued to be used by fighter units until the end of the war.

With the ever increasing efficiency of fighter aircraft, there developed a new class of military hero—the fighter ace. By the end of the war many of these aces were better known to the general public than were the army commanders. For Germany the top aces included Baron Manfred von Richthofen with eighty victories, Ernst Udet with sixty-two, Erich Loewenhardt with fifty-three, and Werner Voss with forty-eight. The premier French aces were Paul-René Fonck with seventy-five victories, Georges-Marie Guynemer with fifty-four, Charles Nungesser with forty-five, and Georges Felix Madon with forty-one. Leading the way for the British were Edward "Mick" Mannock with seventy-three victories, William A. "Billy" Bishop with seventy-two, Raymond Collishaw with sixty, and James T. B. McCudden with fifty-seven. Both Bishop and Collishaw were Canadian born. Willie Coppens with thirty-seven victories was the fighter ace for Belgium, while Alexander A. Kazakov with seventeen, Godwin Brumowski with forty, and Maggiore Francesco Baracca with thirty-four set the pace for Russia, Austria, and Italy, respectively. Although only in the war for a few months, the American Air Service contributed such fighter aces as Edward V. Rickenbacker with twenty-six victories, Frank Luke with eighteen, Raoul Lufbery with seventeen, George Vaughan with thirteen,

Field E. Kindley with twelve, Elliott W. Springs with twelve, and David Putnam with twelve. Of those Americans who flew only with the RFC/RNAS/RAF, William L. Lambert with twenty-one victories, Francis W. Gillet with twenty, Harold A. Kullberg with sixteen, Oren J. Rose with sixteen, and Clive Warman with fifteen were top aces.

Approximately three hundred Americans joined the Royal Flying Corps, the Royal Naval Air Service, and the Royal Air Force. Most of these young men journeyed to Canada, where they enlisted and did part of their ground and air training. After three or four months they were sent to the United Kingdom, where they underwent still more training. Of the three hundred pilots, most were assigned to British units on the western front, where they flew combat against the Germans. Of this American group that flew only with the British, no less than twenty-eight became aces. In fact, of the twenty-three Americans who scored ten or more victories, some thirteen flew only with the British air squadrons. Unfortunately, the American public in the 1980s knows very little about such air aces as William C. Lambert, Francis W. Gillet, Oren J. Rose, Harold A. Kullberg, Frederick Libby, Louis Bennett, Clive Warman, A. T. Iaccaci, P. T. Iaccaci, Kenneth Unger, Eugene Coler, James W. Pearson, and Alvin A. Callender.

Why did such a large number of United States citizens join the RFC, the RNAS, and the RAF in the first great air war? Many of them enlisted with the British air units before the United States entered the war on 6 April 1917. Several joined because they had a real desire to help save the English people. Still others joined because they were fascinated with flying. Many enlisted with the British after America entered the war because they felt the English planes and air squadrons were much more advanced than those of the United States at that time.

Because many of the young American flyers felt that they might lose their American citizenship by joining the British air forces, they sometimes listed their birthplace or citizenship as Canadian or English. Consequently, when the war was over they could return to the United States without divulging they had flown for another nation.

Only a few of the American pilots who were assigned to the British air squadrons participated in the Somme campaign in the last several months of 1916. Several, including Lts. Francis Peabody Magoun, O. C. LeBoutillier, and D. F. Hilton were engaged in the Cambrai offensive in November and December of 1917. However, a great many fought against the enemy in the five German offensives in the first six months of 1918. These German drives included the Somme campaign of 21 March to 4 April, the Lys offensive from 9 April until 29 April, the Aisne drive covering the period 27 May to 6 June, the Noyon-Montdidier struggle of 9 June through 12 June period and the German push on the Champagne-Marne front from 15 July to 17 July. In addition, several were engaged in the Aisne-Marne counteroffensive covering the period 18 July to 6 August. The big British drive in the Amiens-Arras area during August 1918 found many fighter pilots involved in strafing and bombing troops, dive-bombing, and air combat. Very few American pilots assigned to the RAF units participated in the St. Mihiel and Meuse-Argonne campaign on the French end of the battle front during September, October, and November. However, most of the American Air Service squadrons based in the St. Mihiel and Meuse-Argonne area were heavily engaged. The Americans serving with the RAF were fiercely involved in the Somme and Flanders sector during the last several weeks of the war.

According to the Directorate of History in the National Defence Department, Ottawa, Canada, of the Americans who flew only with the British forces in World War I some fifty-one were killed in combat, thirty-two were wounded, thirty-two became prisoners of war, eight were listed as missing and five others were injured or hospitalized in non-combat activities. Indeed, these aggressive young pilots paid a high price for their service with the British, and they certainly deserve to be recognized by the American public. It is for this reason this book has been written.

Frederick Libby (center) with Capt. Stephen Price (right)
and unidentified man leaving Buckingham Palace
after being awarded the Military Cross
Courtesy Ola Sater

Capt. Frederick Libby

Frederick Libby was born in Sterling, Colorado, on 15 July 1891. Raised as a cowboy, young Libby had just turned twenty-three when World War I broke out. Libby was described as "stocky, slightly bandy; had jet black hair; unblinking eyes and reddish colouring . . . one would have traced a Red Indian pedigree if one had gone very far. He was very quiet, serious and unassuming."[1] Libby was in Canada when the war began and immediately joined the Canadian Army. After several months of training, he was shipped to France. The ex-cowboy found life in an ambulance unit in the rainy spring of 1916 to be "more than he could stand. When the Royal Flying Corps sent out a call for observers by circulating bulletins in the trenches, Libby jumped at the chance to get away from the rain, mud and muck."[2]

Libby was among the first to be accepted as a machine gun-ner–observer and was posted to No. 23 Squadron, which was then flying FE-2B two-seater pushers.[3] In the FE-2B–type ma-chine, "the observer sat in front of the pilot in an open nacelle." Years later Libby described the dangerous situation:

> When you stood up to shoot, all of you from the knees up was ex-posed to the elements. There was no belt to hold you. Only your grip on the gun and the sides of the nacelle stood between you and eternity. Toward the front of the nacelle was a hollow steel rod with a swivel mount to which the gun was anchored. This gun covered a huge field of fire forward. Between the observer and the pilot a second gun was mounted, for firing over the FE-2B's upper wing to protect the aircraft from rear attack. . . . Adjusting and shooting this gun required that you stand right up out of the nacelle with your feet on the nacelle coaming. You had nothing to worry about except being blown out of the aircraft by the blast of

air or tossed out bodily if the pilot made a wrong move. There were no parachutes and no belts. *No wonder they needed observers.*[4]

At the time Libby joined No. 23 Squadron of the Royal Flying Corps, "the possibility was held out that successful applicants would be made second lieutenants in the RFC after a probationary period. To Private Libby, this was a substantial inducement. He did not know that, at the time he volunteered, the life expectancy of an observer was a scant ten operational hours." On 15 July 1916, while flying his first mission as an observer, Libby and his pilot Lieutenant Hicks, along with another FE-2B crew, shot down a twin engine enemy plane in flames. After landing at Le Hameau, No. 23 Squadron's home airfield, Libby was greeted by Colonel Shephard, the wing commander, who grabbed his hand and pumped it furiously. Colonel Shephard commented "First flight, first fight . . . wonderful, wonderful. When they go down in flames, Libby, by God, they don't come back up again."[5]

Frederick Libby served with No. 23 Squadron until 4 August 1916 when he transferred to the FE-2B–flying No. 11 Squadron, also based at Le Hameau some ten miles west of Arras.[6] During the next three months young Libby, appointed a second lieutenant on 26 September 1916, became an aggressive gunner and observer in No. 11 Squadron. According to Arch Whitehouse, a noted air historian, by 27 August 1916 Libby had "racked up his fifth, which certainly made him the first American Ace in that war."[7] He, indeed, was the first American to shoot down five enemy aircraft in aerial combat. "Only the fact that he performed this feat as an observer instead of a pilot prevents his occupying the historic spot of first American Ace."[8] Even though there is still much debate over whether an observer really qualifies for acedom, Libby continued his combat success with No. 11 Squadron. On 14 September while on a photography mission he brought one hostile machine "down in smoke, another two driven down. Tracer ammunition could very easily be seen going into hostile machine."[9]

While on an offensive patrol at 10,500 feet on 10 October, Libby and his pilot Lieutenant Harvey drove down a hostile aircraft out of control.[10] One week later, Second Lieutenant Libby and Capt. S. W. Price, his pilot, sent an Aviatik down out of control.[11] Three days later, Libby and Captain Price dived on a hostile aircraft and fired "two double drums at close range. The hostile machine was seen going down steeply and sending out a great amount of smoke and was subsequently seen by several of the No. 11 formation pilots on the road between Douchy and Ayette." [12]

During his assignment to No. 23 and No. 11 Squadrons, Lieutenant Libby was credited with no less than ten aerial victories, and on 26 September he was awarded the Military Cross "for Conspicuous Gallantry in Action. As an observer, he with his pilot attacked 4 hostile machines and shot one down. He has previously shot down 4 enemy machines." [13] On 8 November 1916, Libby returned to the United Kingdom for pilot training at the School of Aeronautics located in Reading. [14]

On 18 April 1917, after the completion of his pilot training, Fred Libby was posted to No. 43 Squadron, then flying Sopwith two-seaters. This squadron was based at Auchel. [15] According to one source, Lt. Libby's

> aerial victories as a pilot began on the very day he arrived for duty with his new squadron—he shot down an enemy Albatros fighter in flames near the French town of Messines. Libby's squadron leader, Major Sholto Douglas (an Air Chief Marshal of the Royal Air Force during World War II), confirmed this victory. [16]

On 6 May 1917 Libby and his observer, Lt. J. L. Dickson, sent a hostile aircraft crashing into the vicinity of Petit Vimy. [17] Late in the afternoon on 23 July, while on patrol, Lieutenant Libby and his observer, Lieutenant Pritchard, intercepted three Albatros scouts near Lens. Libby's combat report stated, "when on the same level, attacked E.A. [enemy aircraft] again with front gun following him down to about 3000 feet. E.A. was evidently hit as he was doing a series of stall spins then going into nose dives. Was last seen at about 1000 ft Northeast of Lens." This kill was confirmed as decisive by others in the No. 43 Squadron formation. [18] On 26 July Libby was appointed a flight commander in No. 43 Squadron and was promoted to captain. [19]

In early August 1917 Captain Libby was transferred to the DH-4–flying No. 25 Squadron. The DH-4 two-seater, powered by a 240 horsepower engine, was capable of a speed over 120 miles per hour at sixty-five hundred feet and approximately 110 miles per hour at fifteen thousand feet. It was armed with one Vickers and one Lewis machine gun. Many of the later models of the DH-4 were powered with the famous 400 horsepower "Liberty" engine. Perhaps the greatest weakness of the De Havilland aircraft was its vulnerability to tracer machine-gun fire and its likelihood of becoming a "flaming coffin." On 9 August 1917 Captain Libby and his observer, 2nd Lt. O. H. Hills, drove down an enemy two-seater "apparently out of control." Later on the same day, Libby and Hills were credited with an Albatros. Four days later, the ex–Colorado cowboy was "credited with an LVG."[20]

At 5:20 A.M. on 14 August 1917, Libby and Hills, while on a line patrol from Hulloun to Scarpe, spotted a German DFW two-seater doing artillery observation over the town of Lens. Libby

> dived on the hostile machine and opened fire at close range, firing about 40 round. He then turned the machine enabling his observer, 2nd Lt. Hills, to fire a drum at point blank range. The hostile [aircraft] was seen to stall, then go into a nose-dive and was last seen falling vertically in a nose dive at about 700 feet east of La Bassée, a heavy ground mist then hid the machine from view.

Anti-aircraft observers saw the German plane going down pursued by the DH-4, but the ground mist prevented them from seeing the actual crash. Nonetheless, the squadron considered this a victory for Libby.[21]

At 12:15 P.M. on 15 August, Libby and his observer attempted a photographic mission in the Cambrai area. Unfortunately, the weather proved unsuitable for photography, but the DH-4 crew sighted a hostile aircraft a little northwest of Cambrai and immediately attacked it at about seven thousand feet. "Libby fired 60 rounds with front gun and, on machine coming into range of observer's gun, 2nd Lt. Hills fired 40 rounds into it. The enemy machine was followed down and was last seen nose diving to the ground by Boquet St. Quentin." The DH-4 received heavy anti-aircraft fire from guns on the ground, and "flaming onions" were sent up in great numbers, in groups of five. Libby and Hills managed to "recross the battle lines safely, however, at 4000 feet."[22]

Some thirty minutes later, after bombing gun positions north of Courrières, a DFW two-seater was observed at about six thousand feet. Libby "dived after it, firing about 50 rounds at long range, when the enemy disappeared in the clouds." A German Albatros was then observed at about four thousand feet over Lens. The American "dived on it and fired about 50 rounds with the front gun, 2nd Lt. Hills, his observer, also fired as the DH-4 followed the hostile machine down. This scout was seen to turn over on its back and crashed near a block of red houses near Vendin Le Vieil." [23]

Although Captain Libby continued to fly combat missions for No. 25 Squadron until 15 September 1917, he was not credited with the destruction of any other German aircraft during this period. He did, however, inflict damage on several enemy planes. On 17 August he and his observer, Lt. O. H. Hills, fired several rounds into an enemy two-seater "when a quantity of white smoke was observed coming out of the hostile machine, which immediately dived east. Both pilot and observer considered that the engine of the machine was badly damaged." [24]

At 9:15 A.M. on the next day, Libby and Hills fired about a hundred rounds from their front and rear guns into an enemy observation plane. Apparently, the German was not seriously damaged, for "the hostile machine turned east and made off at great speed." [25]

Shortly after the United States entered the war, Frederick Libby was presented with an American flag by one of his squadron mates. His commanding officer suggested the Colorado cowboy cut the flag into strips and use it as streamers on his plane. "The idea was that the flag would be carried over the German lines every day by an American pilot, thus signifying to the enemy that the United States was in the war." [26] When Libby, at the request of Gen. Billy Mitchell, left the RFC on 15 September 1917 and joined the American Air Service, he took the flag with him. On his return to the United States, the Aero Club of America auctioned off the flag at a Liberty Loan drive at Carnegie Hall. The historic flag brought some $3,250,000 into the Liberty Loan coffers, but Libby contrived to retain possession of the relic. [27]

Libby's transfer to the U.S. Air Service was, in the view of General Mitchell, much needed because of his great combat experience. After his participation in the Liberty Loan drive in the auction of 1917, he was assigned to No. 22 Squadron, U.S. Air Service at Hicks Field, Texas. Unfortunately, Libby became very ill "from a circulation and spinal impairment, and soon thereafter was found to be permanently disabled and medically unfit for further military service." Indeed, Frederick Libby "remained a cripple for the rest of his life, and on 9 January 1970 he died at

Los Angeles, California—an almost forgotten American hero of the First World War."[28] He never flew combat for the American Air Service. Consequently, he is considered to belong in the category of those Americans who performed as combat fliers only with the British.

Even though Frederick Libby is not accepted as the first American to become an ace by the august American Fighter Aces Association because he scored his first victories as an observer, he was indeed the first to shoot down five enemy planes. According to several sources, Libby shot down ten planes as an observer and fourteen more as a pilot for a total of twenty-four.[29] Bruce Robertson, in his book *Air Aces of the 1914–1918 War,* lists Captain Libby as having fourteen kills. Most combat reports and official documents seem to credit him with seven victories as an observer and seven more as a pilot for a total of fourteen kills.[30] Whatever the real score was, there is no question Frederick Libby, the Colorado cowboy, was one of the top American aces of the first great air war.

Capt. Clive W. Warman
Courtesy Ola Sater

TWO

Capt. Clive W. Warman

C live Wilson Warman, who was awarded the British Military Cross and the Distinguished Service Order while flying with the Royal Flying Corps during World War I, was born on 30 June 1892 in Norfolk, Virginia. When the Kaiser's armies, following the Schlieffen Plan, swept into France in August 1914, Warman was a practicing civil engineer in his native state of Virginia.[1] Like many hundreds of other young Americans, young Warman felt something must be done to save England and stop German aggression in western Europe.

Although there was some question with regard to the possible loss of American citizenship, Warman closed down his civil engineering operation, and on 5 September 1914 (during the middle of the First Battle of Marne) he enlisted in the Princess Patricia's Canadian Light Infantry Regiment in Valcartier, Canada. After some three months of training, he proceeded to England in January 1915. A few weeks later, in February 1915, his unit moved to the battle front in France.[2] In the fierce fighting in the Second Battle of Ypres (22 April–25 April 1915),[3] Warman was wounded in action and returned to England. After spending several weeks in an English hospital, he was posted to the mechanical transport unit on 5 August 1915. Three weeks after Warman joined this outfit it was sent to Ireland, where it was involved in putting down the Easter Rebellion at Dublin in 1916.[4]

Warman, fed up with the mud and gore of ground combat, returned to England on 10 June 1916 and was commissioned in the Royal Flying Corps on 18 August 1916. He attended the School of Aeronautics at Oxford University from 20 August through 20 September 1916 and graduated with honors. He was posted to the Central Flying School on Salisbury Plain on 23 September, and on 28 October he was assigned to the Hythe School of Aerial Gunnery. After two weeks of intense aerial gunnery training, he was granted a three months leave. Warman returned to England and Central Flying School on 15 February 1917. He graduated with first class honors, and on 5 April 1917 he was posted to Turnberry Aerial Fighting School as an instructor.[5]

Although he realized the importance of instructing young pilots in the art of aerial warfare, Warman wanted desperately to serve as a combat aviator himself. His desire was fulfilled when, on 13 June 1917, he was posted to France. Three days later he was assigned to No. 23 Squadron[6] flying Spad-7 fighters out of La Lovie airdrome, located some sixteen miles southeast of Dunkirk.[7]

Lieutenant Warman considered himself extremely lucky to have been assigned to No. 23 Squadron, one of the top pursuit outfits on the western front. At the time, the squadron was commanded by Maj. Alan M. Wilkinson, a nineteen-victory ace, who had much sage advice to give the recently assigned pilots.[8] Before the war was over, No. 23 Squadron had destroyed or sent down out of control some 247 aircraft and more than a score of enemy observation balloons.[9]

During his first three weeks with No. 23 Squadron, Warman scored no victories over the enemy but gained considerable combat experience. On 2 July, while cruising at eleven thousand feet, he spotted a German two-seater about two thousand feet above. Due to his own engine "sputtering and missing," he was unable to catch the hostile aircraft but fired a burst with his Vickers machine gun without success.[10] Four days later, Lieutenant Warman, as a part of a five-ship patrol, attacked nine Albatros Scouts with "indecisive" results.[11] The following afternoon, while serving as an escort for a friendly photography plane, he was more successful when he fired seventy rounds into an enemy Albatros. This machine "spun down and appeared out of control." During the dogfight, he was attacked by two other Hun fighters and was unable to observe the results of his attack on the Albatros.[12]

Warman's learning experience continued over the next several days. On 11 July he was a part of an eight-plane patrol that engaged ten Albatros Scouts and three Aviatik two-seaters just north of Comines. The hostile aircraft were chased down to four thousand feet, but no decisive results were reported.[13] Three days later, he participated in another wild affair over the Menin–Houthulst Forest–Ypres area. Warman became separated from his patrol for a few minutes and, while rejoining his formation, he saw three enemy two-seaters. Two of them turned away, but one Rumpler continued on course. Warman's report stated,

> I dived on him and when within about 50 yards, opened fire in a long burst, closing the range to about 10 yards. I then did an Immelmann turn and attacked again; he then turned East and proceeded in a steep glide without his engine in the direction of Comines, where he made a forced landing in a field, his machine running into a fence just north of the canal. . . .[14]

This aircraft was probably damaged beyond repair. In an air battle between No. 23 Squadron Spads and eight Albatros fighters on 22 July, "three E.A. were seen to go down in spins" but were listed as unconfirmed by squadron and wing headquarters.[15]

The Virginia boy certainly was polishing his air combat skills as the combats piled up. Warman's indecisive battle against a DFW two-seater observation plane, which took place on 23 July, is described as follows:

> While waiting to try and intercept an E.A. which has been in the habit of coming over our lines early at a low altitude, I saw him approaching above me. I turned east and got between him and his lines. Being lower than him and in poor light he had not seen me. I then climbed up under his tail and fired a short burst at close range from below. The E.A. immediately dived and tried to regain his lines. I maneuvered to cut him off, firing bursts as opportunity offered. Having succeeded in this I then commenced to drive him west and down. I got him down to 500 feet and would soon have forced him to land, as he had no chance of getting back to his own lines, when I was hit in the engine by a bullet fired from the ground. Several machine guns were opening fire at the time. I was at once covered with oil and was forced to break off and make for my aerodrome. I am under the impression that the observer was hit in my first burst, as he made no attempt to fire at me, though I could see him in his seat.[16]

On 27 July Warman sent an Albatros down "with smoke pouring from the fuselage." This dogfight occurred at eleven thousand feet over the town of Menin and was considered a down-out-of-control victory even though the American was unable to witness the actual crash "as I was at this point attacked in turn myself."[17] At high noon four days later, Lieutenant Warman, while on a special mission, "planed down through the clouds" and found himself over the town of Westroosbeke at twelve hundred feet. In his words:

> I observed an Albatros Nieuport in front of me and as he had not seen me, I got on his tail and followed him until in a suitable position for attack, i.e., some twenty-five yards behind him. I then fired a burst and he immediately stalled, then glided down gradually, sideslipping to the right. I fired again, but he appeared out of control and crashed in a field. . . about ½ mile s.w. of Westroosbeke.

This combat marked his fourth victory in the month of July.[18]

During August 1917, Clive Warman became the hottest pilot in No. 23 Squadron by shooting down eleven enemy aircraft and balloons. On 8 August he, along with three squadron mates, engaged two DFW observation planes escorted by several Albatros fighters, and, in the ensuing dogfight, Warman sent one of the enemy aircraft down out of control.[19] At 12:45 P.M. on 12 August, Warman, using small scattered clouds to stalk two enemy fighters, "got into favorable position above and behind without being seen and dived on the rearmost of the two, firing a short burst at about 50 yards range." The German dived vertically and was confirmed by ground observers as having crashed just behind Polygon Wood for Warman's sixth "kill".[20] Later on the same day, he scored his seventh victory by shooting down an Albatros Scout in the vicinity of Gheluvelt.[21]

During the three days between 15 August and 18 August 1917, Warman established himself as one of the top pilots of the First World War and won the Distinguished Service Order, the second highest award for gallantry given by the British government. Early in the morning of 15 August, eight Spads of No. 23 Squadron became involved in a series of dogfights with some forty Albatros Scouts and several German two-seater observation planes. Early in the fight, Warman had to retire with a gun jam and, being engaged by three enemy aircraft, "only escaped by firing all his Very lights [signal flares] at them at close quarters, and eventually throwing his machine gun hammer at one very near him." He eventually managed to maneuver his way through three hostile formations, reaching his own airdrome with his machine badly damaged by enemy fire.[22] Late in the afternoon of the same day, Lieutenant Warman, using a borrowed Spad, attacked and shot down two enemy fighters in the Houthulst Forest–Zonnebeke area. These kills were confirmed by ground observers.[23]

At 8:30 P.M. on 17 August, Warman attacked an enemy observation plane northeast of the city of Ypres and drove it down to approximately one thousand feet, where he lost it "in growing darkness."[24] On the following day, at 7:40 P.M., while trailing an offensive patrol, Lieutenant Warman sighted two patrols of four enemy aircraft each. In his report he stated,

> my formation attacked and I singled out the nearest one, who was straggling. I got within eighty yards of him, opened fire, giving him a burst of about 30 rounds, which appeared to go straight into him. He turned sharply, then nose dived and spun, finally going absolutely vertical to the earth.

The enemy machine, an Albatros fighter, crashed near Passchendaele,[25] some eight miles northeast of Ypres and the site of one of the big land battles fought several months later.

On a gloomy, cloudy 20 August, Warman, now a captain and flight commander, fought his last air battles of the war. Between 7:15 A.M. and 7:50 A.M., he dodged in and out of heavy clouds to attack three different enemy formations. After firing several bursts into one enemy aircraft at fifty yards range, the machine dived vertically into the clouds below, which made it impossible for Warman "to observe whether he crashed." Five minutes later, the American fired another burst into an Albatros but, once again, was unable to ascertain whether the enemy was destroyed. After circling the area for a few minutes, he spotted two Aviatiks and fired a short burst into one of them. Because of the poor visibility, he was not able to observe the results.[26] Later on the same day, Clive Warman was severely wounded in aerial combat but managed to land his Spad on the British side of the battle lines. He was admitted to a military hospital a few hours later.[27] During the two months Warman had served with No. 23 Squadron, he was officially credited with the destruction of ten enemy aircraft and two kite balloons, "some under specially gallant circumstances."[28]

Captain Warman was not discharged from hospital care until 28 June 1918 and, two days later, was appointed to a post in the Air Ministry. In September he was declared fit for flying again. On 18 December 1918 he relinquished his Air Ministry appointment to go on a mission to Italy. On his return from Italy in February 1919, he returned to active duty as a flight commander in the newly organized No. 1 Squadron of the Canadian Air Force.[29]

Capt. Clive Wilson Warman's promising Air Force career came

to an end on 12 May 1919 when he died at Edmonton Military Hospital, from injuries received in an airplane accident that occurred on 8 May. According to his obituary, he had been doing a series of stunts over the Edmonton Sewage Farm when the plane went out of control and crashed.[30]

Lt. D'Arcy Fowles Hilton
Courtesy Mrs. Helen Douglas

THREE

Lt. D'Arcy Fowles Hilton

D 'Arcy Fowles Hilton was born in Youngstown, New York, in 1890 and, during his high school years, was a noted athlete in swimming and track. In January 1914 he married a Canadian girl from St. Catherines, Ontario. In May 1916 a son, William DeVeaux Woodruff Hilton, was born.[1] Hilton was accepted as a Royal Flying Corps candidate during a 1916 recruiting drive in Canada and sailed from Montreal on the ship *Scandinavian* on 10 November 1916. He received his ground school training at Reading, after arriving in the United Kingdom. D. F. Hilton's flight training began at Doncaster, and in January 1917 he was "posted to a scout training unit in Lincoln." On 8 June 1917 Second Lieutenant Hilton, who had been commissioned the previous November, was posted to No. 29 Squadron, then located at Izel le Hameau on the British end of the battle front.[2]

Hilton had trained in the Avro 504B, the RE-8, the Bristol Scout, and the Sopwith Pup but had never flown the Nieuport Scout, which No. 29 Squadron was then flying in combat. Consequently, during the first few days of his new assignment, he was to have real problems. On 11 June, while on his first patrol, he became lost in the clouds and ended up making a forced landing at Cauroy. He became lost again the next day, and on 13 June he landed at No. 8 Royal Naval Air Service Squadron at Izel-Hameau and, in doing so, damaged his machine.[3]

Slowly, Lieutenant Hilton began to get acquainted with the Nieuport biplane's pecularities, and on 27 June 1917 he became involved in his first real air combat. While on a patrol at nine thousand feet over the town of Pronville, he ran into three Albatros Scouts, and, in his words, "I fired a half drum at the nearest at 50 yards range. I drew closer, but at 25 yards my gun jammed. The [enemy aircraft] dived away, but under control."

Hilton managed to remedy the jammed gun (the Nieuport 17 had only one Lewis gun) and followed the Albatros down to three thousand feet. "Then I was attacked by two [enemy planes] from above, but they dived past me. As they went past I fired a burst at them." He then returned to No. 29 Squadron's home airdrome and reported his air battle. The squadron commander listed the combat as indecisive. Despite his not getting credit for shooting down an enemy machine out of control, Hilton was beginning to build his self-confidence and would very shortly establish himself as a real fighter.[4]

On 24 June Captain Holt, commander of "C" flight, was killed in action, and Capt. C. M. B. Chapman took over his position. Four days later, Lieutenant Hilton was promoted to deputy leader of "C" Flight, a position he was to hold for several months.[5] During the month of July 1917, No. 29 Squadron, flying the Nieuport, suffered several losses. On 13 July, Lt. A. W. B. Miller was reported missing and "subsequently reported dead." Lt. Frederick W. Winterbothan, who would write the classic book *The Ultra Secret* dealing with intelligence work in World War II, was also reported missing on the same day. A few days later, he was listed as a prisoner of war. Four other pilots from No. 29 Squadron were lost in the next two weeks.[6]

Lieutenant Hilton scored his first victory over the Germans on 31 July 1917. As one of the "five machines of No. 29 Squadron sent to attack Enemy Kite Balloons 2nd Lt. Hilton fired at a Balloon near Polgon Race Course. The observer jumped out and the Balloon rose to 12,000 feet pursued by 2nd Lieut. Hilton who eventually shot it down." A little later on the same day, Hilton "attacked an Albatros scout at 500 feet which was driven out of control and crashed near Westhoek."[7] The New Yorker was now on a successful run against enemy aircraft and would win considerable recognition in the next few months.

At 5:30 P.M. on 9 August, a formation of Nieuport scouts from No. 29 Squadron intercepted eight Albatros Scouts at twelve thousand feet over Langemark. Lieutenant Hilton saw an enemy pursuit plane get on the tail of one of his No. 29 Squadron colleagues and banked his Nieuport sharply to the left, firing two bursts of about thirty rounds each at close range. "I distinctly saw my tracers hitting the E.A.'s engine and entering the side of his fuselage. He went down completely out of control, side-slipping for some distance and then going into a spin." A second Albatros tried to get on Hilton's tail, but the American "did a quick flat turn and fired a few rounds at about 50 yards range. He at once dived away, but under control." Lieutenant Hilton fired the remainder of his "drum at a third [enemy aircraft] while maneuvering to get into a favorable position but observed no results." Later, after changing the drum on his Lewis gun, he was "unable to push the gun up hard enough to get it to catch." Capt. C. M. Chapman, the squadron's commanding officer, credited Hilton with one down-out-of-control victim and two indecisive dogfights.[8] This ran Hilton's score to three.

Two days later, at seven P.M. on 11 August, a No. 29 Squadron patrol engaged some six Albatros Scouts at ten thousand feet a little east of Houthulst Forest. In the wild dogfight that lasted several minutes, three enemy machines were brought down. Lt. D'Arcy Fowles Hilton described his own combat in the following fashion:

> I attacked one of the . . . [enemy planes] firing about 20 rounds into him at long range, he dived East and got out of my range. I then attacked a second E.A. and fired a burst of 20 rounds into him at 50 yards range. Lt. F. W. Wilson then fired several bursts into him at very close range and I observed the E.A. to go down completely out of control—turning over and over. Another [enemy aircraft] dived on me from above. I maneuvered and got a burst into the side of his fuselage, and when he put his nose down I fired 50 rounds into his tail at very close range. The E.A. went down rolling over and over—completely out of control. His elevator was moving about uselessly from side to side. I must have shot his controls away.

A short time later, he spotted four large aircraft "thought to be Gothas" and fired several bursts at them from long range. His Lewis gun jammed, and he was forced to return to his home base. He was credited with one Albatros down out of control and two indecisive battles.[9]

During the next four days, Lieutenant Hilton and his No. 29 Squadron mates were involved in several air combats while on offensive patrols. On 13 August Hilton spotted an Albatros attacking an Allied machine over Houthulst Forest and plunged down on it firing a drum into the German from about seventy-five yards range. "I saw my tracers entering his fuselage. He did a vertical dive and I lost sight of him. I had just changed my drum when an [enemy aircraft] got on my tail. So I put my machine upside down, spun, and got away."[10] Hilton was credited with damaging the enemy machine, but the battle was written up as indecisive. Several other pilots from No. 29 Squadron were involved in dogfights at the same time, but no one was credited with a "kill." At 9:15 on the following morning, Lts. Hilton and J. D. Payne battled several Albatros pursuit planes some four miles east of Houthulst Forest but scored no victories. Hilton did manage to damage one enemy aircraft.[11] On the next day, Hilton "dived and attacked enemy troops in shell-holes from 400 feet— scattering them in all directions."

Early in the morning on 16 August, Lieutenant Hilton was to have one of his most successful air combats. While on ground patrol with a Lieutenant Machaffie over the town of Zonnebeke, Hilton saw three Albatros Scouts slightly above:

> They dived below us, and one got on the tail of one of our two seaters. I dived at this E.A. and opened fire at 50 yards range. He turned to the right, which left me right on his tail, and I fired a drum at him at close range. I clearly saw a number of my tracers hit the enemy pilot, and entering the fuselage. The machine turned over on its side and dived, obviously out of control to about 100 feet from the ground, right into our barrage. . . . I think he must have crashed just behind the enemy lines. I could not see him crash because of the smoke.

A short time later, Hilton got on the tail of a second Albatros and fired a drum at close range. In Hilton's words, "I am sure I hit the pilot, as he made no effort to get away from me but simply did a slow spiral and then fell over on his side and disappeared into the smoke on the ground." Lieutenant Hilton then spotted German troops going west along the road from Westroosbeke to Zonnebeke and dived to about one hundred feet, firing a burst of fifty rounds straight down the road. The troops scattered, "but some were left lying on the road. In my second dive I fired along the ditch where I saw the troops kneeling. After 40 rounds my gun jammed." Major Chapman credited Hilton with two decisive victories, running his score to six.[12]

Despite the fragile nature of the Nieuport Scout, Lt. D. F. Hilton, having learned its capabilities, continued a very active and effective combat role. Late in the afternoon of 22 August, the No. 29 Squadron patrol he was leading intercepted five Albatros Scouts and an Aviatik two-seater over Houthulst Forest a little to the southeast of Westhoek at six thousand feet. The German formation was slightly above the No. 29 Squadron flight. Consequently, Hilton climbed toward them and "fired 25 rounds at one and 30 rounds at another at long range." The Albatros Scouts dived away to the east. Lieutenant Hilton then attacked the Aviatik over Menin Road just east of the battle lines at four thousand feet. In his combat report Hilton stated, "I fired about 50 rounds at close range, and distinctly saw my tracers hitting the observer. He did not fire at me, and I am confident that he was badly hit. The machine went down in a steep dive, apparently under control. I did not follow it lower than 2000 feet as my drum was empty." One of his wing men. Lt. A. J. B. Colin, also fired two bursts into the Aviatik observation plane. The squadron commander listed the combat as indecisive but did indicate the two-seater was damaged.[13]

According to No. 29 Squadron's commanding officer, Lt. D. F. Hilton on 28 September 1917 "attacked and drove down one enemy balloon." Two days later, he attacked and drove down a second German observation balloon, "from which the observers were seen to jump." On the next day, 29 September 1917, he strafed a "hostile motor transport going along a road, from a height of 1000 feet." During the month of October, the New York pilot continued to shoot up German transports and troops on the ground. He was particularly effective on 26 October when he attacked the enemy trenches "firing a drum into them from under 1000 feet. Later he attacked a hostile battery and observed gunners run into their dugouts. He noticed the battery fire again, and although he was under severe A.A. and M.G. fire he again attacked the battery and silenced it."[14] Lts. D. H. Robertson and D. F. Hilton engaged an Albatros Scout and a two-seater observation plane at low altitude over Houthulst Forest on 30 October 1917. Robertson managed to shoot down the Albatros out of control, while Hilton took on the two-seater at approximately five hundred feet over the forest. The observation plane did a spiral turn, but Hilton "got on his tail and fired a whole drum into him at close range. The observer fired about 20 rounds, and then stopped. The machine went down out of control," but, in Hilton's words, "in zooming up to change my drum I lost sight of it, and so could not observe it crash."[15]

At approximately 9:30 A.M. on 9 November, Capt. A. G. Jones-Williams and Lts. J. M. Leach and D. F. Hilton became involved with a large number of Albatros Scouts and observation planes in the vicinity of Roulers. Although one German machine was driven down, Hilton's combat was declared "indecisive," even though he fired a whole drum of ammunition into one of the Albatros Scouts from approximately fifteen yards. On 13 November, four days later, he attacked an Albatros at six hundred feet over Roulers and fired fifty rounds into it from a range of fifty yards. "He immediately went right down out of control, into a cloud." This was confirmed by Capt. W. E. Molesworth but was, nonetheless, marked as indecisive on his combat report.[16]

According to No. 29 Squadron's commanding officer, Hilton had driven "down 6 enemy machines out of control, one of which was seen to crash, and driven down 3 enemy balloons." In addition, "He has had many indecisive combats. His action on many occasions has been most conspicuously gallant, and by his fine example has greatly helped to increase the dash of other pilots of the Squadron."[17] Lieutenant Hilton was to receive the Military Cross on 14 December 1917, for his action on 30 October in battling six enemy aircraft and forcing one down, and the Air Force Cross on 3 June 1919. There has been considerable disagreement on just how many aerial victories Lieutenant Hilton achieved. His squadron commander listed nine kills for him. Bruce Robertson's *Air Aces of the 1914–1918 War* shows him with six victories, while still other sources indicate that he scored only five decisive kills.[18]

Hilton flew his last patrol in France in the middle of November 1917, and, in the late summer of 1918, he returned to Canada and became a flight instructor at Deseronto, Ontario. He was attached to the Royal Air Force (Canada) Headquarters at the end of the war where he was involved with the demobilization program. Unfortunately, his marriage broke up in 1924, and his wife did not hear from him again until 1940 when their only son was killed in air combat in the Second World War. D'Arcy Fowles Hilton died in the United States shortly after the end of World War II.[19]

The Sopwith Camel
Courtesy Headquarters Army Air Forces

FOUR

Capt. Oliver C. LeBoutillier

Oliver Colin "Boots" LeBoutillier was born 24 May 1894 in Montclair, New Jersey, and grew up in that city.[1] According to an oral interview at Nellis Air Force Base, Nevada, on 7 January 1970, LeBoutillier had all of his training at Montclair and "went to high school there, and of course I was always vitally interested and with the boys in school would try to make gliders and what have you."[2] In 1916 young LeBoutillier began his pilot training at Mineola, a little flying school on Long Island. His flight instructor was Howard Rhinehart, who later became a test pilot at Dayton, Ohio. "Boots" LeBoutillier made his first solo flight in a two-propeller Wright Model B pusher-type aircraft on 3 July 1916.[3]

Shortly after his first few solo flights, LeBoutillier crossed into Canada and joined the Royal Naval Air Service. He was not particularly interested in the war but was very interested in gaining more flying experience. Because he had had some five solo flights at Mineola, the Royal Naval Air Service almost immediately sent him on to England for further flight training. The journey on board an old freighter took some two weeks, but, on arrival in the United Kingdom, he was assigned to ground training at a place called "Crystal Palace outside London," where he remained for approximately two months.[4] After completing basic training, "Boots" was sent to Redcar in Yorkshire, northeast England, and located on the North Sea. Here he flew Maurice Farman and French Caudron planes. During his first solo flight in the Caudron, in which he had virtually no experience, he crashed but was not injured. The base commander apparently blamed the accident on the lack of instruction on the part of his flight instructor and assigned LeBoutillier to another individual.

From this point on, the Montclair boy progressed rapidly. After Redcar, the pilots in training were sent to Cromwell in Lancashire, where they trained in the Bristol Bullet, the French Nieuport 17, and in the Sopwith Pup.[5]

From Cromwell, LeBoutillier and several other pilots were sent to Dover, "the checkout point for pilots flying single seaters before they went to France." LeBoutillier stated, "I didn't think I was advanced that far enough, but there was such a crying need for pilots in France at that time that they were pushing all the boys through." Actually, Leboutillier had only nine hours of instructional flying and only twenty-nine hours of solo when he was sent to France. He had flown the Sopwith Pup and the Camel while at Dover.[6]

In April 1917 Sublieutenant LeBoutillier was assigned to the Sopwith Triplane and the Camel, while flying with No. 9 Squadron of Royal Naval Air Service.[7] Since the Sopwith Triplane's and the Camel's rotary engines developed tremendous heat, they used pure castor oil instead of ordinary engine oil. Consequently, pilots flying these aircraft found the castor oil fumes "pretty hard to get used to, because when you started these engines the fumes and everything would come right back into the cockpit and you were breathing castor oil all the time."[8]

During the early weeks of his assignment, "Boots" LeBoutillier did mostly patrol work over the North Sea while "protecting the British Navy and their commerce." Most Sopwith Camels operated by RNAS Squadrons were powered by the 150 horsepower Bentley rotary engines instead of the 130 horsepower Clerget engines. The Bentley-powered Camel performed very well at 17,500 feet while the Clerget engine Camel operated best at about 12,500 feet.[9] On 26 May 1917 LeBoutillier brought down an LVG "out of control off Ostend" for his first air victory.[10] A few days later, on 5 June, seven aircraft of No. 9 Squadron took off to try to intercept German raiders returning from bombing attacks on Essex and Kent. According to the squadron's history,

> three of the party encountered about twelve Albatros Scouts which were apparently waiting to escort the enemy bombing machines back to their base. A general engagement followed in the course of which three Albatros Scouts were driven down out of control by F/S/Ls Tanner, LeBoutillier and J. W. Pinder.

This combat marked "Boots" LeBoutillier's second kill.[11]

34

On 28 July 1917, the New Jersey lad scored his third victory when "about 4 miles over the lines [his patrol spotted] three enemy aircraft at 2000 feet below." His formation dived toward the German planes but were interfered with by some eight other enemy aircraft. LeBoutillier "singled out one, an Albatros Scout, on the tail of a British triplane and fired 150 rounds into it. The E.A. nose dived, turned on its back, and went down out of control." The Naval Summary of the day lists the LeBoutillier victim as destroyed.[12] This kill was also listed in the Royal Flying Corps Communiqué.[13]

During the next several months, Oliver C. LeBoutillier performed many offensive patrols between the North Sea and the German/British battle lines. In the spring of 1918, he became commander of the squadron's "B" Flight and, on 1 April, the day that the RNAS and the RFC combined to become the Royal Air Force, LeBoutillier was promoted to captain.[14] On this same day, RNAS No.9 Squadron became No. 209 Squadron in the RAF. Because of the big German push in the Somme River area, No. 209 Squadron was moved closer to the battle front and became involved in the air fights in that area. The squadron's new base was located near the Amiens-Albert Road, approximately ten miles behind the battle line. According to LeBoutillier, "the Germans and Richthofen were stationed in a little place called Cappy, I'd say approximately the same distance on the other side of the German line." Consequently, No. 209 Squadron, among others, and Richtofen's *Jagdgeschwader I* would be contesting the sky over the battle front for the next several weeks.[15]

Sunday morning on 21 April 1918 dawned sunny with excellent visibility. Consequently, a large number of aircraft from both sides of the battle lines ventured into the sky. The previous week had been dominated by cloudy and rainy weather. In LeBoutillier's words, "that Sunday morning we [No. 209 Squadron] were doing a squadron patrol on the front lines. We knew it was a heavy combat area, we knew that things were going to be pretty tough that day."[16] Indeed, the Richthofen *Jagdgeschwader* had every intention of destroying the Sopwith Camels of No. 209 Squadron, which was patrolling the front lines in three flights of five planes each. Capt. Roy Brown commanded "A" Flight, Captain LeBoutillier led "B" Flight, and Captain Redgate was commanding "C" Flight. Each flight maneuvered back and forth in a different sector over the Somme River valley and the Bray-Corbey woods.[17]

LeBoutillier's flight was working on the southern flank of the Somme River while Brown's flight patrolled the northern sector and Redgate's flight handled the center sector. "Boots" LeBoutillier's "B" Flight was attacked by several German aircraft but suffered no casualties while shooting down an enemy two-seater in flames. At this point, LeBoutillier became aware of a large number of German pursuit planes attacking the Brown and Redgate flights.[18] An intense aerial dogfight immediately erupted. Capt. Oliver C. LeBoutillier's plane was hit several times, and he pulled out of the dogfight until he could check his aircraft's maneuverability.[19] As soon as he completed the check, he spotted a Camel diving toward the Somme Valley with a red triplane pursuing from close behind. As it turned out later the Camel was being flown by Wilfred "Wop" May, flying one of his first combat missions, and the pursuer was none other than Baron Manfred von Richthofen, an eighty-victory German ace. According to his combat report, LeBoutillier stated "he fired on the red triplane which was shot down by Captain Roy Brown and crashed our side of the lines."[20] It is quite true that Capt. Roy Brown was, indeed, chasing the red Fokker triplane in a desperate effort to save young Lieutenant May. Although machine gunners on the ground were also shooting at the Red Baron, according to LeBoutillier it was Captain Brown who actually shot Richthofen down. In his words "I looked over and it was Roy Brown because you could tell by his markings. They all had different markings and he came down at a 45 degree angle on that triplane. . . . you could see [Brown's] tracers going into the [Red Baron's] cockpit."[21] Brown pulled up from the chase as the red Fokker crashed near the Australian anti-aircraft battery. Richthofen had been hit high in the right shoulder, and the bullet exited through his heart.[22] There was, indeed, much controversy over whether Richthofen was shot down by machine gunners on the ground or by Captain Brown. Lt. Wilfred "Wop" May, the pilot the Red Baron was chasing, stated that "the bullet could not have been fired from the ground, and Brown was given official credit."[23]

At approximately ten A.M. on 22 April, Captain LeBoutillier and his "B" Flight intercepted an Albatros two-seater at eight thousand feet over the city of Albert. The Camel formation dived on the enemy observation plane "getting off good bursts." The German "turned over on his wing and then nose dived and when about 1000 feet from the ground he broke up." The "pilot and observer were killed." "Boots" LeBoutillier shared in the air victory for his fourth kill since joining the No. 209 Squadron.[24]

On 9 May 1918 Captain LeBoutillier encountered a formation of enemy aircraft and "got on the tail of one, firing about 150 round into it at 50 yards range. The E.A. went down in vertical nose dive and was later seen crashed on the ground."[25] The New Jersey boy had finally reached acedom after approximately a year with his naval unit—now numbered as 209 Squadron.

One week later, on a fine weather day, LeBoutillier and Lt. R. M. Foster attacked a German LVG at thirteen thousand feet at 9:40 A.M. in the vicinity of Villers Brettoneux. The pair fired several bursts into the enemy plane and saw flames and smoke coming from the LVG. LeBoutillier then fired an additional "200 rounds at it in steep glide near Bayonvillers," and the plane went down out of control.[26] This victory marked LeBoutillier's sixth kill. For his success as a fighter pilot he was cited in the *London Gazette* on 3 June 1919.[27]

Capt. Oliver C. LeBoutillier was wounded on 14 June 1918, some four weeks after his last air victory.[28] He was transferred out of the RAF in February 1919 and returned to the United States.[29] On returning to his home country after the war, he became a barnstormer like so many other World War I ex–fighter pilots. LeBoutillier also flew SE-5 aircraft in skywriting "missions" until 1925. In addition, "Boots" performed as a pilot in no less than eighteen Hollywood movies, "which included such films as *Hell's Angels, Eagle and the Hawk, Wings* and many others." As an instructor, he gave Amelia Earhart her first dual instruction in a twin engine aircraft and acted as a test pilot for Howard Hughes for several months.[30] Later, he was CAA Inspector in charge of Colorado and Wyoming and left aviation with nineteen thousand flying hours. In 1956 LeBoutillier moved to Las Vegas, Nevada, "where he formed a wholesale drug firm, Associated Researchers, and raised thoroughbred horses as a hobby." He died on 12 May 1983 after a lifetime in aviation.[31]

The SE-5A, with Lt. William L. Dougan in the cockpit,
summer 1918.

Courtesy Mrs. Helen Dougan

FIVE

Lt. Jens Frederick "Swede" Larson

Jens Frederick Larson was born in Waltham, Massachusetts, on 10 August 1891. His parents were living in Stockholm, Sweden, when he enlisted in the First Canadian Overseas Contingent in February 1915. Shortly thereafter he went to France as a member of the Canadian infantry force. Larson was commissioned as a lieutenant in August 1916 and was assigned to a Canadian artillery regiment a few months later. During his tour of duty with the infantry and the artillery, he became fascinated with the combat aircraft performing overhead, and in October of 1916 he joined the "Preliminary School" for air training at Oxford. In May 1917 he began his elementary flight training at Netheravon and, a few weeks later, was assigned to No. 34 Squadron's advanced training at Tern Hill. At this location he flew Avro aircraft, Morane Parasols, Sopwith Pups, and SE-5A machines. His date of graduation was listed as 12 July 1917.[1]

On 21 September 1917, he was posted to No. 84 Squadron, then based at Estrée Blanche on the British end of the battle front. Lieutenant Larson was assigned to Capt. J. M. Child's "C" Flight but was to do his first war flying, a line patrol, with Capt. K. M. Leaske's "A" Flight on 12 October 1917.[2] Maj. Sholto Douglas, who would be a marshal of the Royal Air Force in World War II, was then the commander of No. 84 Squadron. Major Douglas, who had flown two-seaters the previous year, was very impressed with the Squadron's SE-5A single-seaters, as was everyone else in the outfit.[3] Larson had fallen in love with the SE-5A, because of its great stability, while in his final stages of advanced flight training.

On 22 November 1917, Lieutenant Larson was transferred to Capt. E. R. Pennell's "B" Flight and was made deputy leader. Four days later, while leading an early morning patrol at eight thousand feet between Cambrai and St. Quentin, Larson spotted two enemy single-seaters about five hundred feet below. The Massachusetts man dived on the highest German machine and got a burst from both guns into him. In Larson's report he stated, "He dived under me, passing under Lieut. Brown who then opened fire on him. I then continued my dive on the second machine, setting well on his tail, giving him a long burst from both guns. He dived vertically with engine full on, probably out of control." Larson and Brown were now over two enemy airdromes at six thousand feet and started to attack the German machines on the ground, but saw a large number of enemy planes climbing up to cut off the two SE-5s. The No. 84 Squadron pair then dived toward the west and their home airfield. Maj. Sholto Douglas listed Larson's victim as a decisive "down out of control" kill.[4]

The month of December 1917 was basically plagued with bad weather, and most fighter squadrons on both the British and German sides were able to get in very little air combat. Nonetheless, squadrons attached to the 22nd Wing of the RFC endeavored to keep the whole army front clear of enemy aircraft up to the line Lesdain-Villiers-Outereux-Beaurevoir-Ramecourt-Sequehart. "All machines were to work in pairs. From dawn to 10:30 A.M. No. 54 Squadron (Sopwith Camels) were to patrol; from 10:30 to 12:30 No. 48 Squadron (Bristol Fighter); and from 12:30 to dusk No. 84 Squadron (S.E.5)." In accordance with these orders, three pair of SE-5s left their airdrome on offensive patrol at 12:30 on 3 January 1918. Three other pairs went up at approximately two P.M. Five of these patrols proved more or less uneventful. "One, however, proved fruitful." It consisted of Lt. J. F. Larson and 2nd Lt. A. W. Beauchamp Proctor. About three P.M. they spotted two enemy two-seaters coming from the east.[5] In Larson's report he stated, "I was in the sun, so charged one of them head on, both guns going. I fired till within 20 yards of E.A., then zoomed up and "Immelmanned" back onto E.A. tail, and got in another burst. The [enemy aircraft] burst into flames and spun down." Larson than saw 2nd Lt. Beauchamp Proctor shoot down the second German plane.[6] Larson's kill would mark his second victory since joining No. 84 Squadron.

The weather during January 1918 turned out to be rather poor for high altitude flying. Nonetheless, No. 84 Squadron remained rather active in low-level strafing and bombing. On 28 January Lieutenant Larson led his first full-size "B" flight patrol over the lines. Not being able to find targets in the air, he turned his attention to the ground and "brought back a report of railway movements behind the enemy lines which proved of great value."[7]

At 10:20 A.M. on 16 February, Lieutenant Larson's formation saw four large V-Strutters over the town of La Fère and immediately dived on them. Larson "turned in under them, chose one, got well under his tail, pulled down the Lewis gun and put a drum into him. It seemed as if the pilot was hit as he stalled, fell over on his back, and then went into a vertical nose-dive." Larson then attacked several other enemy machines and circled underneath, giving them short bursts with his Lewis gun, but without effort. Shortly thereafter, he "saw a large two-seater being archied over our side of the lines. I made after him and got well under him at short range. But on opening fire with my Lewis I got a stoppage." Since his Vickers gun was not working either, he had to break off combat. Larson was credited with shooting down one V-Strutter out of control for his third victory.[8]

Capt. R. A. Grosvenor took over the command of "B" Flight from Captain Pennell on 17 February,[9] and on the next day he and Lt. J. F. Larson became involved in an air combat with five German planes at fourteen thousand feet in the vicinity of Homblieres. While Captain Grosvenor attacked a two-seater, Larson fired a long burst into an enemy aircraft attacking his flight leader. The machine "stalled and fell out into a very steep dive, without finishing his dive on Captain Grosvenor." In Larson's combat report, the "V-Strutter" he shot off the tail of Captain Grosvenor was listed as "driven down." Captain Grosvenor, without a doubt, was grateful for Larson's performance.[10]

While on an offensive patrol northeast of Ribemont on 15 March, Lieutenant Larson and Lt. A. E. Clear intercepted six Pfalz Scouts at eighteen thousand feet. Larson and Clear attacked the upper group of three enemy planes, and each RFC pilot chose a target. In Larson's words, "I fired at one with both guns; he went into a spin, but flattened out lower down and went northeast." Another German attacked Larson and they maneuvered for position, and while the American was on top of a turn his engine cut right out forcing him to fall into a short dive. According to Larson's report, the enemy

dived on me quickly at an angle to my machine. I pulled out of the dive, turned quickly, and fired a good burst from both guns into his nose. His machine then fell into a vertical dive, then started to sideslip, and finally went into a spin. After watching him a bit I made for the lines as I had no engine.

Larson managed to land safely on the Allied side of the battle lines. Lieutenant Clear reported Larson's opponent had gone down out of control. An Allied anti-aircraft battery also reported seeing the Pfalz go down but lost sight of it in the haze near the ground. Douglas, No. 84 Squadron commander, marked the German plane as down out of control.[11]

On 18 March 1918, a fine clear day, Lt. J. F. "Swede" Larson and No. 84 Squadron pilots encountered "between forty and fifty Fokker Dr1 triplanes & V-Strutters" in a wild dogfight at ten thousand feet over Le Cateau. In the tremendous air battle, Larson "dived at a triplane, which rolled and then spun a short distance going east." He then attacked another triplane and fired a long burst with both guns. "The triplane then fell into a slow spin" and seemed to be going down in the vicinity of Le Cateau. Larson was unable to observe whether the enemy machine actually crashed. Maj. Sholto Douglas credited him with a down-out-of-control victory for his fifth kill since joining the squadron.[12]

The Royal Air Force came into being on 1 April 1918, as a new independent service ranking with the Army and the Navy. On that beautiful sunny day, with great visibility, Lieutenant Larson, accompanying his flight commander, Captain Grosvenor, was to score his sixth victory in the air war. At 1:30 P.M., he dived from fifteen hundred feet to drop his bombs on the village of Denuin. As he released his bombs, he observed a two-seater, probably an LVG, "underneath me going south." The enemy immediately turned east and dived with the observer firing. In his report Lieutenant Larson commented: "I fired a good burst into the E.A. at about 50 yards range, and he went into a steep spiral dive, after which the observer did not fire. I fired at the E.A. down to 400 feet, and then left it. I saw it still going down completely out of control at about 200 feet." At this point Larson was forced to climb because of intense ground fire. Major Douglas, later that day, wrote on the combat report, "1 enemy two-seater shot down completely out of control."[13]

J. F. "Swede" Larson had been granted a leave to visit London on 21 March 1918 but was recalled by the squadron commander ten days later because of the German Somme offensive. Despite his vacation being cut short, "Swede" Larson was eager to get back into combat. Not only did he score a kill on 1 April, but he achieved even greater success on 3 April. Low clouds and rain made flying difficult, but, while leading an offensive patrol in the Rosieres area at approximately one P.M., "Swede" Larson met "two formations of Pfalz and V-Strutters in the clouds at 7000 feet." He led his patrol of four SE-5s into the clouds and then dived onto the enemy formation. His first machine-gun burst apparently was unsuccessful, and a real dogfight developed with two Sopwith Camels from No. 65 Squadron also becoming involved. Lieutenant Larson continued to maneuver and reported, "I got well on the tail of one at close range, firing with both guns. The E.A. turned under me; but I again got on his tail and fired both guns. The E.A. went down vertically, pulled out stalled and started to spin." Due to being attacked by another Pfalz, Larson did not actually see his victim crash. Larson then got on the tail of one of the "V-Strutters, firing long bursts from both guns into him. . . . The [enemy aircraft] fell into a spin, and I saw him crash into the ground about one mile east of Rosieres." The No. 84 Squadron commander credited Larson with one enemy plane crashed and one down out of control.[14]

In spite of low clouds and rain, a considerable amount of flying took place on 6 April. At 11:20 A.M., Lt. J. F. Larson and Lts. H. W. Saunders, C. L. Stubbs, and H. O. McDonald caught an LVG two-seater at eleven thousand feet over the city of Hangard. The German had strange markings, and the SE-5A pilots did not attack until Larson flew in close enough to spot the black crosses inside of a circle. Larson then shot the enemy observer, and the other three SE-5s began firing long bursts into the German plane. After the enemy went into a vertical spin, Larson fired another long burst into the machine. The LVG crashed straight into the ground a little north of Hangard on the Allied side of the battle lines. All four of the No. 84 Squadron pilots shared in the kill.[15]

Four days after the 6 April air battle, Lt. J. F. Larson left No. 84 Squadron for the United Kingdom, where he became a flight instructor. According to one source, Larson was injured while instructing pilots in advanced training on 3 September 1918.[16] There has been considerable disagreement over how many enemy aircraft Larson shot down during his tour of duty with No. 84 Squadron. The combat reports now housed in the Public Records Office and signed by Maj. Sholto Douglas indicate he had at least eight kills. Bruce Robertson's *Air Aces of the 1914–1918 War* does not list Larson at all. Combat records in the public archives in Ottawa, Canada, show him to have nine victories. After the First World War ended, J. F. Larson returned to the United States and, shortly thereafter, became an architect. Apparently, he was still practicing his profession in the 1970s.[17]

Lt. Francis Peabody Magoun
Courtesy Mrs. F. P. Magoun

SIX

Lt. Francis Peabody Magoun

F rancis Peabody Magoun, Jr., an air ace and winner of the Military Cross while flying with the British during the First World War, was born in New York City on 6 January 1895. Because his father, Francis Peabody Magoun, was economically well off and very interested in the cultural development of his son, young Francis received a fine education. He attended St. Andrews School in Concord, Massachusetts, and the Noble and Greenough School in Boston. After completion of his preparatory school work, Magoun attended Harvard University where, in 1916, he received the Bachelor of Arts degree. In February of that year, he joined the American Ambulance Field Service and sailed for France. He served as a volunteer ambulance driver during the period 3 March 1916 to 3 August 1916. His unit was cited for outstanding work in French Divisional Orders on 15 July 1916.[1] Like many other idealistic crusaders wishing to save Western Civilization from the imperialist "Hun," Magoun found service in the mud and gore on the western front something less than pleasant. The occasional aerial dogfight he witnessed in skies above the trenches began to intrigue him, and he returned to the United States to plan his future role in the war.[2]

In February 1917 Magoun returned to London and, in March, enlisted in the Royal Flying Corps. He attended the School of Military Aeronautics at Oxford, England, and did his elementary flight training at the Royal Naval Air Service School. His advanced training was done at Catterick, Yorks, and at the School of Aerial Gunnery at Turnberry, Scotland. On 4 July 1917 Magoun was commissioned a second lieutenant in the RFC.[3]

Lieutenant Magoun was attached to No. 1 Squadron, a veteran fighter outfit, on 14 November 1917.[4] Bad flying weather prevailed during the last weeks of 1917, and "the final Christmas of the war was a drab one," in spite of the effort of the pilots to make the best of it,

if only to try and forget for a day the static slugging match that had now been in progress for over forty months. But the temporary respite from operations only served to give time for personal feelings of nostalgia and it was almost with relief that the pilots went forward into the New Year determined to make the most of improving weather and do their best to end the war as soon as possible.[5]

January of 1918 saw the squadron pilots resume their offensive patrol efforts that had been pretty well abandoned in December. However, No. 1 Squadron had some problems in the new year. Capt. Tom Hazell, one of their flight commanders and already a nineteen-victory ace,[6] was transferred to No. 24 Squadron, and this caused a leadership gap. But an even more serious problem was the fact that the Germans were now beginning to equip *Jagdgeschwaders I* and *II*, located in the area, with Fokker Dr-1 Triplanes. It was obvious to No. 1 Squadron pilots that this highly maneuverable fighter would completely outclass their very fragile Nieuport 17 biplanes.[7]

Lieutenant Magoun, along with the rest of No. 1 Squadron fighter pilots, was greatly relieved in late January when he learned that the outfit was to be reequipped with the SE-5A biplane. This aircraft, designed at the Royal Aircraft Factory, was powered by the two hundred horsepower water-cooled Wolseley Viper engine and had a top speed of 122 miles per hour with a ceiling of twenty-two thousand feet. Furthermore, because of its broad wing, it had good maneuverability. In addition, the SE-5A had good fire power with a Vickers machine gun mounted on the cowl, synchronized to fire through the propeller, as well as a Lewis gun situated on the center section of the top wing. The Lewis gun could be hauled down by the pilot and reloaded while in flight.[8] The squadron was removed from the front line in late January to reequip it with the new machine. After a brief conversion course and a few days of gunnery training, No. 1 Squadron was moved back into the front lines[9] and stationed at Bailleul near Armentières.

The twenty-three-year-old Magoun scored his first aerial victory on 28 February 1918 when he and Capt. W. D. Patrick fired three hundred rounds into an Albatros Scout at one hundred yards range. The enemy aircraft "toppled over and dived straight for the ground, last seen at 500 feet still diving vertically." The victory, which took place in the Westhoek-Gheluvelt area, was listed as a "decisive" by squadron and wing headquarters.[10]

At 7:30 A.M. on 10 March, Lieutenant Magoun, flying alone, spotted an enemy observation balloon at three thousand feet over the Roulers-Menin road about fifteen miles east of the city of Ypres. "After firing my first burst from very close range," he wrote in his report, "the observer jumped out. I then fired several bursts from very close range, 500 rounds in all. The balloon went down slowly in a greatly deflated condition." This action was listed decisive and marked the Harvard man's second "kill" of the war.[11]

On 15 March, a three-ship patrol from No. 1 Squadron led by Capt. W. D. Patrick attacked a DFW Aviatik observation plane being escorted by an Albatros fighter. Second Lieutenants Magoun and L. W. Mawbey concentrated on the two-seater. Magoun described the combat as follows: "opening fire at 150 yards, I fired a long burst up to within 20-30 yards. I fired 150 [rounds] Vickers and 97 Lewis, and 2nd Lt. Mawbey 50 Vickers. The machine stalled along and then toppled over in a vertical dive. It crashed south of Ledeghem. . . ." At the same time Captain Patrick shot down the Albatros. Both victories were confirmed.[12]

On 21 March 1918 the Germans launched a massive offensive toward the Somme River in the Albert-St. Quentin sector and, after a few hours of intensive bombardment, broke through the Allied lines in several places. Every available squadron of the RFC was thrown into the battle area to harass the advancing German forces with bombs and machine-gun fire. During the first few days of the offensive, No. 1 Squadron pilots were in the air from daybreak until sunset.

> From dawn on 26th March until dusk on 3rd April, the squadron was detached on a daily basis to reinforce the 10th (Army) Wing, which was heavily engaged with advancing German infantry in a serious breakthrough to the south of Arras, on what became known as the Bapaume front.

The squadron's SE-5s were flown south to Bruay, some twenty-five miles northwest of Arras, each morning and returned, "battle scarred and weary, to their own airfield at night." Three aircraft were lost in the first day's action.[13]

Lt. Francis Peabody Magoun was heavily engaged in the air

effort to stop the German advance. In recommending Magoun for a decoration, Maj. H. Adams, commanding officer of No. 1 Squadron, wrote,

> He is a most brave and gallant officer. . . . on 26-3-18 he dropped two bombs on Bapaume from 200 feet causing general panic. Later, he with four other officers bombed a camp at Sapignies and attacked the troops from very low altitudes with machine gun fire causing a stampede. On 27-3-18 he dropped two bombs from a very low altitude on a column of troops coming up Cambrai-Arras road and obtained two direct hits. He then dropped two bombs at Sapignies and fired 300 rounds at troops along the Bapaume-Albert railway. Continuing along he engaged a field gun at Achiet-LeGrand with machine gun fire. At 3:30 the same day he dropped 2 bombs on troops massed in a field near Ervillers and dispersed them. Later he dropped 4 bombs on hutments at LeSars and fired 150 rounds into trenches east of Fampoux.

On the next day, he continued his low-level bombing and strafing activities.[14] For this highly dangerous but very effective effort, he was awarded the British Military Cross.[15]

In addition to his highly successful bombing and strafing work while operating out of Bruay, Lieutanent Magoun was also involved in two low-level dogfights. At 8:35 A.M. on 28 March, he attacked a black and white Albatros fighter "east of Arras and after pursuing it East for some time [he] secured a favorable position behind and fired 3 long bursts. The enemy aircraft turned North, and then went down and crashed in a marsh." Five minutes later, Magoun and Capt. G. B. Moore engaged a LVG two-seater over Gavrille. "Each fired two or three bursts. The observer stopped firing and the machine went down without engine and crashed in a field north of Oppy (near Douai)."[16] With these confirmed victories, Magoun became a five-victory ace.

As the German drive neared Bailleul, No. 1 Squadron was forced to change its base of operations. On the night of 28 March, the unit was moved to St. Marie Cappel approximately fifteen miles to the northwest. Nonetheless, squadron pilots continued to fly out of Bruay during the daylight hours. They "flew into St. Marie Cappel at night too tired to care much about their new surroundings and snatched a few hours of sleep before returning to Bruay at dawn." Fortunately, the German offensive on the Bapaume front lost momentum on 4 April and, due to an abundance of targets near St. Marie Cappel, no more operations were flown from Bruay.[17]

When the Royal Flying Corps and the Royal Naval Air Service were combined to become the Royal Air Force, the honor of becoming the senior squadron in the new independent air force went to No. 1 Squadron; but its significance was, at the moment, lost on the "very tired men in Flanders."[18]

Even though the German push, now known in the area as the Battle of Lys, had slowed in early April, No. 1 Squadron continued to pay a price. On 10 April two pilots were shot down and taken prisoner while three others, including Lt. Francis P. Magoun, were wounded by ground fire.[19]

Young Magoun spent several weeks in a military hospital and, in the summer of 1918, he returned to the United States on a furlough. After being declared fit for flying duty, he rejoined his old squadron, now based at Senlis airdome located about six miles west of the city of Albert. On 27 October he sent an enemy aircraft down out of control for his sixth official victory.[20]

Magoun remained on active service with No. 1 Squadron until 1 January 1919 and was demobilized at Folkestone, England, on 10 January. He immediately enrolled for graduate work at Trinity College, Cambridge, England. In the summer of that year, he returned to the United States where he continued his quest for a graduate degree.[21]

In 1923, Magoun completed the PhD degree in English at Harvard University, where he remained in the English department for some thirty-eight years. His principal teaching field included Old and Middle English, and during his career as a professor he published over a dozen books and numerous scholarly articles. After his retirement in 1961, he became interested in the Finnish language and, shortly thereafter, translated the *Kalevala* into English.[22] Francis Peabody Magoun, Jr., died in 1979.[23]

Capt. George W. Bulmer (second from right)
with members of No. 22 Squadron RAF
Courtesy Aviation Photo Service, Syracuse, New York

SEVEN

Capt. George W. Bulmer

George William Bulmer was born in Dixon, Illinois, on 1 September 1898 of British parents. When his father was transferred to Toronto, young Bulmer moved to Canada prior to 1910. George W. Bulmer was always considered a serious young man and became an accountant before being accepted by the Royal Flying Corps in Ottawa in April 1917.[1] After a few weeks of training in Canada, he was sent to England where he finished his pilot instruction. On 29 December 1917 Bulmer joined No. 22 Squadron, then flying the Bristol Fighter.[2]

Lieutenant Bulmer was attracted to the Bristol Fighter. This two-seater fighter had arrived on the western front in April 1917 but was used defensively and was not a success. Once used offensively, and flown by a good team of pilot and gunner, it became a formidable opponent.[3] Although large and somewhat heavy on the controls, the Bristol Fighter, frequently called the "Brisfit," was fast and strong. It usually was flown in the same manner as the single-seater scout, with the pilot utilizing his two forward-firing Vickers machine guns, while the observer guarded the tail with a pair of Lewis guns.[4] Powered with a 250 horsepower Rolls-Royce engine, the Brisfit was capable of 125 miles per hour at sea level and approximately 105 miles per hour at ten thousand feet.

Despite the atrocious weather on the western front, young Bulmer flew several combat missions in January and February of 1918. The first air victory he was involved in occurred at 11:15 A.M. on 6 March. In his combat report Lieutenant Bulmer stated,

> while on patrol east of La Bassée at 16000 feet. . . . the formation was attacked by 9 E.A. Leader dived on our tail at close range and my observer [Lt. S. J. Hunter] put a burst into it at about 50 yards

range and drove it down out of control. The enemy aircraft continued to dive to the east. My machine being badly shot about I retired.[5]

Although Bulmer did not shoot down the Pfalz Scout engaged in the battle, he was, indeed, very pleased that his observer had been successful.

Ten days later, on 16 March 1918, the nineteen-year-old Bulmer scored his first personal victory. While flying an offensive patrol at fifteen thousand feet in the vicinity of Hénin-Liétard at 10:30 A.M., Bulmer and his observer Lt. P. S. Williams spotted several Pfalz and Albatros scouts camouflaged "silver, blue and dark green and one machine with blackish coloured body with a red nose." Some five minutes later, Lieutenant Bulmer dived his Bristol Fighter on two Pfalz scouts between Hénin-Liétard and Dourges. In Bulmer's combat report, he commented "the machine I dived on went down completely out of control and as I pulled out of the dive my observer fired on a second machine which also went down completely out of control."[6]

On 23 March 1918, two days after the Germans began their big Somme offensive, Lieutenant Bulmer was to score his second "kill." The air battle occurred over Bussy, a small town between Arras and Cambrai, at ten thousand feet. Despite cloudy weather Bulmer and his observer, Lt. P. S. Williams, spotted approximately ten Albatros scouts. Their combat report stated that one of the Albatros "machines passed immediately under ours" and Bulmer and Williams fired about fifty rounds into it, "when it spun down and . . . crashed."[7]

Although the weather during the week of 6–12 May was relatively bad, air combat tended to intensify. During the seven days, the RAF officially claimed eighty-four enemy aircraft brought down and twenty-four others driven down out of control. Some twenty-eight British planes were lost during this period.[8] At 6:25 P.M. on 6 May, a No. 22 Squadron flight braved low clouds, mist, and rain while patrolling northeast of Arras near Fresnoy. During this mission, Bulmer and his observer, Lt. H. E. Elsworth, became involved in a dogfight with several Pfalz pursuit planes. In Bulmer's words,

I picked out one Pfalz scout and dived twice on it. After the second dive the enemy machine was seen by my observer to lose speed and sideslip very steeply toward the ground completely out of control. As we continued the fight with the other two machines we were not able to see E.A. actually crash.[9]

This victory marked young Bulmer's third "kill" since joining No. 22 Squadron.

At 10:15 A.M. on 8 May, Lieutenants Bulmer and Williams, while on an offensive patrol at twelve thousand feet over Brebières, intercepted a half-dozen Pfalz pursuit planes. Bulmer immediately dived on one of the enemy machines and fired a long burst from his Vickers guns. The enemy sideslipped into a nose dive and fell completely out of control. "This machine's tail was seen to crumple up" by another Bristol Fighter pilot. Lieutenant Bulmer was credited with his fourth victory and was now recognized as one of the most aggressive Brisfit pilots in No. 22 Squadron.[10]

The weather on the British-German battle front during the week of 13–19 May proved to be rather good. Consequently, air combat casualties were relatively high. According to Royal Air Force reports, some 130 enemy aircraft were shot down, and another thirty-two were driven down out of control. The RAF lost fifty-two of their own machines during the week.[11] On 16 May, during a fine visibility day, BF-2B pilots Lts. Bulmer and B. C. Budd, while returning from an offensive patrol, observed several German observation balloons near Neuf Berquin. Both pilots began a strafing attack on the balloons. In his combat report, Lieutenant Bulmer wrote "the second balloon I dived on was seen to give way in the center and both ends fold up and it immediately fell to the ground. Other balloons were drawn down along the line but none were seen to be actually damaged." The destruction of the German balloon moved George W. Bulmer into the ace category.[12]

On 17 May the weather was again fine "but the visibility was not so good."[13] Nonetheless, Lieutenant Bulmer and his observer, Lt. P. S. Williams, flew an offensive patrol and escort mission in the Douai-Villers area. On returning from escorting the DH-4s on a bombing patrol, Bulmer stated, "I observed an E.A. machine coming from the west and losing height through the clouds." The American circled around until he had his Bristol Fighter in a favorable position to attack. He then "dived firing about 150 rounds to the enemy machine. The E.A. pulled nose up and did one turn of a spin then nose-dived to the ground and crashed, southeast of Douai near Villiers." The "kill" was witnessed by another No. 22 Squadron crew flying in the same area.[14]

During the next several weeks of relatively good weather on the British-German battle front, Lieutenant Bulmer continued to fly offensive patrols and escorted missions with DH-4 bombing planes. Although he did not shoot down any enemy aircraft, he was highly successful in protecting the bomber formations. His last air victory occurred on 9 July 1918, when he and his observer, Lt. J. M. McDonald, caught an Albatros two-seater at approximately ten thousand feet a little north of Bois de Pinlenpin. Bulmer immediately maneuvered his fighter on to the tail of the Albatros and fired a long burst into it. The German machine "did a close turn of a spiral and then burst into flames dropping through the clouds." The "flamer" was seen by Bulmer's observer as it plunged toward the forest below.[15]

On 16 September 1918 the *London Gazette* published information on Lt. G. W. Bulmer's receipt of the Military Cross. The account read as follows:

> The King has been graciously pleased to confer the undermentioned reward in recognition of gallantry in flying operations against the enemy:—Military Cross T/Lt. George William Bulmer, Gen List, and 10th Wing No. 22 Sqn. RAF. For conspicuous gallantry and devotion to duty as a fighting pilot. In recent operations he destroyed seven enemy machines and an observation balloon. By his tenacity and zeal he set a magnificent example in his squadron.[16]

Certainly, young Bulmer was regarded as one of the most aggressive pilots in No. 22 Squadron.

Bulmer was promoted to temporary captain on 29 May 1918 and frequently led No. 22 Squadron patrols over the western front. After completing his tour of duty with the Brisfit squadron, he was transferred to the "Home Establishment" on 20 August 1918.[17] On 13 April 1919 he left the Royal Air Force and, shortly thereafter, returned to his accountant's job in Canada.[18]

Young George Bulmer, a devout Methodist, was much disturbed that his parents had separated and eventually divorced. For several years, he refused to see either parent. In fact, his father died before any reconciliation. In 1925 a relative urged Bulmer to return to the United States, so he returned to Dixon, Illinois, and lived there and in Chicago for some forty years. In the spring of 1970 he moved to Phoenix, Arizona. His son became one of the first officers on the USS *Nautilus*, a nuclear submarine.[19]

Lt. John Sharpe Griffith
Courtesy Stewart K. Taylor

EIGHT

Lt. John Sharpe Griffith

L t. John Sharpe Griffith, born on 26 November 1898 and
educated in Seattle, Washington, joined the SE-5A–flying
No. 60 Squadron at La Gorgue airdrome near the city of Armentières on 14 February 1918. Due to atrocious weather during that
month, there was relatively little air activity. Although young
Griffith managed to make some half dozen flights, he was not
able to inflict any real damage on the German forces.[1]

On 8 March No. 60 Squadron moved a few miles north to
Bailleul airdrome and, with the improving weather conditions, a
"lot of very valuable work was done, mostly low bombing." Unfortunately, the airdrome was shelled during the whole time No. 60
Squadron was based at Bailleul and was severely bombed on the
last two nights. Luckily, "there were no casualties."[2]

While flying at nine thousand feet in the vicinity of Menin at
11:10 A.M. on 9 March, Griffith's flight spotted approximately a
dozen enemy aircraft a few hundred feet below. A general dogfight developed, and Griffith managed to attack an Albatros
fighter, shooting it down out of control over Menin. The enemy
machine was "confirmed by A.A. [an Allied anti-aircraft battery]
as absolutely out of control."[3] This kill marked the American's
first victory since joining No. 60 Squadron. Some nine days later,
on 18 March, Lieutenant Griffith "attacked and shot down out of
control an Albatros Scout over Roulers at 10,000 feet." The victory was confirmed by a Lieutenant Christie of No. 60 Squadron.[4]

With the big German offensive underway during the last week
of March, No. 60 Squadron was hurriedly moved to Bellevue,
some ten miles southwest of Arras, on 27 March 1918. After
three days stay at Bellevue, the squadron was moved to Fienvillers, approximately a dozen miles further to the southwest and
out of range of the German drive.[5]

Shortly after the squadron arrived at Fienvillers on the morning of 30 March, Lts. Griffith, W. J. A. Duncan, and J. O. Priestley took off on an offensive patrol in the Albert area. At 11:50 A.M., while flying at four thousand feet, the three pilots spotted an LVG two-seater "firing a white Very light and apparently doing contact patrol work." In his combat report Griffith stated, "I attacked and fired 150 rounds at 25 yards. Lieutenant Duncan also attacked at the same time." Duncan described the combat "with Lieutenant Griffith I attacked the L.V.G. 2-seater and fired 150 rounds into it followed it down to 500 feet from ground and saw it crash in Village of Becourt." The commanding officer of No. 60 Squadron divided the victory between the two pilots involved in the combat.[6]

On 1 April 1918, the day the RFC and RNAS were combined to become the Royal Air Force, Lieutenant Griffith was involved in an offensive patrol. Unfortunately, his SE-5A developed a radiator leak, and he was forced to return to his home airfield. Despite "a considerable bank of clouds over the lines at about 2000 feet" on the afternoon of 2 April, Griffith was again engaged in an offensive patrol in the vicinity of La Motta, a small town south of Hamel. At 6:40 P.M., he became involved with an Albatros Scout, managed to out-turn the enemy machine, got on its tail, "and fired 150 rounds at range of 150 yards. E.A. turned sharply to the left and went down but appeared to be under control. Could not see him land as I was being 'archied'". The combat was listed as indecisive.[7]

In spite of low clouds and rain, a considerable amount of flying took place on 6 April, and many RAF squadrons "were out engaging with their machine guns enemy troops which were massing Northeast of La Motta."[8] Lieutenant Griffith, a part of an offensive patrol staged by No. 60 Squadron, observed an enemy Albatros Scout "cross the line to ground strafe. Dived on him firing a short burst when he retired east into the clouds." This air combat also was listed as indecisive.[9]

The squadron left Fienvillers on 12 April 1918 and moved to Boffles airdrome, some ten miles north, where they remained until the unit moved forward with the British advance in September. According to the squadron's history,

> very good work was done in April, May, and June both low bombing and offensive patrols during which a large number of enemy machines were brought down. Capt. Belgrave, Capt. Copeland,

Capt. Duncan, Lieut. Whitney and Lieut. Griffith were the most successful pilots at this time.

Maj. J. B. McCudden, winner of the Victoria Cross, the D.S.O., and the Military Cross, was posted as squadron commander on 9 July 1918; unfortunately he was killed in an airplane accident while flying out to the squadron, "a very severe loss to No. 60 and the RAF."

Maj. C. M. Crowe, a Military Cross holder, took command of the squadron on 13 July.[10] Although John Sharpe Griffith participated in no less than ten offensive patrols during the three weeks following No. 60 Squadron's transfer to Boffles, he was unsuccessful in destroying a German plane. However, on 6 May, he and Lt. W. J. Duncan braved "low clouds, mist and rain"[11] while on a "roving commission" in the Albert area. The two No. 60 Squadron pilots, while circling at eight thousand feet,

> saw a machine diving toward our lines and thinking it to be our machine which was in trouble, we flew over it toward the Archie but as the machine passed below us we noticed it was an Albatros Scout with black crosses inside circle. We immediately attacked it at about 7000 feet. As we dived on E.A. he kept turning under us—this continued until we were firing continuously. The E.A. dived vertically and crashed just behind some trenches.

As the RAF pair climbed away from the enemy trenches, Lieutenant Griffith's plane had one flying wire broken and the front main spar shot through. Fortunately, he was able to nurse his machine back to his home airdrome. Griffith and Duncan shared the destruction of the enemy aircraft.[12]

One week later, while on a "roving commission," Griffith met an Albatros two-seater,

> apparently doing artillery work and attacked. Fired two bursts at 200 yards range. E.A. circled around and then flew east. I followed him down to 200 feet from the ground and two more two-seaters came overhead and I was Archied and machine gunned from the ground so broke off and flew back.

Even though the American had inflicted some damage on the Albatros, the combat was labeled as "indecisive."[13]

"The sky was overcast, with occasional clear gaps" on 14 May. Despite the weather, Lts. Griffith and H. K. Whitney took off on an offensive patrol in the Moreuil sector at approximately seven

A.M. Thirty minutes later, the pair observed two Albatros two-seaters "camouflaged light green with circles of white around crosses." Griffith and Whitney quickly maneuvered behind, and slightly below, one of the enemy machines. Each fired over one hundred rounds into its tail section. The German plane managed to slip into the cloud bank and fled to the east. The No. 60 Squadron pair were disappointed that the enemy had escaped into the clouds but could not find the Albatros. The combat, of course, was listed as indecisive.[14]

The Royal Air Force Communiqué described 15 May 1918 as fine weather all day. While searching for enemy aircraft at ten thousand feet a little north of Villers Brétonneux, John S. Griffith suddenly observed an enemy observation plane pass over his head "about 300 feet above me going east. I zoomed up and fired about 200 rounds at 200 yards range." The enemy continued on to the east and Griffith "could not climb up to him." Once again, the American was required to describe the combat as indecisive even though he did inflict some damage on the enemy machine.[15]

The following day also dawned clear with good visibility and, at 8:45 A.M., Lts. Griffith and H. G. Hegarty, while cruising in the area south of Arras at two thousand feet, spotted two LVG observation planes and an Albatros Scout coming toward the Allied lines. Hegarty fired a short burst at the Albatros then joined Griffith in an attack on the LVG two-seater. The No. 60 Squadron pair fought the observation plane "for about 5 minutes till, when very close to the ground, he [the German pilot] put his nose down and crashed at Fampoux, turning over on his back with smoke coming from him." Griffith and Hegarty were credited with an enemy plane destroyed since the German crashed inside Allied lines.[16]

During the next several days, the Seattle youth was involved in minor combats with enemy aircraft, but in no case did he significantly damage one. On 18 May he was forced to return to his home airdrome because of engine trouble. On 5 June at 9:55 A.M., he attacked two enemy observation balloons southeast of Bapaume with Captain Duncan but did not notice the result of the combat. He then flew north to Arras and crossed enemy lines at four thousand feet,

> zig-zagging in the general direction of an enemy balloon which
> was at Cherisy. I was heavily "archied" on approaching the balloon

and observer jumped out in white parachute. I then fired about 150 rounds from a range of 200 yards. Pulling out I noticed balloon going down slowly and it looked to me as if it was deflating.

Because of intense fire from the ground, Griffith was not able to witness the actual destruction of the kite balloon but was credited with a "decisive driven down damaged" victim.[17]

During the next twenty-five days, young Griffith flew no less than sixteen missions over the front. On four occasions he participated in actual aerial combat. Unfortunately, all of the dogfights resulted in indecisive actions.[18] On most of these flights Griffith acted as patrol leader.

After over three weeks of frustration, John S. Griffith had a highly successful day on 1 July. The weather was fine, and visibility was excellent during the morning hours. At 8:40 A.M., while on an offensive patrol in the LaMotte area, he saw an enemy observation plane flying at a very low altitude. Griffith dived his SE-5A toward the enemy aircraft but lost it in the ground mist. He then noticed a silver-colored enemy balloon a short distance away and banked his fighter in that direction, opening fire with his Lewis gun's Buckingham ammunition. The German observer "jumped out and the balloon went down slowly and did not come up again." While climbing up from the heavy ground fire, he spotted an Albatros D-5 with silver wings some one thousand feet below. In Griffith's report he stated, "I dived to attack and fired two bursts at E.A. [enemy aircraft] from about 200 yards range from directly behind his tail. E.A.'s nose went down and he was diving vertically. I then pulled out owing to double feed and lost sight of E.A. in ground mist." Lieutenant Daley of No. 24 Squadron confirmed the Albatros crashed and phoned the report to wing headquarters. Both the silver-colored balloon and the enemy aircraft were confirmed as decisive kills.[19] These victories ran Lieutenant Griffith's score to eight and established him as one of the leading pilots in the squadron.

During the next seventeen days, Lieutenant Griffith flew no less than thirteen offensive patrol missions over the battle lines. At high noon on 2 July, Lieutenants Griffith and Whitney became engaged in combat with five blue-tailed Fokker D-7s at fifteen thousand feet over the village of Wiencourt. The enemy aircraft "were so well handled," according to Griffith, "that we could observe no decisive results."[20] Young Griffith had to land at No.

56 Squadron airdrome because of "over heating."[21] Two days later, Griffith led a patrol of six SE-5s in the vicinity of Marcelcave and engaged three Fokker D-7s "with bright blue fuselage, blue tail, speckled wings." The Seattle man "dived on one which was a little apart from the other two reserving my fire until within 100 yards range. I surprised the E.A. [enemy aircraft] and he did not attempt to get out of my line of fire. E.A.'s nose went down and I pulled up. On looking for E.A. I lost him beneath the clouds." No doubt the Fokker was heavily damaged but Griffith was unable to get a firm confirmation.[22]

On 7 July, Lieutenant Griffith became involved in two dogfights with German aircraft. At 10:55 A.M., he, along with Lieutenant Whitney, battled an Albatros two-seater for several minutes without decisive results. Approximately forty-five minutes later, while over Achiet Le Grand, he noticed a second two-seater below the cloud level and rolled his SE-5 over and dived on the observation plane, "surprising the E.A. and got short bursts from Lewis and Vickers on his tail at 100 yards range. E.A. turned several times with observer firing. I continually maneuvered on his tail firing short bursts. Engine of E.A. appeared to stop and he tried to land and turned over and crashed." This "kill" was confirmed by Allied anti-aircraft batteries and in Royal Air Force Communiqués.[23]

Due to a broken cam rod, Lieutenant Griffith had a forced landing on 8 July, and, one week later, he was forced to land at Izel-le-Hameau airdrome, due to an oil shortage in his plane. During the period 8 July to 18 July, he was engaged in three air combats with indecisive results. However, in all three battles, he managed to inflict damage on the enemy aircraft.[24] The commanding officer of No. 60 Squadron, on 8 July 1918, wrote a strong recommendation in behalf of Lt. John Sharpe Griffith in which he stated:

> He has at all times shown the greatest determination and gallantry. I particularly point out the height of his decisive combats which, in nearly every case, are not above 4000 feet and the manners in which he has pressed home his attacks cannot be too highly commended. On several occasions this officer has led his flight formation and always with great credit. He has fought a great number of engagements and has frequently returned with his machine shot about. Lieut. Griffith has been a splendid example of keenness to all.[25]

On 23 July 1918, Lieutentant Griffith was awarded the British Distinguished Flying Cross.[26]

While on patrol on the clear but windy 18 July 1918, Lt. John S. Griffith's SE-5A fighter was hit by anti-aircraft fire. He crashed near Fortel on the Allied side of the battle lines. Griffith was wounded and suffered a concussion as result of the crash. He was admitted to a hospital shortly after the disaster and did not return to active combat duty before the Armistice on 11 November 1918.[27]

Even though World War I had come to an end, Griffith was still involved in combat. He journeyed to Archangel to participate in the White Russian war against the Reds in the spring of 1919. Between 5 May 1919 and 24 July 1919, he carried out no less than forty bomb raids and reconnaissance missions. On 3 June he dived to within one hundred feet of the ground with a Sopwith Camel and destroyed an enemy balloon, as well as several of its attendants. For this action, he won a bar for his British DFC. The History of 60 Squadron RAF credits Griffith with the Russian Order of Grand Duke Vladimir and the Order of St. Stanislaus for his service in the Russian campaign. Following the Russian struggle, Griffith went to Egypt where he rose to the rank of captain.[28] Leaving the RAF in 1921, Griffith came home and joined the U.S. Army, "where a lack of Air Corps openings forced him briefly into the infantry."[29]

Griffith was able to work his way back into the Army Air Corps, and in 1929 he was to perform a spectacular record-smashing dawn-to-dusk flight from Kelly Field in San Antonio, Texas, to Seattle, Washington, in a Curtiss P-1 fighter. "At the 1931 Cleveland Air Races he led the Three Turtles," a stunt flying team. In 1934 he "accompanied General (then Colonel) Henry H. (Hap) Arnold from Washington, D.C. to Fairbanks, Alaska, on a mass flight of 10 bombers that brought international headlines." As a test pilot in 1936, Griffith flew an experimental plane when the engine caught fire. He managed to extinguish the fire and saved the lives of several passengers as well as the plane. For this action he was awarded the American DFC.[30]

During World War II, Griffith, now a colonel, in 1944 headed a military mission to the Soviet Union, which established air bases there for the bombing of targets in Germany.[31] Colonel Griffith retired from the U.S. Air Force in 1951, after a long and successful career. Most accounts credit Griffith with having shot down seven German aircraft and one observation balloon in the First World War.[32] Some sources credit him with seven planes shot down and two balloons destroyed. John Sharpe Griffith died on 14 October 1974 in Rivermead, Long Island, at the age of seventy-five. He was survived by his widow, Beatrice.

Capt. Eugene S. Coler (bottom left)
Courtesy S. K. Taylor

NINE

Capt. Eugene Seeley Coler

E ugene Seeley Coler was born on 13 January 1896 at 375 Park Avenue, New York City. At the time he enlisted in the Royal Flying Corps in Canada, he lived in Newark, New Jersey.[1] After several weeks of training, he was commissioned a second lieutenant and embarked for overseas on 29 October 1917. On arriving in England, he was given further flight training, and on 12 March 1918 he was posted to No. 11 Squadron, then based at Vert Galand some fifteen miles northeast of Amiens.[2]

At the time Lieutenant Coler joined No. 11 Squadron, it was flying the Bristol Fighter. Actually, No. 11 Squadron had the distinction of being the first British fighting squadron in France. It had started the war with Henri Farman and Vickers FB-5 planes early in 1915. In September 1915 the squadron was stationed at Villers Brétonneux from where a flight was detached to operate from Auchel airdrome during the battle of Loos. The work at Loos was very limited, owing to bad weather, and the flight rejoined the rest of the squadron at Villers Brétonneux as soon as the offensive stopped. The work from Villers Brétonneux consisted chiefly of long reconnaissances "over Ham, St. Quentin and Peronne about 30 miles over the lines, but these were rarely interfered with by enemy aircraft." No. 11 Squadron moved to Bertangles in November of 1915, and in early 1916 the unit moved to Savy, where it finally gave up its Vickers fighters and replaced them with DH-2s. At the end of the Somme campaign, the scouts were given to No. 60 Squadron, and No. 11 Squadron now operated with FEs, which proved ineffective. In May 1917 the FEs were replaced by Bristol Fighters.[3] One of the first Bristol pilots posted to No. 11 Squadron was Lt. A. E. McKeever, who quickly ran his victory score to thirty kills and was awarded the Distinguished Service Order and the Military Cross.[4] In November 1917 the squadron took a prominent role in the Cambrai offensive. The weather was terrible, and the Bristol Fighters were compelled to work with mist and clouds at about three hundred feet. Luckily, the "casualties were light and the results achieved excellent." Work during the next several months consisted mainly of long distance reconnaissance for the British Third Army. At this time Coler became a pilot in the outfit.[5]

During March, April, and May, No. 11 Squadron continued its long distance reconnaissance activity. The work was "interesting but not many Huns were encountered and the fighting spirit of the Squadron was not given much opportunity to show itself."[6] However, on 9 May, Lieutenant Coler and his observer, Lt. C. W. Gladman, while doing a reconnaissance mission a few miles south of Albert, became involved with some fourteen Pfalz scouts. In Coler's combat report he stated,

> I dived on one and fired a burst of 20 rounds at a range of 15 yards. E.A. went down in a vertical dive, side-slipping and stalling out of control, as my gun had a No. 4 stoppage I was unable to watch E.A. down to the ground. While rectifying this stoppage my observer engaged another E.A. that was slightly above and on my tail. After a burst of 50 rounds E.A. went down diving beyond the vertical. My observer watched him diving for about 6000 or 7000 feet, when I engaged another E.A. which was coming at me nose on. I opened fire at a range of about 50 yards, after a short burst E.A. immediately rolled over on his back and went down out of control side-slipping and diving.[7]

Lieutenant Coler was credited with two kills in this fight and Gladman with one by the squadron's commanding officer. Because of its great fire-power, the Bristol Fighter was beginning to establish itself as one of the best Royal Air Force combat planes of the First World War.

On 7 June 1918 two Bristol Fighters, piloted by Lts. E. S. Coler and N. B. Scott, spotted two enemy observation balloons in the Pelves and Fontaine area. Coler's observer, Lt. G. W. Gladman, fired a drum into one of these balloons, and it was seen going down in smoke. Lt. J. P. Y. Dickey, Scott's observer, sent the second balloon down in smoke. The balloon observers were apparently killed, for in neither case did they parachute from the burning balloons. Maj. W. E. Davey, No. 11 Squadron commander, confirmed both victories.[8]

With the Allied offensive in the Amiens sector, which began on 8 August 1918, the air war changed, and "the Huns with the newly introduced Fokker biplane D-7 became a serious factor again." Scarcely a day passed when large formations of enemy aircraft were engaged over the battle front. Even though the German squadrons were wary of attacking large Allied formations and "preferred to cut off stragglers,"[9] they, nonetheless, frequently were involved in tremendous dogfights.

At eight A.M. on 13 August, some five days after the Amiens offensive had gotten underway, Lt. Eugene S. Coler and Lt. G. W. Gladman, his observer, became involved in one of the fiercest dogfights of the war. Several Bristol Fighters from No. 11 Squadron were escorting a formation of DH-4s from No. 57 Squadron in the vicinity of Peronne when twenty Fokker D-7s appeared on the scene. The enemy fighters were flying north at different heights; Coler was not sure the No. 11 Squadron leader had seen them. He quickly fired a red flare and immediately dived on the enemy formation. Coler commented in his combat report, "I singled out a Fokker biplane with a red nose and yellow fuselage. At a range of about 10 yards I fired a short burst from both Vickers & Lewis guns (the latter being fitted on the top center section) E.A. burst into one huge sheet of flame." Lieutenant Coler then attacked another Fokker and fired a short burst before the enemy machine went down in a dive out of control. The American then had to level out in order to correct a stoppage in his Vickers guns:

> Meanwhile numerous [enemy Fokkers] got on my tail and my observer Lieut. Gladman put a burst into one which turned over on its back and went down vertically. By this time I was surrounded by Fokker biplanes on all sides one of them crossed my front at about 50 yards distance. I immediately fired a burst of about 60 rounds and this E.A. emitted clouds of black smoke and burst into flames.[10]

Shortly afterwards, another Fokker got on the tail of the Brisfit and wounded Lieutenant Gladman in the right shoulder while he was changing an ammunition drum. Gladman "immediately recovered and maneuvering the Lewis gun with his left arm he managed to fire a drum into this [enemy aircraft] at very close range. E.A. fell into a vertical side-slip and was noticed by both of us to burst into flames." In this blazing air battle, Lieutenant

71

Coler was credited with three victories, and his observer was confirmed as having made two other "kills."[11] Indeed, very few individuals were to score such a success in a single air combat during the war. This episode moved Coler into the ace category.

Late in the afternoon on 30 August, No. 11 Squadron braved a cloudy situation while escorting a formation of DH-4 bombing planes from No. 57 Squadron. A short distance northeast of Havrincourt Wood, the Bristol Fighter pilots saw four formations of enemy scouts flying from almost every direction and at various heights. The Bristol Fighters quickly dived on some eighteen enemy machines while they attacked the DH-4s. Lt. Eugene S. Coler singled out

> a Fokker biplane with a red nose and yellow body who was coming towards me. I then put in a burst of about 30 rounds at 100 yards range. E.A. did a kind of half roll underneath me and tried to get on my tail. I immediately did a short Immelman turn and got on the E.A.'s tail. After a burst of about 70 rounds E.A. went down in a vertical dive emitting thick clouds of black smoke.

Coler then did a sharp climbing turn and got underneath a Pfalz Scout "with a yellow nose and tail and black fuselage." After he fired approximately one hundred rounds of machine-gun bullets into the enemy plane, it went down and "appeared to break up, being last seen in a very flat spin."[12] This marked Coler's seventh victory since joining No. 11 Squadron.

In the Royal Air Force communiqúe the weather on 6 September was described as "fair," but there was strong wind and, in some areas, low clouds. Relatively little air activity took place on that miserable day. However, during the late morning, Coler and Lt. D. P. Conyngham, his observer, ventured into the sky on a reconnaissance mission. While circling over Cambrai they were attacked by several Fokker D-7s. In Coler's words,

> The first thing I noticed was a Bristol Fighter diving with 2 E.A. on his tail. I immediately went down on these E.A. opening fire at the one nearest to the Bristol. This one dived away. I then put a long burst from my Vickers gun into the other E.A. which immediately went down in a vertical dive and crashed into a house in the western outskirts of Cambrai.

Almost at the same time, Coler and Conyngham were attacked from below by three Fokkers. The observer fired a burst into one which "went down completely out of control, falling from side to side with its tail down."[13] Coler, now a captain and a flight leader, had pushed his victory total to eight.

The week of 9–15 September saw air activity somewhat restricted by rain and low clouds. Nonetheless, the RAF officially claimed eighty-two enemy aircraft brought down and some twenty-nine others driven down out of control. In addition, five enemy observation balloons were destroyed. Thirty-seven of the RAF's own planes were missing. On 15 September, a fine weather day, Capt. E. S. Coler and his observer, 2nd Lt. E. J. Corbett, were on reconnaissance when they were "attacked by five Fokker biplanes, one of which was shot down by the observer. On the return journey Capt. Coler dived on another Fokker which was also brought down."[14] On returning to No. 11 Squadron's home airdrome, Captain Coler received considerable attention; he was now one of the unit's top air aces.

Early on the morning of 16 September, Captain Coler and Lieutenant Corbett took off for a reconnaissance mission, a little east of Cambrai. At 8:30 A.M., while flying at eighteen thousand feet, they were attacked "from behind by about 25 to 30 Fokker biplanes and Pfalz scouts." Coler quickly turned east to assist another RAF machine under attack from behind. In his combat report he wrote,

I fired a short burst into one machine at close range, but was unable to observe the results as I was then attacked by six or seven Fokker biplanes. My rear patrol tank was pierced and my Aileron controls shot away, so I went into a vertical dive with engine full on. I pulled out at about 1000 feet over Cambrai, and a Pfalz scout and a Fokker biplane which had followed me down, overshot me in their dive. I gave the Pfalz a burst from both guns at very close range. He immediately burst into flames and fell in the streets of Cambrai. By this time the Fokker biplane had got on my tail and my observer fired about 4 drums into him. He crashed about half way between Cambrai and the line.

By this time, Coler's Bristol Fighter was down to five hundred feet and receiving heavy ground fire. Coler now crossed the battle lines at 150 feet near the village of Marquion but his engine had quit and "the machine suddenly fell out of control, but I managed to do a slow sideslip and crashed."[15] Captain Coler was wounded and was removed from No. 11 Squadron. On 20 September he was returned to a hospital in England.[16] He was awarded the British Distinguished Flying Cross for his performance on 13 August when he and his observer shot down five enemy aircraft in a single air combat. According to the citation, "Capt. Coler was bold in attack and skillful in maneuver, he never hesitated to engage the enemy regardless of disparity in numbers." [17]

According to most studies, Capt. E. S. Coler scored ten confirmed victories during his seven months with No. 11 Squadron. However, Bruce Robertson's *Air Aces of the 1914–1918 War* lists him as having twelve kills. Whatever the score, Captain Coler was one of the top American aces who flew only with the Royal Air Force during the First World War. During World War II, Coler served in the medical branch of the U.S. Army Air Force.

Lt. William C. Lambert
Courtesy W. C. Lambert

TEN

Lt. William Carpenter Lambert

William Carpenter Lambert, the son of William G. and Mary Pierce Lambert, was born in Ironton, Ohio, on 18 August 1894.[1] When he was only fifteen years old, a pilot flying a "Wright Flyer" visited Ironton for the Fourth of July celebration. From that moment on, Bill Lambert became fascinated with the airplane. When the Wright Flyer's pilot prepared to leave the Ohio town, the frail engine refused to operate. For the next several days young Lambert ran errands for the pilot and was accepted as a good friend. When the pilot finally was able to get the engine to function properly and was ready to leave, "he rewarded the fifteen-year-old with a five minute ride. Soaring above the Ohio River and the small river town, young Lambert fell in love with flight—a love that was to change his entire life."[2]

Upon graduating from Ironton High School, he traveled to Buffalo, New York, where he obtained a job as a chemist in the Lackawana Steel Company. At a nearby flying school, he became acquainted with several pilots and occasionally managed to hitch an airplane ride. Despite the fact Lambert was very efficient as a chemist at the Lackawana Steel Company, he was very interested in participating in the war. In 1915 he traveled to Canada with the intention of enlisting in the artillery. When the Canadian recruiting officer learned Lambert had been working in a laboratory, he offered the young American a job as a chemist in a high explosive ammunition plant at Nobel, Ontario. Since the pay "was twice what he was making at Buffalo and the hours were much less, Lambert accepted."[3]

The Ironton, Ohio, boy worked at the Canadian ammunition

plant, some two hundred miles north of Toronto, until the fall of 1916 when he read in a newspaper that the Royal Flying Corps was establishing a program to recruit and train pilots in Canada. He immediately went to Toronto for "an interview, was accepted and signed up."[4] On reporting for duty in early 1917, he was sent to ground school at the University of Toronto. Following the completion of his ground school training, he began his flight training in the "Canuck," the Canadian version of the JN-4 "Jenny," at Long Branch, Camp Borden, Mohawk, and Rathbone. After completing his flight training in the early autumn of 1917, he was then assigned as a flying instructor at Deseronto for approximately one month. Lambert then received his overseas orders and arrived in England in December of 1917.[5]

Lambert was first sent to Stockbridge outside London, where he trained on Avro 504s, Sopwith Pups, Sopwith Camels, and Spads. These were "war machines," but the airplane which won his heart was the SE-5A. In his view, the SE-5A was far superior to anything he had ever flown. During his training in this plane, he put it through its paces and "so impressed those on the ground with his skill that he was later asked to demonstrate it for a visiting general."[6]

Upon completion of his advanced flight training at Stockbridge, he was on 9 March 1918 transferred to Turnberry, Scotland, for gunnery training. Unfortunately, it was raining when he reached Turnberry; the rain continued for the next five days. Because of heavy combat losses, No. 24 Squadron, operating on the British battle front, requested four pilot replacements, and Lieutenant Lambert was immediately sent to France without gunnery instruction. He and three other pilots were posted to No. 24 Squadron on 16 March 1918. This assignment was a pleasing one for Lambert, for No. 24 Squadron was flying the SE-5A, the airplane he most wanted to fly in combat. Young Lambert was assigned to "C" flight, then commanded by Capt. G. E. H. McElroy, one of the ranking Royal Flying Corps aces of the war.[7] According to Lambert,

> George McElroy, without a doubt, was one of the most fearless men I have ever met. He was also most considerate of the pilots under him and at all times tried to keep his pilots out of trouble. He would not allow me to go out until he felt I was ready and I think I owe my survival to his teaching.[8]

Lieutenant Lambert did four or five combat patrols with McElroy before the latter transferred to No. 40 Squadron. McElroy, the forty-six-victory ace, was killed on 31 July 1918.[9]

No. 24 Squadron had been in active service on the western front since early 1916. It was, indeed, one of the first fully-equipped single-seat fighter squadrons to participate in the great air battle with the "Fokker Scourge" and such top German aces as Max Immelmann and Oswald Boelcke. The No. 24 Squadron fought its early air battles with the DH-2 pusher pursuit plane, then the fastest scout-type aircraft in the Royal Flying Corp. The DH-2 and the squadron's commanding officer, Maj. Lanoe G. Hawker, brought real success to the unit in its early days in combat. Hawker won the Victoria Cross, but on 23 November 1916 he was killed by the "Red Baron," Manfred von Richthofen, becoming his tenth "kill" of the war. In May of 1917 No. 24 Squadron was reequipped with the DH-5 aircraft. Unfortunately, this machine did not live up to expectations, and, in late December of 1917, the outfit was given SE-5A fighters, the aircraft many pilots believed to be the best plane of the war.[10]

Shortly after Lieutenant Lambert was posted to No. 24 Squadron, the Germans launched a massive offensive along the Somme River front. Consequently, the squadron was forced to move from Matigny, to Moreuil, to Bertangles, and finally to the airdrome at Conteville-sur-Somme near the city of Abbeville. During the first two weeks of Lambert's assignment, he received ground duty and did not get to fly.[11]

Since William Lambert had not been able to train at the gunnery range at Turnberry, Scotland, his first flights with No. 24 Squadron consisted of gunnery practice at ground targets. On 1 April, the day the RFC and RNAS combined to create the Royal Air Force, Bill Lambert flew his first combat mission along with McElroy and three other pilots.[12] During this mission, on a bright, sunny day, McElroy shot down one enemy aircraft. Like most newcomers, young Lambert did not see the three other German machines involved in the dogfight.[13] During the next several days, McElroy, "C" Flight commander, took Lambert and other new pilots over the battle front on familiarization patrols.[14]

On 7 April 1918, Lambert scored his first aerial victory when he got separated from his No. 24 Squadron teammates and ended up in the middle of a group of German fighters. The Ohio boy had "to fight with all his skill to escape with his life."[15] As he wrote in his log book,

> I was completely surrounded by huge black crosses. Scared! I was paralyzed with fear. Four Albatros and two Pfalz fighters. I gave B-79 [his SE-5] everything she could take, kicked the rudder bar right and left, shut my eyes, fired both guns and trusted to luck. I finally chanced a look around and saw one Albatros falling off to the right with smoke trailing behind.[16]

An RAF Bristol Fighter pilot confirmed Lambert's victory, and members of his own "C" Flight also witnessed the performance, saying "you made the damnedest maneuver that we ever saw anybody do in an airplane."[17]

For the next several days, rain, ground fog, and mist greatly impaired air combat activity in the Somme area. On 12 April the weather was clear, and "C" Flight, now commanded by Capt. G. O. Johnson, McElroy's replacement, became involved with a large number of Albatros and Pfalz machines. Lambert became engaged in a duel with an Albatros which had cut across in front of him: "I pressed the button and could see my bullets spattering the fuselage under and slightly behind his seat. I know I had hit the pilot who then did a very strange thing. He turned and opened fire at me from the left side, fell into a dive then spun into the ground."[18]

A second Albatros attacked Lambert, but the American managed to out-turn the German and shot off the enemy's right aileron. The German landed in a nearby field without further damage.[19] During the wild dogfight, no less than eight enemy aircraft were shot down, and several were damaged. No. 24 Squadron lost no planes, but most of those that participated in the fight suffered some damage.[20]

In the next few days, the weather over the western front remained poor. Nonetheless, pilots of No. 24 Squadron plus fliers from several other units continued low bombing and ground strafing activities in an effort to stop the German drive in the Somme area. Fortunately, the weather on 21 April turned out to be nearly perfect. Pilots of No. 24 Squadron spent much of the day searching for and shooting up enemy observation balloons. Because much of this combat activity occurred in the territory patrolled by Richthofen's *Jagdgeschwader I*, RAF pilots were constantly on the alert. What the No. 24 Squadron pilots didn't know was that the Red Baron had been shot down and killed a little earlier in the day.[21] Capt. G. O. Johnson and Lieutenant Lambert fired on an enemy kite balloon and watched it being pulled down in a smoking condition. Unfortunately, this victim was not confirmed in the Royal Air Force Communiqué.[22]

During the last week of April, rain, ground fog, and low clouds complicated No. 24 Squadron's combat efforts in the Roye, Albert, Villers Brétonneux area. However, the pilots armed with small bombs and machine-gun ammunition continued their low-level attacks on the German infantry and artillery units. Capt. I. D. R. McDonald of "A" Flight did manage to shoot down a Pfalz scout during this period.[23]

According to Lambert, the terrible weather continued on into May. There were "low clouds and heavy mist everywhere." The German offensive had been underway since 21 March 1918 and, by early May, "the strength of the Germans had just about spent itself. The drive slowed down but was not over. Their leaders were a stubborn lot. The plan had been to drive a wedge between the British V Army. . . . and the French to the South. . . ." The RAF squadrons were instructed to bomb and strafe everything from low altitude in order to stop the enemy's drive. Of course, this type of combat was extremely dangerous, and most fighter pilots prayed for the day they could get back to air-to-air combat.[24] Indeed, a chill ran up Lieutenant Lambert's spine when he performed the dangerous task of "trench strafing."[25]

On 4 May six No. 24 Squadron pilots challenged seven Pfalz and six Fokker triplanes at eight thousand feet over Bray, a small town on the Somme River. Capt. G. O. Johnson, "C" Flight commander, managed to send one of the Fokkers down out of control. Lambert "with another S.E. dived on one of 4 Pfalz over Meziere at 6:45 [P.M.] at 5000 feet. Lt. Lambert fired 25 rounds at 150 yards range simultaneously with the other S.E. and the Pfalz was seen to spin down and was lost sight of at about 800 feet."[26] The Royal Air Force Communiqué did not mention this victory. Nonetheless, No. 24 Squadron gave Lambert credit for his third victory on this occasion.

Late on a hazy afternoon five days later, eleven SE-5A pilots intercepted some eight enemy planes at ten thousand feet over the town of Hangard. In the swirling dogfight, three of the German planes were shot down and several others were heavily damaged. Lts. T. T. B. Hellett and William Lambert dived on an enemy aircraft:

> firing 160 rounds and 100 rounds respectively from 200 to 25 yards range. The E.A. spun away starting at 5000 feet and was seen down almost to the ground by Lt. Hellett, and seen to crash in a field in the open by Lt. [J. A. E. R.] Daley. Lt. Lambert was then attacked from below and got on the E.A.'s tail firing 70 rounds without effect.[27]

Lambert had now run his victory total to three and one-half victories and greatly increased his prestige in "C" Flight.

For the next six days, the weather over the Somme sector continued to be misty, foggy, with low heavy clouds. On 16 May the weather was fine all day, and enemy aircraft were active over the whole area. Five "C" Flight pilots, while escorting DH-4s, engaged five Albatros D-5 at eight thousand feet over Warfusee at 11:30 A.M. In the dogfight, Lieutenant Lambert "fired 70 rounds from 300 to 75 yards range on an E.A.'s tail. Another E.A. fired on Lt. Lambert but his first spun away." Neither side lost a plane in the battle, but at least four of the Germans were damaged and turned toward their home base.[28]

On the following day, "C" Flight performed an offensive patrol early in the morning in the area north of the Somme River. During this mission, Lieutenant Lambert's SE-5A developed engine problems, and he was forced to glide back toward his home airdrome at Conteville. Due to a heavy gust of wind, he had to land in an open field a few hundred yards from his air base. He made a perfect landing, but the plane ran into a small ditch and nosed over. In his words, "after a perfect landing, we were upside down. . . . after loosening my belt, I had fallen to the ground from the upside down cockpit. Nothing was hurt but my pride. Nor was there any serious damage to 1082 [his plane] but her propeller was gone and there was a slight bend in her rudder." Fortunately, the machine was not seriously damaged and was back in flying condition in a day or two.[29] On 19 May 1918, Lambert, flying a new SE-5A, was involved in an offensive patrol late in the afternoon and "fired 30 rounds at a German Pfalz which was attacking a DH.9. The E.A. cleared off." The No. 24 Squadron patrol scored some eight indecisive hits and forced one of the enemy machines to land, but achieved no "kills."[30]

Thirteen pilots from No. 24 Squadron took off on an early morning mission on 20 May, escorting DH-4 bombers. In the vicinity of Chaulnes-Albert, at 8:30 A.M., the SE-5A flyers engaged ten Pfalz scouts, three two-seaters, and two enemy kite balloons. Lambert fired fifty rounds into a "Pfalz at about 25 yards range. The E.A. fell over and dived vertically for 2000 feet, after which it began to spin slowly and was last seen spinning rapidly about 5000 feet down." No. 24 Squadron credited Lambert with shooting the plane down. Two other German planes were listed as being shot down out of control and two balloons were considered driven down. Lt. R. T. Marks of No. 24 Squadron suffered heavy damage, crash landed, and burst into flames.[31] On the following morning, Lambert and five other pilots from No. 24 Squadron attacked three DFWs at twenty-five hundred feet over the town of Warfusee. One of the enemy planes was forced to land, but young Lambert, although he fired thirty rounds into the fuselage of one of the two-seaters, received no credit for the damaged machine.[32]

In a wild dogfight on 28 May, Lambert drove an enemy aircraft off of the tail of his friend, Lt. J. A. E. R. Daley, and, a few minutes later, saved Lt. J. Palmer by firing twenty rounds into an attacking German fighter. In neither case was he credited with a victory. Nonetheless, he was warmly congratulated by the No. 24 Squadron pilots involved.[33]

On the last day of the month, Lambert was once again engaged, along with seven other No. 24 Squadron pilots, in a dogfight with nine German machines in the locality of Moreuil. Several of the enemy were damaged in the combat, but no "kills" were recorded on either side.[34]

On 1 June at 8:45 A.M., "C" Flight, led by Capt. G. O. Johnson ran into one LVG and one DFW at ten thousand feet over Aubicourt. Lambert, at first, "mistook the L.V.G. two-seater for a Frenchman until the observer opened fire. Lt. Lambert then dived firing 20 rounds without effect." Shortly after this action, Lambert, Johnson, and two other members of "C" Flight attacked a German observation balloon at six thousand feet. The balloon was pulled down to one thousand feet, but did not catch fire. Consequently, no RAF pilot received credit for destruction of the balloon. The two-seater aircraft were driven off but, apparently, were not seriously damaged.[35] Late in the afternoon of the same day, five pilots from No. 24 Squadron, while on an offensive patrol, became engaged with some twenty Albatros D-5s and Pfalz

Scouts. According to the combat report written that night, "our patrol saw the E.A. climbing to the DH-9s so dived on a formation of 8. Capt. McDonald fired 25 rounds, Capt. Lowe 100, Lt. Dawe 40, Lt. Crossen 30, Lt. Lambert 200, all at fairly long range, as the E.A. all at once dived east out of range. Lt. Lambert saw his adversary land." Although eight of the enemy machines were considered to have been driven down and one forced to land, the Royal Air Force Communiqué for the day did not credit No. 24 Squadron pilots with a kill. Still, the squadron credited Lambert with having driven down one aircraft.[36]

The next day dawned bright and clear with good visibility and, late in the morning, some nine No. 24 Squadron pilots took off from Conteville Airdrome on an offensive patrol. At approximately 11:15 A.M., the patrol, made up of pilots from all three flights, intercepted a dozen enemy aircraft near the battle lines. Lambert was attacked by two scouts and fired fifty rounds at one "which dived away and then fired 200 rounds at a second at 20 yards range, after getting on his tail, following down to 5000 feet from 13,000 feet. At 8000 feet he started to spin and crashed near Davinscourt. This E.A. was brown with a blue tail."[37] According to the No. 24 Squadron record book, this enemy machine was a Fokker biplane.[38] Lieutenant Daley and Captain MacDonald sent enemy machines crashing to the earth in the same dogfight, while eight other German planes were damaged, but they were listed as indecisive.[39] Lieutenant Lambert's SE-5A was damaged during the combat but was repaired in time for the next day's activities.[40]

Although Lt. William C. Lambert made several offensive patrols and escort missions during the next several days, it was not until 5 June that he was again involved in a real air battle. Five pilots from "C" Flight, led by Captain Johnson, dived on three new type LVG two-seaters at seven thousand feet over the town of Mézières. Lts. Lambert and W. Selwyn fired fifty and forty rounds respectively into one of the German planes at long range and watched it diving to the east "almost on the ground."[41] The combat report listed this enemy machine as damaged but indecisive.

The weather on 15 June was cloudy, but with fair visibility. Lambert spent the late morning hour as a "balloon sentry" in the Warfusee area. At 11:35 A.M., three Albatros D-5s dived on him.

He managed to out-maneuver the attackers and got on the tail of one of the enemy machines. Lambert followed the Albatros for some "5000 feet, firing 100 rounds at 200 to 40 yards range, and coming out below the clouds. The E.A. went into a spin and was last seen in a slow spiral at 2000 feet as though about to land near Demuin." The German was considered "drive down damaged."[42]

The weather on 16 June was variable—"some rain, fair intervals" with considerable activity on the French battle lines and north of the British front. Once again, "C" Flight from No. 24 Squadron attempted an offensive patrol in the early morning. Unfortunately, the heavy clouds kept the five-plane patrol at approximately one thousand feet. Captain Johnson, the flight leader, attacked two DFW observation planes and fired one hundred rounds. The other pilots in the patrol got in a few rounds, but the Germans managed to flee to the east at fifty or one hundred feet. No victories were scored.[43]

The following day proved to be a real air battle. Between 11:50 A.M. and 1:50 P.M., no less than ten SE-5A pilots from No. 24 Squadron became involved in combat with approximately the same number of Fokker D-7s. Lambert, the Ironton, Ohio boy

> had a long fight with one of them firing 100 to 150 rounds, until the right side of the tail doubled up and he went into a spin. Lt. Lambert then had a fight with another E.A. firing 200 rounds. The E.A. emitted a puff of blue black smoke and went down in a vertical nose dive, ending in a spin smoking heavily. Lt. Lambert then had an indecisive fight with a third E.A.

Lambert was credited with two victories in the dogfight. The other pilots in his patrol inflicted heavy damage on some half dozen other enemy aircraft and two No. 24 Squadron pilots had forced landings as a result of the air duel.[44]

Capt. G. O. Johnson was transferred out of No. 24 Squadron on 19 June and was replaced as "C" Flight commander by Capt. W. Selwyn. On 25 June, on an overcast and poor visibility day, a mixed group from all three flights of No. 24 Squadron engaged some twelve Fokker biplanes and triplanes and a couple of two-seaters at fifteen thousand feet. Two of the enemy were knocked down, and two others were driven down in a damaged state. Lieutenant Lambert "drove a Fokker biplane down in a spin and was then attacked by a triplane which he turned on and fired 80 rounds."[45] Lambert, however, was not credited with a victory in the combat report, while other sources give him credit for a plane driven down.[46]

Two days later, on a clear and sunny day, eight No. 24 Squadron pilots led by Captain Selwyn flew a late afternoon offensive patrol and ran into fourteen Fokker D-7s, Triplanes, and Albatros D-5s in the vicinity of the town of Chippilly. Lambert "got on the tail of a blue D.V. diving down, and opened fire at 50 yards getting to point blank range firing 70 rounds. The pilot was seen to fall forward and after Lt. Lambert pulled out he saw him spinning." Young Lambert then turned sharply and got on the tail of a second plane, firing ten rounds without effect. No. 24 Squadron managed to shoot down three German machines out of control and damaged several others. Lambert was credited with sending one plane down out of control for his eleventh victory, according to the squadron's record book.[47]

On 29 June, a rather poor visibility day, four No. 24 Squadron fighter pilots attacked some ten Fokker D-7s and Fokker Triplanes at fifteen thousand feet over Rosieres. In the wild dogfight, Captain Selwyn shot one down out of control, Lieutenant Daley sent one down in flames, and William Lambert fired seventy-five rounds into an Albatros that crashed near the town of Rosieres. He also bounced a Fokker biplane lagging behind the others and fired some fifty rounds into the enemy machine. The German aircraft, however, was not fatally damaged and dived away toward the German lines. According to squadron records, this combat ran Lambert's score to thirteen "kills" for the three months he had been in combat.[48]

"C" Flight, under the leadership of Captain Selwyn, became involved in a dogfight with several Albatros D-5s and Fokker D-7s on 30 June. Although Lt. W. C. Lambert managed to fire on two or three of the enemy machines, he was not able to shoot one down. When his Lewis gun ran out of ammunition, he pulled it down to change the drum. In his words, "as I lift it off I swing my arm out too far. The wind catches it broad-side, slaps my right arm down hard on the rear of the cockpit, jerks the drum out of my hand and sends it sailing off to the rear. For some seconds I think my arm is broken as I have no feeling in my hand or arm." Fortunately, things returned to normal, and he was able to reload the gun and continue in the combat.[49]

Perhaps William Lambert's greatest day in air combat occurred on 4 July 1918 when ten No. 24 Squadron pilots staged an offensive patrol and then attacked ground targets near Warfusee. Combats on a large scale took place between the No. 24 Squadron fliers and twenty hostile machines, consisting of fourteen Fokker D-7s, two Pfalz Scouts, and four Albatros D-5s. One enemy aircraft was brought down by Captain Selwyn and two by Lieutenant Lambert, while one other was driven down out of control. The No. 24 Squadron combat report stated

while Lt. Lambert was attacking ground targets near Bayonvillers at 9:00 A.M., 3 Fokker biplanes appeared. He half rolled on the tail of one firing 100 rounds at 40 yards range. The enemy aircraft did one turn of a spin and crashed. . . . Lt. Lambert zoomed on the tail of the third and fired a single shot and got a number stoppage. The E.A. zig-zagged down steeply and crashed. . . .

In addition, No. 24 Squadron pilots listed ten enemy machines as damaged. The Royal Air Force Communiqué indicated "all our machines returned undamaged."[50] The Ironton, Ohio, pilot had now run his victory total to fifteen.

Shortly after his 4 July success, Lambert was given a leave. During the next sixteen days, the Ohio boy, along with three or four other pilots, "lived it up" in London. During this period, Lambert had downed some twelve enemy aircraft and was notified that he had won the British Distinguished Flying Cross, which was to be awarded by King George V at Buckingham Palace.[51] "Not wishing to expose himself to a nerve-racking experience because of the presence of British royalty, Lambert simply did not show up. But, he only delayed the inevitable. Upon arriving at the British Embassy in 1919 he was presented the award by the Prince of Wales."[52]

On arriving back with No. 24 Squadron, still based at Conteville, Lambert was stunned to learn his good friend Lieutenant Daley "had a bad accidental crash on July 7 and died in the hospital the next day."[53] He also learned that Maj. "Mick" Mannock, the top British ace, was reported missing on 26 July and his ex-flight commander, George McElroy, had been killed on 31 July.[54]

Despite his depression over the losses during his leave, Lambert and Lt. H. L. Bair, an American who had joined No. 24 Squadron in early July, flew an aerial sentry operation over Aubigny in the late afternoon of 1 August. As the pair reached the lines, they saw five enemy aircraft shoot down four kite balloons. "They were however at 12,000 feet over Amiens and could not get within fighting distances so fired 75 & 50 rounds each at long range but did not observe any result except that the E.A. were diving East." Although Lambert and Bair were not able to inflict damage on the Fokker D-7s, they did manage to drive them away from the Allied balloon line.[55]

At approximately eleven A.M. on 4 August, a rainy and low clouds type of day, seven aviators from No. 24 Squadron engaged some ten enemy aircraft at three thousand feet over the Somme River. During the swirling air combat, Bill Lambert made three dives on an LVG two-seater and fired two hundred rounds. "After the last attack the E.A. went down spinning slowly and crashed in the water. . . . A Fokker biplane then came up and attacked Lt. Lambert. After a short fight in which he [Lambert] fired 200 rounds the E.A. went down and landed intact in a field. . . ." During the murky poor visibility combat, No. 24 Squadron managed to crash two German machines, sent one down out of control, forced one to land damaged, and drove down two observation balloons. Lambert was credited with having "crashed" one plane and forced another to land in a damaged state.[56]

The next two days were stormy with low clouds and considerable rain. Consequently, there was little air activity on either side. On 7 August, the weather improved, but ground mist prevailed, and, on the whole, visibility was poor. Despite this weather condition, Lambert was sent out on an "aerial sentry" mission in the Warfusee area. At 1:15 P.M., he spotted a DFW observation plane and immediately attacked it firing some fifteen rounds and "silencing the observer." The Ohio boy got in two more dives on the enemy machine firing one hundred rounds, "but had to break off on account of engine trouble." The DFW then escaped by diving toward its home base. Needless to say, Lambert was disappointed in the results of the combat; he felt, with the observer out of action, he would have no difficulty in destroying the German machine.[57]

The big French-British offensive in the Amiens area got underway on 8 August. In spite of the mist and fog during the early morning hours, Allied planes were very active in strafing and dive-bombing of the retreating German infantry. Lambert, along with most other pilots from his squadron, spent most of the day attacking ground targets. At 11:25 A.M. Lieutenant Lambert spotted an enemy kite balloon at five hundred feet and, in two dives, immediately fired seventy-five rounds at close range. The balloon "went down to the ground in a deflated condition and remained there." The No. 24 Squadron listed this as a "decisive" victory for the American pilot.[58]

A little later in the day, while Lambert was trying to warn an Allied convoy that was pushing into a German ambush, an enemy soldier rose up from a trench and fired at him. The bullet punctured the SE-5A's fuel tank. Gasoline began spewing back, soaking Lambert. Because of the great danger of fire, the Ohio man "cut his ignition and looked for a place to land. He selected a field that at takeoff time had been British. Unfortunately, it had been taken by the Germans." After landing, Lambert suddenly spotted several enemy soldiers running toward his plane. He quickly pulled out his service revolver and fired at the approaching Germans. One soldier grabbed at his stomach and fell to the ground. Despite being soaked with the volatile fuel, he noticed that his prop was still turning and immediately flipped his ignition switch on. The engine started, and he pushed the throttle forward and took off:

> But while only 100 feet in the air, the S.E.5a was hit once again by ground fire and the engine stopped. Lambert barely made it across the lines. Because of his low altitude, he did not have time to select a choice landing site. As a result, he landed among shell holes and tore off the landing gear. As the S.E.5a skidded to a stop on its belly, Lambert jumped out and ran.

A few moments later, he returned to the plane and pulled its clock from the instrument panel. Since he was now in British territory, he managed to escape.[59]

On 9 August the German Air Force was able to shift considerable air reinforcements into the Amiens-Somme sector. After heavy ground target activity in the morning hours Lts. T. T. B. Hellett and W. C. Lambert became involved in air combat with several Fokker D-7s and Pfalz D-3s, who were attacking RAF DH-4 bombing planes. Both No. 24 Squadron pilots managed to get in several rounds on the attackers, and one of Lambert's foes "went down as though to land." Results of the combat were considered indecisive.[60]

The morning of 10 August dawned with a few clouds but with

good visibility. Eight pilots, led by Capt. T. F. Hazell, an individual who would score forty-one victories before the war was over, took off from Conteville on an offensive patrol over the rapidly changing battlefront. While flying at twenty-five hundred feet at 1:50 P.M., the No. 24 Squadron fliers spotted approximately fifteen enemy pursuit and observation planes. A general dogfight took place, and for a few minutes it was a flaming chaos. Lieutenant Lambert

> got onto a Fokker biplane at 500 feet near Fouquescourt and fired 80 rounds at 100 to 50 yards range. This E.A. went down in a spin and was last seen practically on the ground spinning. Lt. Lambert at this point saw several others above but could not reach them but attacked a Hannoveranner or Halberstadt firing 150 rounds vertical. This E.A. crashed N.E. of Parvillers.

In the air battle, No. 24 Squadron was credited with two down out of control and three others crashed or down in flames. Lambert was credited with one down out of control and one crashed, making him one of the top pilots in the outfit.[61] Earlier in the day, he had shared an enemy "kill" with three other No. 24 Squadron pilots.[62]

The Allied drive that began on 8 August was successful in pushing the German army back several miles. Because of this, No. 24 Squadron, on 13–14 August, changed their home base from Conteville, where they had spent the last five months, to Bertangles. The move placed the squadron much closer to the battle lines.[63]

After nearly five months of almost daily air fighting, Lt. William C. Lambert was suffering from "combat fatigue." While on a mission on 19 August 1918, Lambert became lost and ended up landing at a French airdrome. It was noon, and he was invited to join the French pilots for lunch. "Although he asked for water with his meal, he was served red and white wine instead. By 2:30 P.M. he was feeling the effects of the heady substitute. Somehow he was able to get his S.E.5a off the ground" and back to his home airdrome. Shortly after returning to the No. 24 Squadron base, "Lambert discovered he was bleeding from one of his ears. He was sent immediately to a British General Hospital at Dieppe and then transferred to a hospital in London. Because he was in a coma practically all the time, he never learned what his illness was or what caused his condition."[64] Very likely the reason for the ruptured ear drum was the extreme changes in altitude to which he was constantly subjected in air combat. For whatever reasons, his air combat days were over, and in November 1918 he was allowed to return to Ironton, Ohio, to recuperate. When the war ended on 11 November, Lambert decided there was no use to return to England. "Strangely the RAF did not object," and he continued to draw his military pay until September 1921 when he was finally released.[65]

In 1919 Lambert became a "barnstormer" flying Curtiss JN-4 "Jennies" around the country, especially in the midwest and in the south.[66] However, in December of 1920, he married Chlo Ann Hall of Ashland, Kentucky. She immediately "grounded" him and indicated that she did not want him to fly anymore, and they settled down in Ironton, Ohio. In 1922 he bought into an automobile dealership—a business he was to run until 1932. After the state of Ohio constructed an overpass in Ironton's west end and disrupted Lambert's automobile business, he went into the refrigeration business. During the period between the two World Wars, he served in the Air Corp Reserve. When World War II broke out, he planned to join the Royal Canadian Air Force, but when he was not offered the rank he wanted he declined to join. In September 1942 he was called to active duty as a captain by the U.S. Army Air Corp. "Not able to qualify for flying, he was assigned as engineering officer at Rome Air Base, N.Y. . . . He tried hard, but never got an overseas assignment." He rose to the rank of major and was released from active duty in August 1946. "Returning to civilian life, Lambert remained in the Air Force Reserve until August 18, 1954 when he retired at the age of 60 as a lieutenant colonel."[67] Lambert died in his hometown of Ironton, Ohio, on 19 March 1982 at the age of eighty-seven.

Certainly William Carpenter Lambert was one of the top American fighter aces of the First World War, but there has been much confusion as to how many victories he really achieved. According to *Air Force Magazine*, he was credited with twenty-two official kills. Glasebrook's *American Aviators in the Great War, 1914–1918* cites the British Ministry of Defence as having confirmed his victory score at twenty-two. No. 24 Squadron's record book places his victory total at nineteen. In the Directorate of History, Department of Defence, Ottawa, Canada, there is a document that indicates he was officially credited with seventeen enemy machines and seven unofficial victories. According to

George Williams, editor of *Over the Front,* Maj. V. A. H. Robeson, commanding officer of No. 24 Squadron, stated Lambert had ten destroyed, four out of control, and four shared with other squadron pilots. On 3 January 1968, W. J. Trunton of the Royal Air Force Air Historical Branch wrote Dr. Royal D. Frey of the U.S. Air Force Museum that Lambert was credited with eighteen and a half enemy airplanes and two enemy observation balloons for a total of twenty and a half victories. In addition, he shared in the destruction of three balloons and forced another plane to land in a damaged state. Lambert, in his oral history interview with Robert J. Smith, states he had twenty-one and a half kills. Even with only twenty and a half official victories, Lambert would rank second to Edward Rickenbacker's top American victory score of twenty-six. Unfortunately, until recent years, Lambert, like other Americans who flew only with the British, has had little publicity.

Capt. Frederick Ives Lord
Courtesy Stewart K. Taylor

ELEVEN

Capt. Frederick Ives Lord

Young Frederick Lord, then a lieutenant and only recently assigned to a Sopwith Dolphin[1] in No. 79 Squadron, Royal Air Force, adjusted the throttle on his fighter to conserve fuel as he searched the clear sunny sky over France for a possible enemy target. It was 7:30 A.M., 28 May 1918, and he was quite annoyed that he had not yet had the opportunity to score against hostile forces. Suddenly, he spotted two German observation balloons some three thousand feet below, approximately over the village of Comines. He quickly banked his Dolphin to the left and began a long dive toward the kite balloons, which were being rapidly pulled down. In his report, written later that day, he stated,

> I fired about 20 rounds at one kite balloon at about 200 feet range without result, and overshooting this one I saw the second directly in front of me. This kite balloon was only a few hundred feet above the ground. I fired about 30 rounds into it from very close range and the balloon caught fire emitting black and yellow smoke. Fire from the ground was extremely accurate and active and my machine was hit in several places.

Fortunately, the damage to his Dolphin was not serious and he gleefully returned to his airdrome at St. Marie Cappel with his first victory.[2]

Frederick I. Lord was born in Manitowoc, Wisconsin, in 1900, and at the age of sixteen he joined the Texas National Guard and served several months in "A" Company of the Third Texas Infantry Regiment. When U.S. Army officials discovered he was underaged for military service, he was given an honorable discharge and dropped from the army rolls. Young Lord, now living in Houston, Texas, and eager to participate in World War I, was unwilling to wait until he reached the legal age to serve. Using a "doctored" birth certificate, he traveled to Canada, where he joined the Royal Flying Corps.[3] He went overseas in October of 1917 and, after flight training, was posted to No. 79 Squadron on 21 March 1918.[4]

No. 79 Squadron was formed at Gosport, England, on 1 August 1917 but did not go to France until February of 1918. Under the command of Maj. W. W. Noel, the squadron began combat operations on 6 March and scored its first aerial victory on 21 March. The squadron was ineffective in its first few weeks on the battle front; not until the unit was stationed at St. Marie Cappel on 16 May did it begin to function efficiently.[5]

During the next several months, Frederick Lord became one of the most daring and effective fighter pilots in No. 79 Squadron. At nine A.M. on 7 June 1918, "Tex," as Lord was called by his fellow pilots,[6] scored his second "kill" when he shot down an Albatros Scout over the village of La Bassée. His combat report described the action in succinct terms:

> I turned on an Albatros Scout which was following the formation and engaged it. The E.A. (enemy aircraft) at once went down in a series of side-slips, and Lt. Howse and myself followed it down firing bursts into it when at 5000 feet he flattened out and I fired a burst into it at very close range. The E.A. went down out of control and was seen to crash near La Basse Ville by Lt. Howse and myself.[7]

Perhaps Lord's most successful mission of the war occurred on 27 June 1918 when he destroyed two enemy fighters and sent another down out of control. In his combat report Lord stated,

> While on patrol by myself N.E. of Armentières I saw 4 Bristol fighters[8] above me fighting with 5 Pfalz Scouts which they drove down in front of me and I fired a short burst into one of them at close range as he passed. He went down spinning. On the way back I saw 4 Pfalz Scouts and one Triplane (A Fokker DR1) over Neuve Eglise. I dived on them firing from long range. The E.A. dived, but the triplane was behind the others, and I over hauled him. When about 8000 feet I again opened fire and he dived very steeply and broke up at 7:30 P.M. I climbed back to our lines rejoining the formation and signalled to the leader that I could see E.A. The formation followed me down and I attacked, firing on the leader. After a short burst he fell out of control and crashed by a road between Neuve Eglise and Plugstreet Wood . . . at about 7:45 P.M. I then returned owing to shortage of ammunition.[9]

Two of the kills were confirmed by Royal Air Force communiqués.[10] For his 27 June action, Frederick Lord was awarded the British Distinguished Flying Cross.[11]

Because of his flying skills and aggressive leadership, Lord was made commander of No. 79 Squadron's "C" Flight and promoted to captain on 10 August 1918.[12] Since young Lord was only eighteen years old at the time of his promotion, he probably was the youngest flight leader in the RAF. Due to the "doctored" birth certificate, it is doubtful RAF officials were aware of his age.

Despite his youth, Captain Lord continued his aggressive leadership. At 8:20 P.M. on 21 August, he scored his fifth official victory when he shot down a hostile two-seater a short distance northwest of the city of Armentières. The air battle took place at very low altitude, and the enemy aircraft "hit a clump of trees and crashed."[13]

No. 79 Squadron, commanded by Maj. A. R. Arnold since 22 June 1918, now became one of the hottest fighter outfits on the British front. Several factors contributed to this success. Engine mechanics had become experienced in maintaining the Dolphin's Hispano-Suiza engine. In addition, the squadron had, since May of 1918, been able to operate out of the same airdrome—St. Marie Cappel. No longer was there the confusion of having to move planes and repair facilities almost weekly.[14]

In a wild dogfight between a patrol from No. 79 Squadron and a formation of Fokker D-7s, on a hazy afternoon of 5 September, Lt. F. W. Gillet[15] shot down a German fighter in flames while Captain Lord attacked another. Lord's victim "fell over its back, and a large object, which would appear to have been the pilot, was seen to leave the machine which was last seen falling on its back within 200 feet of the ground." This Fokker was confirmed for Captain Lord's sixth victory.[16]

"Tex" Lord continued his victory streak when, on 17 September, he sent a Fokker D-7 crashing into the Lys River near Comines.[17] Three days later, at 6:55 A.M., he fired about 150 rounds into a Hanoveraner two-seater with "bronze colored wings and grey tail." The enemy machine "went into a steep dive and crashed north of Houbourdin in a large open field." His ninth and last kill came at 1:15 P.M. on 28 September when he was bounced by an enemy fighter at about two hundred feet. In Captain Lord's words, "the Pfalz Scout attacked me from in front hitting my machine in several places. We fought in and out of some trees for about 10 minutes, when we eventually met nose on, both firing a burst. E.A. went underneath me and dived straight into the ground and crashed." This low level combat took place in the vicinity of Werquin.[18] During the same day, No. 79 Squadron pilots were to have their greatest success, downing seven German aircraft.[19]

Capt. Frederick Ives Lord's World War I combat career came to an end when, on 17 October 1918, he was shot down and wounded. Fortunately, the combat took place on the British side of the front lines, and he was admitted to a hospital on the same day.[20] No. 79 Squadron, led by such individuals as Capts. R. B. Bannerman, Francis W. Gillet, and J. H. McNeaney, continued to run up its score against the German Air Force right up to the end of the war. In its eight months in combat, the unit was to down sixty-four aircraft and nine hostile observation balloons.[21] The top individual scorer was Capt. Francis W. Gillet with at least seventeen victories.[22] Certainly, Capt. Frederick Lord, with his nine official victories and through his active and aggressive leadership, made a real contribution to the squadron's success.

On 19 November 1918, some eight days after the official end of the First World War, Lord, the restless adventuresome soldier of fortune, was posted out of No. 79 Squadron and, shortly thereafter, found another war to fight—this time in Russia. Early in 1919 he volunteered for service with the White Russians, then in a life and death struggle with the Bolshevik rebels. For a time, he commanded the Pinega front air service made up of an assortment of aircraft ranging from Sopwith 1½ Strutters, DH-9s, Sopwith Snipes, and RE-8s.[23] While flying one of the RE-8 two-seaters biplanes, on the morning of 27 June 1919, he spotted a Red Army force near the Pinega River, preparing to attack the town of Pilegori, and "attacked the moving column from a height of 200 feet with such effect that their transport was stampeded and their expected attack broke down without any casualties being sustained by [White Russian] forces."[24] In the action, his aircraft was damaged, and he plunged into the river. For two days, he tramped "through forests and swamps and made his own lines again where General [Edmund] Ironside recommended him for the D.S.O and the Russians gave him the Order of St. Stanislaus, the White Army Medal, the Russian Service Cross, and the Russian rank of Colonel."[25]

Lord returned to the United Kingdom in the early fall of 1919 and, in late October, returned to the United States on the *Minnekahda*. His home destination was given as Houston, Texas.[26] In Texas he became the owner of a fleet of three biplanes in which he spent the next few years barnstorming and working in the oilfields. In 1926 he went to "Europe found it still peaceful, so returned here [the United States] and got a job as an oil-well supply salesman" in Trinidad, British West Indies. Bored with that job, he obtained the distributorship for Stearman Aircraft in Texas. He even managed to sell a few of these sturdy biplanes in Mexico City[27] and, for a short time, served as combat advisor to the Mexican government.[28]

Always seeking a new challenge, Lord started an airline business between San Antonio, Texas, and Monterey, Mexico, using Bellanca aircraft. According to one source, most of his passengers were "Prohibition's drought-stricken Americans" who flew to Mexico "where they spent their all" and had to be "dead-headed back." Consequently, the airline project became a losing proposition for Frederick Lord. He then joined Curtiss-Wright Company in 1930 and spent approximately a year with that organization. The restless flier then purchased an old Sikorsky plane and tried his hand at an airline effort between Nantucket and Cape Cod. This, too, proved a failure, and he lost most of his investment. However, he did acquire a wife during this episode in his life.[29] As a major in the Army Air Corps Reserve, Lord managed to get two-week active duty tours annually in 1932, 1934, and 1935.[30]

With the outbreak of the Spanish Civil War in 1936, Frederick Lord had an opportunity once again to fight for "world peace and democracy." In November of that year, Lord and several other Americans joined the Spanish Loyalist government in its struggle against Franco's Fascist forces. The Loyalist equipment consisted of a motley collection of old military and hastily-acquired commercial aircraft such as Breguet XIX's, Miles Falcons, Fokkers, and Farmans. Flying out of Bilbao on the Basque front, Lord, the old fighter pilot, flew several bombing missions. His fighter escorts at the time were frequently Russian "Reds," the people he had fought against in 1919.[31]

Actually, Lord spent only a few weeks with the Spanish Loyalists and, in January of 1937, he and his wife, Mildred, established residence in Paris. Here he convalesced from a bad throat and learned that his "U.S. Army Reserve Commission had been revoked due to his Spanish service."[32] By May of 1937, Lord was back in the United States, where he sold articles to the pulp magazine *Flying Aces* and to *The New Masses* and attempted to drum up support for the Loyalist cause. His combat efforts in Spain and his crusade for support for the Spanish government received attention in *The Literary Digest*, *The Daily Worker*, and *Life*.[33] In addition, he launched a successful lecture tour in which he narrated stories of his war experiences in Spain and pushed for aid to the Loyalists.[34]

When World War II broke out, Frederick Lord once again "doctored" his birth certificate and managed to talk his way back into his old fighter outfit, No. 79 Squadron of the Royal Air Force. The English authorities soon caught up with him, however, and he was posted to the A.T.A. where he was assigned to ferry bombers.[35]

There is little question Frederick Ives Lord's love of flying pulled him into the First World War. In addition, he no doubt looked upon the British effort against Germans as a crusade for freedom and democracy. The love of combat flying may have been a factor in his participation in the Spanish Civil War, but it is quite likely the soldier of fortune's mercenary spirit also played a role. His attempt to become a fighter pilot again, after more than twenty years, in the early days of the Second World War probably was a return to his original idealism.

Lt. Emile John Lussier
Courtesy Ministry of Defence, Gloucester, England

TWELVE

Lt. Emile John Lussier

Emile John Lussier, the son of Joseph Emile and Louise Swalwell Lussier, was born in Chicago, Illinois, on 10 October 1895.[1] He spent the first fifteen years of his life in that city and received much of his education there. However, in 1910 his father took a job building a string of railroad stations from Winnipeg, Canada, westward toward the Pacific Ocean; subsequently young Lussier spent much of the next seven years in Alberta and the western provinces in Canada. With the bloody World War I underway, Emile John Lussier, using Medicine Hat, Alberta, as his home address, enlisted in the Royal Flying Corps and won his second lieutenant's commission as a pilot on 29 November 1917. Early in 1918 he was sent overseas, and, on 24 March of that year, he was assigned to the No. 73 Squadron flying Sopwith Camels and operating on the southern end of the British front between Cambrai and St. Quentin.[2]

No. 73 Squadron was heavily engaged in the Allied attempt to halt the German offensive between Cambrai and St. Quentin. Low strafing was carried out "continuously to the exclusion of all other work." When the battle lines became stable again, No. 73 Squadron resumed its offensive patrol duties and moved back to a central position on the British front. During the German drive in the Lys valley in April, the squadron spent much of its time in offensive patrols over the battle area. From the end of April until early June, the Camel squadron continued its patrol activity and bombing escort missions over the entire British sector from "north of Ypers to Amiens." In June, No. 73 Squadron moved south to the French sector and took part in the operations on the Noyon-Montdidier front. Low strafing and a great number of offensive patrols were carried out, and, during the nine days the battle was at its height, twenty-four enemy aircraft were destroyed or driven down out of control.[3]

Lieutenant Lussier was very active in the strafing and offensive patrol work during the April–June period. No. 73 Squadron, unlike most fighter outfits, had moved frequently on the battle front and had been involved in a great variety of combat duties. In late June, the unit moved back to the British front and resumed its offensive patrols and bombing escort missions. However, a few days later the squadron was again shifted to the French front and "took part first in the German attack between Château-Thierry and Rheims and subsequently in the French offensive on the whole of the Soissons–Château-Thierry–Rheims Salient."[4]

On 25 July 1918 young Lussier scored his first aerial victory on an offensive patrol in the Villers area at approximately seven P.M. Although there had been showers earlier in the day, the weather was fine at the time of Lussier's combat with several Fokker D-7s. In his combat report, written after his return to his home airfield, Lussier wrote,

> three Biplanes were attacking a Camel, and I dived on one of them, firing 100 rounds. He then went down out of control. I was then attacked by the scarlet Biplanes, and we fought from 13,000 ft. to 8,000 ft. He then went vertically down, and crashed into a wood south of Villers. I fired 700 rounds at him.

The Royal Air Force Communiqué confirms the plane that crashed, but does not mention the one down out of control.[5]

Five days later, Lussier and Lts. A. McConnell-Wood and Norman Cooper, while escorting low-flying French planes, saw a "German L.V.G. 2-seater painted yellow with camouflaged" wings and immediately brought on an air combat: "He immediately started north with his nose down, and we all dived on him several times. When at 200 feet he went into a steep side-slip and crashed into the ground. The observer must have been wounded after the first couple of dives, as he did not fire after that."[6] The three No. 73 Squadron pilots shared this "kill," which was confirmed by Royal Air Force communiqué No. 18.[7]

At the beginning of August 1918, No. 73 Squadron was moved back to the British front and was engaged in both offensive patrols and low bombing during the Allied advance in the Amiens drive. "From this time onward the Squadron was attached to the

Tanks Corps for special duties in connection with Anti-tank gun strafing, and took part in a succession of battles on the Third and Fourth Armies Front, moving to whatever sector the tanks were operating on."[8]

Late in the afternoon of the opening day of the Amiens offensive, Lts. Lussier, G. L. Graham, and R. N. Chandler, while engaged in ground strafing in the Nesle area, spotted a dark gray, yellow-nosed two-seater at two thousand feet. In Emile John Lussier's words, the enemy plane "came out of the clouds and began firing at me. The remainder of the patrol dived on him and after a short fight he went down and crashed into the ground. We each fired about two hundred rounds."[9] Once again, the victory was shared by three Sopwith Camel pilots.

While on an offensive patrol at thirteen thousand feet on 19 August at 8:10 A.M.in the vicinity of the town of Combles, Lieutenant Lussier's flight came in contact with eight Fokker D-7s. In his combat report, Lussier stated,

> the fokkers climbed up beneath us and the leader began firing at me. When he was within two hundred yards, I turned and dived on him, firing about 200 rounds. He turned to get away, but went into a spin, and when he came out of it, turned on his back. I watched him for several thousand feet, and he never regained control.

This Lussier victory was confirmed by Captain Graham of No. 73 Squadron.[10]

On the hazy morning of 25 August 1918, Lieutenant Lussier and his Sopwith Camel flight were heavily involved in ground strafing of German troops near Sapignies when they caught sight of two Fokker D-7s at about two thousand feet. Lussier picked out one of the enemy planes and fired some two hundred rounds into it. "He went into a spin, and crashed into the ground near Sapignies" for his sixth kill since joining No. 73 Squadron.[11]

Four days later, on a cloudy day with good visibility, Lieutenant Lussier's flight acted as an escort for several RE-8 aircraft in the vicinity of the city of Arras. At approximately 10:30 A.M., Lussier observed several formations of Fokker biplanes. In his combat report, he commented, "I started climbing but before I got up to their level, eight of them dived on my formation. I fired 300 rounds at one, which was on a Camel's tail, and it turned on its back and went down, turning over and over. I observed it until it went through the clouds at 4000 ft."[12] The victory was confirmed by Lieutenant Trendell but did not appear in the RAF Communiqué for 29 August 1918. Nonetheless, No. 73 Squadron now considered Emile John Lussier to have seven kills to his credit.

During the period August to November, No. 73 Squadron continued its ground strafing and bombing attacks on German troops and military vehicles. During this time, no less than 160,000 rounds "were fired at and 1176 25lb bombs were dropped on ground targets."[13]

Despite the fact No. 73 Squadron spent much of its time in strafing and dive-bombing, its pilots occasionally became involved in aerial dogfights. At 5:45 P.M., on 15 September, Emile John Lussier and a Captain Baldwin observed about ten Fokker D-7s several thousand feet below them and over the town of Aubigny-Au-Bac. Lussier dove his Sopwith Camel on the Fokkers and, after firing at several, "observed a scarlet one to go down in a nose dive. I followed him down firing at him all the time and saw him crash into the ground near Aubigny-Au-Bac." This marked young Lussier's eighth victory of the war.[14] He was to score his ninth and last victory on 18 October when his patrol caught a formation of six Fokker D-7s a little to the northeast of Le Cateau. Lieutenant Lussier singled out one enemy aircraft that was firing on a Camel, "and after firing about one hundred and fifty rounds I observed it to go into a spin. I lost sight of it but it was seen several thousand feet lower falling on its back." This victory was confirmed by Lieutenants Reid and Tyrrell "who both saw this machine falling upside down."[15]

Emile John Lussier received the Distinguished Flying Cross on 15 September 1918.[16] The citation appeared in the *London Gazette* on 2 November 1918 and reads as follows:

> The King has been graciously pleased to approve the following award in recognition of a gallantry and devotion to duty in the execution of air operations: *Distinguished Flying Cross* Lieutenant Emile John Lussier (RFC) 10th (Army) wing 73rd sqn. During recent operations this officer has driven down out of control or destroyed seven enemy machines, and, with the aid of two other pilots, has accounted for a further two. Three of these he destroyed in one day. In these combats he has proved himself an officer of very high courage, eager to attack without regard to the enemy's superiority in numbers.[17]

On 6 November 1918 Lussier was promoted to captain in No. 73 Squadron.

Lussier returned to America early in 1919 and for the next several years operated a farm. During World War II, Lussier was commissioned in the Royal Canadian Air Force and served in No. 1 Wireless School until 1942. Then he was promoted to flight lieutenant and became the commanding officer of No. 1 and No. 4 Wireless Schools from January 1942. He was then promoted to the rank of squadron leader.[18]

Emile John Lussier was a retired farmer living in Westminster, Maryland, at the time of his death on 11 December 1974. He was survived by his wife Vera Fleming Lussier, four married daughters, fifteen grandchildren, and nine great-grandchildren. He was a much respected individual who had performed outstanding service in two world wars.[19]

Capt. Francis Warrington Gillet
Courtesy Ola Sater

THIRTEEN

Capt. Francis Warrington Gillet

I t was 7:35 A.M., and Lt. Francis Warrington Gillet circled his Sopwith Dolphin at six thousand feet through the broken cloud layer just north of the village of Estaires, a few miles east of his home airdrome of St. Marie Cappel. Suddenly the American spotted a hostile kite balloon several thousand feet below near Le Pt. Mortar. Gillet, who had been assigned to No. 79 Squadron, Royal Air Force, since 29 March 1918, banked his fighter sharply to the left and plunged through the clouds "on to the balloon and fired three long bursts into it, diving from east to west." In his combat report written later in the day, Gillet stated, "I then climbed and on looking back saw a cloud of smoke in the air. I fired 300 rounds of Buckingham ammunition." Captain Mac-Gregor, of No. 85 Squadron, confirmed the balloon went down in flames for Gillet's first official victory.[1]

Francis W. Gillet was born in Baltimore, Maryland, and attended the University of Virginia. At the age of nineteen he entered the U.S. Army Signal Corps at Newport News, Virginia, where he learned to fly, and on 31 May 1917 he was assigned to the School of Military Aeronautics at the University of Illinois. When the United States entered the First World War, Gillet was declared too young to obtain a United States commission and was sent to the Royal Flying Corps in Canada. He was commissioned a second lieutenant in November 1917 and was sent to England in March 1918 where he was assigned to No. 79 Squadron, then operating on the Flanders front.[2]

Although No. 79 Squadron was organized at Gosport, England, in early August 1917, it did not go to the front until February of the next year. Equipped with the Hispano-Suiza–powered Sopwith Dolphin, the squadron did not begin combat operations until 6 March 1918, some three weeks before Gillet joined the organization. The unit was, at first, based at Estrée Blanche Aerodrome, but moved to Champien Aerodrome on 6 March. At the end of March, No. 79 Squadron was forced to move its airdrome because of the German offensive and relocated at Villers Bréton-neux, where it remained only one night. Because of heavy bomb-ing, the unit moved to Beauvois, some twenty-five miles north-east of Abbeville, where it remained for approximately seven weeks. During this period, the squadron had very heavy casu-alties, due to the Dolphin's engine troubles and the necessity of stopping the enemy's ground troops.[3] On 16 May the squadron moved to St. Marie Cappel, located some fifteen miles northwest of Armentières, and, shortly thereafter, Maj. A. R. Arnold re-placed Maj. M. W. Noel as commander of the outfit. "Owing to the fact that mechanics in the squadron had now had consider-able experience" with the Dolphin's engine, and the combat front had stabilized and low-level strafing was no longer required, No. 79 Squadron "commenced to have much greater success."[4]

On 18 August, fifteen days after he scored his first aerial vic-tory, Lt. Francis W. Gillet was again involved in a fierce dogfight. At 12:40 P.M., despite low clouds and high winds, the young American sighted a hostile kite balloon north of Estaires at a height of eight hundred feet. He immediately attacked and fired one hundred rounds at long range, but the balloon did not catch fire. Gillet then dropped two bombs in the neighborhood of the balloon winch and returned to shoot up the kite balloon. At this point, he "observed a Fokker biplane on my tail who fired one burst at me." Gillet then did a sharp right-hand turn, "got above him and on his tail, and fired 100 rounds at close range." The Fokker D-7 dived "straight into the ground and crashed about ½ mile due south of Croix de Bae" for Lieutenant Gillet's second victory.[5]

Some six days after the destruction of the Fokker D-7, young Gillet saw a German

2-seater D.F.W. about 1 mile east of Bailleul at 7:35 P.M. about 2000 feet. I was at 9000 feet and dived on him. The observer at once fired white lights. I did not open fire until I saw his crosses at close range. I then fired two long bursts of 150 rounds at a range of 50 yards. The observer fired three bursts at me.

The enemy aircraft dived east and then suddenly turned over sideways "and crashed about 2 miles east of Bailleul."[6] This marked Gillet's third air kill in the month of August.

On 1 September 1918 Lt. F. W. Gillet became an ace and one of the top pilots in No. 79 Squadron. At 1:20 P.M. he dove through a broken cloud field a short distance northeast of Armentières to attack an enemy observation balloon. As he approached the balloon, he observed an enemy LVG two-seater flying at about fifteen hundred feet. In his combat report, written hours later, Lieutenant Gillet stated, "I opened my throttle and dived upon him, firing about 200 rounds at about 100 yards range. E.A. (enemy aircraft) dived and the observer fired a burst at me. I followed E.A. down and fired another 150 rounds at very close range. E.A. crashed into the ground." Gillet then banked his Sopwith Dolphin west toward the balloon which "was being pulled down and fired 50 rounds into it at very close range, dropping two bombs near the winch. The balloon was hauled down and appeared to be deflating. Balloon was not observed to catch fire. Fire from the ground was very erratic after I dropped my bombs." A few hours later an Allied anti-aircraft battery confirmed that Gillet's balloon victim had fallen in flames.[7]

Although the Sopwith Dolphin was not highly regarded during the spring of 1918, by the end of the summer it had many enthusiastic supporters—one of which was Lieutenant Gillet. Indeed, the Sopwith 5F-1 Dolphin was a most unusual aircraft. Unlike other Sopwith planes, such as the Pup, Triplane, Camel, and Snipe, the Dolphin was a stationary-engine aircraft. As one writer described it, the plane "appeared more like a whale than a slick dolphin."[8] In general, the Sopwith Dolphin was "not an ugly aeroplane and it certainly looked like an efficient fighting machine." One unusual feature was the fact that the pilot was seated with his head level with the upper wing. Since there was no center section, but a strong structural frame of steel tubing, the pilot had an excellent view of everything above his aircraft. Although the Dolphin gave the best possible view upward, it also gave a reasonably good outlook forward and downward. To the rear and downward the view was less good, "because the lower plane got in the way as well as the fuselage and radiator."[9] The Dolphin was normally equipped with two Vickers machine guns and two Lewis guns. However, many pilots, such as Lieutenant Gillet, removed one of the Lewis guns. Unfortunately, the pilot's head protruded above the top wing. Consequently, the aviator might have his neck broken should the aircraft nose over and land on its back. Because of this, some Dolphins were fitted with a "rolling hoop" which went over the pilot's cockpit, and "although it slightly impaired his upward view it gave him an added sense of security, for he felt that the aeroplane could turn over on the ground without his neck getting broken."[10] Even though the Sopwith Dolphin had great firepower and a speed of 130 miles per hour, only four squadrons flew the aircraft in combat. These squadrons were numbers 19, 23, 79, and 87.[11]

During the month of September 1918, Francis W. Gillet continued his hot victory run against the German air pilots. At 6:55 P.M., on 5 September, Gillet, Capt. Frederick Lord, and Capt. H. P. Rushforth caught a flight of Fokker D-7s at twelve thousand feet, a short distance east of the city of Armentières. Gillet attacked one of the Fokkers and fired about one hundred rounds at very close range. The enemy fighter, putting out a heavy cloud of black smoke, went down out of control. Gillet was unable to see the Fokker crash because he was under attack from several other enemy pursuit planes. However, Lieutenant Watson from No. 70 Squadron observed the Fokker crash and burst into flames for Gillet's sixth victory. In this air duel, Captains Lord and Rushforth also scored one victory each.[12]

While on patrol searching for hostile observation balloons in the Harbourdin-Wavrin area on 21 September, Lieutenant Gillet spotted two Fokker biplanes flying east at three thousand feet. He immediately dove his Dolphin through the cloud layer to attack the enemy pilots, who apparently were unaware of his presence. In his combat report, written later in the day, Gillet described the action:

> I fired about 20 rounds at close range into one which immediately spun down. I then fired about 100 rounds into the other, his left wing appeared to collapse and he spun down and crashed near a railway in a woods. I was then attacked by two other Fokkers from above and therefore climbed back into the clouds, being heavily engaged by A.A. fire. The Fokkers flew east apparently engaged by S.E. 5's.

Gillet was credited with his seventh kill as a result of the combat. Unfortunately, the first Fokker that spun down was not confirmed.[13]

Lt. Francis W. Gillet, known in No. 79 Squadron as "Razors,"[14] ran his victory total to nine on 28 September. During the noon hour, while flying on a "low line patrol" in the vicinity of Bousbecque, he caught sight of a German Albatros two-seater flying along the road to the east of the village. Despite the misty rain, Lieutenant Gillet dove his Dolphin to within a few yards of the enemy plane and fired about 150 rounds through its top wing. The Albatros immediately went into a violent spin and "crashed into the ground near a cottage on the road about ½ mile from the village of Bousbecque." On returning to his own lines, "Razors" Gillet met a Halberstadt flying east over Messines, a few miles north of Armentières, and fired some forty rounds into it. The Halberstadt immediately climbed into the clouds and escaped.[15] At 5:50 P.M., a flight of No. 79 Squadron Dolphins attacked some ten Fokker biplanes engaged in shooting up a Royal Air Force Bristol Fighter. In the fight which followed, a white-tailed Fokker got on Lieutenant Gillet's tail. The American climbed sharply, did a half roll, and forced the Fokker to abandon the dogfight. Gillet then chased the enemy aircraft, firing short bursts at close range. The Fokker "crashed about a mile southeast of Passchendaele" for the Maryland boy's ninth kill.[16] No. 79 Squadron pilots destroyed seven German aircraft during the day for their best performance of the war.[17]

On 29 September Lt. F. W. Gillet once again was assigned to patrol duty in the Passchendaele-Roulers area. At 10:10 A.M. he spotted three "slate coloured Fokker biplanes" flying at ten thousand feet a little west of Roulers. Apparently the Fokker pilots did not see Gillet's Sopwith Dolphin until he began firing. In his combat report he stated, "I fired about 20 rounds into one which immediately began smoking from the cockpit. E.A. dived, then stalled and burst into flames and crashed near Menin-Roulers Road." Gillet then returned to his own lines, where he observed three more enemy aircraft shooting up Allied troops near Moorslede. He dived on the German planes, driving them away from the troops on the ground. A few moments later, two enemy planes attacked Gillet from above, forcing him to break off combat.[18] That night, pilots in No. 79 Squadron helped "Razors" Gillet celebrate his tenth victory of the war. In addition to becoming a double ace, Lieutenant Gillet had been awarded the British Distinguished Flying Cross on 16 September.[19]

Heavy rainstorms on 30 September kept No. 79 Squadron pilots on the ground throughout the day. The next day was described as "fine with some clouds," but the squadron scored no victories. However, several RAF bombers and reconnaissance planes were quite active and achieved considerable success. On 2 October the weather was fair in the morning but became cloudy with some rain in the afternoon.[20] Fortunately for Lt. Francis W. Gillet, he was assigned to a low line patrol in the early morning. At 7:10 A.M., while dodging through the broken clouds, he spotted a hostile kite balloon at an altitude of one thousand feet some four miles east of Roulers. In spite of heavy ground fire, he dove on the observation balloon, which was being pulled down, and "fired about 50 rounds at close range" without apparent results. He then "fired another 100 rounds into it and it burst into flames." The destruction of the balloon was confirmed by Lt. J. H. McNeaney of No. 79 Squadron, who observed the kill from a short distance away.[21]

Three days after the balloon episode, Gillet and his wing man observed six Fokker D-7s attacking a Royal Air Force DH-9 in the vicinity of the town of Courtrai. They immediately dived to the rescue of the observation plane, and Gillet fired a burst of fifty rounds into one of the Fokkers at close range. The Fokker "made a vertical turn, turned over and dived into the ground and crashed near Courtrai."[22] This kill ran Lieutenant Gillet's victory total to twelve and tied him with Capt. R. B. Bannerman as the top ace of No. 79 Squadron.

On 8 October pilots of No. 79 Squadron were annoyed to find low clouds and rain dominated the morning hours. Consequently there was little air activity. However, during the afternoon the rain stopped and most of the heavy clouds disappeared. About four P.M., Gillet took off from a muddy field on an offensive patrol looking for enemy aircraft. Some thirty minutes later, he observed several red-tailed Fokker biplanes at about twelve thousand feet over the town of Menin. During the ensuing dogfight, the aggressive American got on the tail of one of the Fokkers and fired about fifty rounds into him at close range. The Fokker "pulled up and stalled, then dived." Gillet "followed him down firing two bursts of about 20 rounds." The enemy pursuit plane crashed in a field. A little later, two Fokker D-7s dived and attacked a Belgian machine. In Gillet's words, "I attacked one firing the remainder of my ammunition into it. E.A. dived down, and on hitting the ground burst into flames near Gullegham."[23] The two late afternoon victories ran Francis W. Gillet's air victory total to fourteen and established him as one of the top American aces serving with the British. Gillet was made a flight leader in

No. 79 Squadron and was promoted to captain. On 13 October he was awarded a "bar" to his DFC.

Capt. Francis W. Gillet ran his victory score to sixteen on 14 October, when he became involved in aerial dogfights at 10:30 in the morning and 2:25 in the afternoon. On the morning patrol, he spotted a Fokker biplane flying at the rear of an enemy formation east of Ingelmunster. The Fokker dived on Gillet's Sopwith Dolphin and, after firing a few rounds, "pulled up, passing over me." At this point, Gillet began firing with his Lewis gun and passed at close range beneath the Fokker. He fired some forty rounds into the enemy aircraft, sending it in a dive for about two thousand feet, "then spun down and crashed near canal east of Ingelmunster."[24] About four hours later, while on offensive patrol, Gillet dived on three "black and grey striped" Fokker D-7s near the village of Dadizeele, but they disappeared in the mist at about one thousand feet. He then turned toward the front lines, where he saw two Fokkers attacking one of the Allied balloons. He then climbed up toward the enemy aircraft firing short bursts from "my top gun." The enemy planes turned east, and Gillet "chased one firing about 150 rounds in short range." The Fokker "dived vertically and crashed in a field near Gits."[25]

During the last two weeks of October 1918, the weather over the front was less than perfect. According to the Royal Air Force Communiqués, "low clouds, mist, rain" was the normal weather condition. Consequently, there was much less air activity than during the summer months.[26] No. 79 Squadron remained at St. Marie Cappel until 22 October, when it moved to Reckem Aerodrome near Halluin on the Lys River and some six miles southeast of Courtrai, due to the advance of British Second Army.[27]

The last big day of air combat during the war occurred on 4 November when No. 79 Squadron pilots shot down four German planes. Captain Gillet downed his last confirmed enemy aircraft—a DFW two-seater, which crashed at Renaix for his seventeenth victory.[28]

While on a special mission in the vicinity of Bekstrom at 6:30 A.M. on 10 November, Gillet sighted a Halberstadt two-seater at about seven thousand feet. According to his combat report, the enemy aircraft turned east, then dived with Gillet firing "several short bursts at short range. The observer of the E.A. after firing two bursts ceased fire, and the machine dived vertically for about 5000 feet." When the Halberstadt leveled out, Gillet "fired another 50 rounds and the enemy dived into the ground, slightly north of Bekstrom." Captain Gillet was then attacked by four Fokker D-7s, into one of which he fired about fifty rounds. He then passed under the enemy aircraft into a cloud. After emerging from it, he "saw two of the enemy aircraft who had dived through the cloud after him collide and fall to the ground N.W. of Bekstrom. One wing was observed to fall off." The three kills mentioned on 10 November were never confirmed by Royal Air Force Communiqués, but were listed in the Public Records Office document "List of Enemy Aircraft Driven Down or Destroyed, 22 March–November 1918."[29] Whether Capt. Francis W. Gillet was credited with seventeen victories or twenty victories, he was indeed one of the top American air aces who flew with the British during World War I and was "decorated by the British and the Belgium governments with the DFC and Bar, Distinguished Service Medal and the Croix de Guerre."[30]

During its nine months at the front, the No. 79 Squadron using Dolphin aircraft was credited with sixty-four enemy airplanes destroyed and nine hostile kite balloons burned. On 26 November, the squadron moved to Nivelles, Belgium, and on to Bickendore near Cologne, Germany, on 20 December 1918 with the Army of Occupation.[31] Captain Gillet, the top Sopwith Dolphin ace, was posted from the squadron on 29 November 1918.

After the war, F. W. Gillet returned to Baltimore, Maryland, and entered business there as president of a liquor importing firm, director of a banking firm, and a director of a realty corporation. He died on 21 November 1969 at the age of seventy-four.[32]

Members of No. 20 Squadron RAF. Left to right: Capt. D. Latimer, Lt. Noble, Capt. A T. Iaccaci, unidentified, Capt. T. P. Middleton

Courtesy E. Hardcastle

Capts. Paul T. Iaccaci
and August T. Iaccaci

P aul T. Iaccaci and his brother, August T. Iaccaci, both from
New York City, traveled to Toronto, Canada, in 1917, where
they joined the Royal Flying Corps. On completion of their preliminary flight training, they were transferred overseas to the
United Kingdom in late December of the same year.[1] After further training in combat-type aircraft, including the Bristol
Fighter, both Iaccaci boys in late April 1918 were posted to the
Bristol Fighters in No. 20 Squadron, then stationed at Boisdingham some eighteen miles southeast of Calais.[2]

No. 20 Squadron, one of the outstanding squadrons of World
War I, was organized on 1 September 1915 at Netheravon.
Shortly afterward, the squadron moved to Filton, Bristol, where it
was equipped with FE-2B aircraft. From this base, it proceeded
overseas to France, arriving on 16 January 1916 at Clairmarais
Airdrome; it became a part of the 2nd Wing, Royal Flying Corps.
Maj. C. W. Wilson became the squadron's commanding officer.
With the formation of the II Brigade, R.F.C., in February 1916,
No. 20 Squadron, with No. 29 Squadron, formed the Eleventh
(Army) Wing. Although No. 20 Squadron was mainly a fighting
unit, it did undertake numerous reconnaissance flights and pho-
tographic missions as required by the British army.[3]

In June 1916 No. 20 Squadron was reequipped with FE-2D
aircraft and, during the next several months, continued to carry
out reconnaissance and photographic duties. The squadron was
heavily engaged in the Somme campaign, which opened on 1 July
1916. During this period, No. 20 Squadron's new commanding
officer, Maj. G. J. Malcolm, was killed in a flying accident and was
replaced by Maj. W. H. C. Mansfield. Major Mansfield, a holder
of the DSO, led the squadron until 1917. The unit was moved to

Boisdingham on 18 January 1917 and in April of that year was stationed at St. Marie Cappel, where it remained until April of 1918. In September of 1917 the FE-2D was replaced with the Bristol Fighter. The squadron continued to carry out many of its reconnaissance and photographic duties, but, with the Bristol Fighter, it frequently dropped bombs and engaged in air-to-air combat. In March and April 1918, during the German Somme offensive, No. 20 Squadron "took part in low bombing and shooting up of enemy troops and transport. At daylight each morning machines were flown to the airdrome at Bruay from which operations were carried out, the machines returning to St. Marie Cappel at dusk." On 13 April 1918 the squadron moved back to Boisdingham and, during the next thirty days, the Bristol Fighter squadron, commanded by Maj. E. H. Johnston, destroyed or shot down out of control some fifty-six enemy aircraft.[4]

The Iaccaci brothers flew several reconnaissance and bombing missions during the first two weeks of their assignment to No. 20 Squadron. On 19 May, during a beautiful clear day, Lt. P. T. Iaccaci and his observer, Sgt. W. Sansome, while on an offensive patrol with ten other Bristol Fighters, spotted about twenty Pfalz Scouts and Fokker Triplanes at fourteen thousand feet over Merville. Paul Iaccaci immediately dove on one Fokker Triplane and "put in a good burst of about 25 shots at 200 yards with the front gun." Iaccaci's gun jammed and was cleared, "but before he could fire again the triplane went down in a vertical dive—came out about 4,000 feet and went into another vertical dive and flattened out near the ground upside down and crashed. . . ." This kill was credited to Lt. Paul Iaccaci and marked his first air victory since joining No. 20 Squadron.[5]

On the same day, and at approximately the same time as Lt. Paul T. Iaccaci's first combat success, Lt August T. Iaccaci and his observer, Sgt. A. Newland, became involved with a Fokker Triplane over the town of Vieux Berquin. A. T. Iaccaci was unable to get the enemy aircraft in his gun sights but did put his observer in position to fire on the enemy plane. Newland emptied one magazine at close range and the German "spun down, leaving behind a trail of smoke, and was seen to crash just to the left of the road south of Vieux Berquin." Even though Lt. A. T. Iaccaci was not credited with the victory, he had, indeed, helped Newland by maneuvering the Bristol Fighter into a postion to destroy the Fokker Triplane.[6] At the end of the day, the New York brothers celebrated their first aerial success.

While flying on offensive patrol at noon on 27 May 1918, Lt. A. T. Iaccaci and his observer were attacked at nine thousand feet by some eight Pfalz Scouts. Despite clouds and poor visibility, a "running fight" developed. Newlands, Lt. A. T. Iaccaci's observer, "put a full drum into one of the Pfalz Scouts and he was seen to go down vertically with large volumes of smoke coming from him. The location was along the road about 3 miles s.w. of Neuve Eglise." This victory was confirmed by a French anti-aircraft battery.[7] Once again, Lt. A. T. Iaccaci had put his observer into a postion to score the kill with the Bristol Fighter's rear guns.

On 31 May, at approximately eight A.M., ten Bristol Fighters from No. 20 Squadron were attacked by fifteen Pfalz and Albatros Scouts a little southwest of the city of Armentières. Lt. Paul Iaccaci saw five Albatros Scouts diving on a Bristol Fighter and immediately went down to the assistance of the Brisfit being attacked. He managed to drive the enemy planes off but was then attacked by several other aircraft. His observer, A. M. Newland, "put about a drum into a Pfalz Scout and it burst into flames and, after gliding a moment, went out of control and crashed just E. of Merville. The observer then put a full drum into an Albatros Scout and it went into a vertical dive, flattening out just before crashing on the canal bank S. of Merville."[8] Meanwhile, Lt. August T. Iaccaci and his observer, Sgt. D. A. Malpas, engaged an Albatros Scout and "put about 150 rounds into him at close range." The enemy plane went down out of control and was credited to Lieutenant Iaccaci.[9] During the big air dogfight, No. 20 Squadron destroyed eight enemy aircraft and drove one down out of control. This ran the squadron's victory list for the month of May to fifty-six. In addition, the squadron had dropped 451 bombs on the Germans, fired 99,790 rounds and took 970 photographs.[10]

The Iaccaci boys continued their aggressive action during the month of June. On 1 June, at approximately eleven A.M., Lt. August T. Iaccaci engaged three Pfalz D-3s near the town of Merville. His observer, Sgt. W. O'Neill, sent one of the enemy planes down out of control.[11] One week later, on a cloudy afternoon, a formation of No. 20 Squadron intercepted some seven Pfalz D-3s at fourteen thousand feet over Wervicq. During this engagement, Lt. A. T. Iaccaci's observer, A. Newland, fired two drums into one of the enemy machines flying a little below and it "was seen to stall and go into a vertical dive and crash near the railway N.E. of Wervicq. . . ."[12] On a cloudy, poor visibility morning six days later, an offensive patrol of twelve Bristol Fighters from No. 20 Squadron ran into some eight Albatros and Pfalz Scouts a little to the northwest of Armentières. During the engagement, Lt. W. Noble, an observer in Lt. Paul Iaccaci's Bristol Fighter, shot down a Pfalz out of control.[13]

Early on the morning of 17 June 1918, both of the Iaccaci youths scored victories while on an offensive patrol with fifteen Bristol Fighters. Several small formations of enemy aircraft were encountered at different times. Since the Huns were split up more than usual, they offered good targets. Lt. August T. Iaccaci and his observer dived on one of the Pfalz Scouts and, "waiting until close up, fired about 200 rounds into it. The E.A. turned slowly over and went down, eventually seen to crash near Houthem."[14] A few minutes later, Lt. Paul Iaccaci maneuvered behind another Pfalz and, from fifty yards range, fired about fifty rounds into it. The Pfalz went down in a steep dive and crashed near the town of Menin. The destruction of the enemy aircraft was confirmed by other members of the No. 20 Squadron patrol.[15]

In the late afternoon on the cloudy 26 June, Lt. Paul Iaccaci and 2nd Lt. F. J. Ralph, his observer, became temporarily separated from the nine Bristol Fighters of No. 20 Squadron flying an offensive patrol mission. Some five Pfalz D-3s "came out of the sun and attacked." Iaccaci fired a burst of twenty rounds into one of the enemy machines and, a few second later, the observer was able to fire some three hundred rounds into it. The Pfalz "went down absolutely out of control directly over Armentières, falling over and over until out of sight in the background of houses." Since both front and rear guns were involved, Iaccaci and Ralph shared the victory.[16]

On 30 June, a day in which the weather was fine and the visibility was good, a patrol of No. 20 Squadron attacked two formations of enemy aircraft, one of nine and the other of seven machines,

two of which were shot down by Capts. T. Middleton and F. Godfrey. Lt. A. T. Iaccaci and Sgt. A. Newland, Capt. D. Latimer and Lt. T. C. Noel, Lts. D. J. Weston and W. Noble, Capt. H. Pale and 2

Lt. E. Hardcastle, of the same patrol, also accounted for an enemy machine each, making a total of six E.A. destroyed.[17]

Despite a strong west wind, 4 July proved a red letter day for Lts. Paul T. Iaccaci and R. W. Turner, his observer, on the late afternoon mission. The offensive patrol of nine Brisfits became separated after dropping bombs on enemy positions east and south of Ypres. Five Albatros D-3 fighters bounced Iaccaci and Turner a little north of Gheluvelt. One Albatros tried to outclimb Iaccaci, but Turner fired one hundred rounds into him "at point blank range, when the enemy aircraft turned over and went into a dive, and was seen to crash just west of Veldhoek." Another Hun attempted to get on the tail of the Bristol Fighter, but the observer blasted him with machine-gun fire from fifty yards. This Albatros "went down completely out of control." Then Lt. Paul Iaccaci joined a formation of Sopwith Camels in a battle with another enemy patrol. He caught one enemy machine out of position and fired a long burst at fifty yards' range. The enemy plane went in a vertical dive and hit the ground near a railway northeast of Zillebeke Lake. In the combat, lasting several minutes, Iaccaci and Turner destroyed three enemy machines.[18]

On 10 July 1918 Paul Iaccaci and his observer, R. W. Turner, braved clouds and rain storms to fly an offensive patrol north of Zillebeke Lake. At 9:20 A.M. they were attacked by five Fokker D-7s. One of the Fokkers dived to within a few yards of the tail of the Bristol Fighter, and Turner fired one drum of ammunition into it but was unable to replace the empty Lewis gun because of "his hands being frozen." Lieutenant Iaccaci dived down to approximately six thousand feet with the Fokker still attacking. From there the observer was able to change drums and, when the enemy plane "was about twenty yards away, fired a burst into it which made it turn over and dive into the ground just east of Zillebeke Lake." The Royal Air Force Communiqué credited the Bristol Fighter crew with two "kills" in this combat, but Iaccaci did not comment on the second victory.[19] According to Frank Bailey and Norman Franks's article in *Cross and Cockade*, Lt. A. T. Iaccaci and Lt. R. W. Turner shot an enemy scout down out of control on 14 July, but this victory was not recorded in "Decisive Combats—Pilots of No. 20 Squadron," nor in the appropriate Royal Air Force Communiqué.[20]

Although No. 20 Squadron was essentially a fighting squadron, between March and November 1918 almost every machine crossing the battle lines carried one 112-pound bomb. In addition to its work "of offensive patrols and aerial fighting, the squadron was called upon to carry out a certain amount of long distance photography and bombing."[21] Indeed, the organization, then commanded by Maj. E. H. Johnston, was a versatile squadron.

According to "Decisive Combats—Pilots of No. 20 Squadron," Lt. Paul T. Iaccaci's observer, on 30 July, shot down a Pfalz Scout which crashed east of Zillebeke Lake.[22] However, this victory does not appear in the combat reports for the day nor is it recorded in the Royal Air Force Communiqué. Both Iaccaci pilots were awarded the Distinguished Flying Cross toward the end of July.[23]

The big Allied Amiens offensive got underway on 8 August 1918. Three days later, working with four other squadrons, sixteen machines from No. 20 Squadron, each carrying a 112-pound bomb, attacked the railway station and sidings at Courtrai. The bombs were dropped at a low level, and direct hits were made on trucks, sidings, and the station. In addition, about nine thousand rounds of machine-gun bullets were fired at German troops and ground targets. On the return from the attack on Courtrai, the No. 20 Squadron leader, Capt. H. P. Lale, fired about 150 rounds into an enemy kite balloon at about one hundred feet from the ground and watched it burst into flames. A short time later, another pilot destroyed a second observation balloon.[24]

No. 20 Squadron was transferred to the V Brigade on 26 August and was moved to the airdrome at Vignacourt, located about ten miles northwest of Amiens. There it came under the orders of the Twenty-second (Army) Wing. On 3 September 1918, Lt. Paul T. Iaccaci engaged a Fokker D-7 over Havincourt Woods; his observer shot down the enemy machine.[25] Three days later, nine Bristol Fighters from No. 20 Squadron, after dropping bombs on Roisel, were at nine A.M. attacked by seven Fokkers a little southeast of the city of Cambrai. Sgt. A. Newland, Lt. A. T. Iaccaci's observer, fired two drums of ammunition into one of the Fokkers. It "went down in a slow spin and was lost sight of in mist and smoke near the ground." At approximately the same time, Lt. A. Mills, the observer in Lt. P. T. Iaccaci's plane, fired several bursts into a second Fokker. It went down spinning and smoking. On hitting the ground between the Cambrai railway and Peronne road, it burst into flames. A few minutes later, Lieutenant Mills "fired a long burst at 1 E.A. which fell in pieces." Lt. August Iaccaci's observer shot down another enemy aircraft which "was seen to crash northeast of St. Quentin, close to the wood near the St. Quentin Canal." Altogether, the Bristol Fighter formation, led by Capt. H. P. Lale, destroyed five enemy planes and drove down three others.[26]

August T. Iaccaci, in September 1918, was promoted to captain and made a flight leader in No. 20 Squadron.[27] On the next day, Paul T. Iaccaci was transferred to No. 48 Squadron, flying Bristol Fighters, promoted to captain and made a flight commander.[28] Unfortunately, Paul Iaccaci was not to shoot down any other enemy aircraft during his tour with No. 48 Squadron. His brother, however, would continue his effective air combat career for several more weeks. While flying in a nine-plane offensive patrol at appproximately 11:30 A.M. on 15 September, Capt. August T. Iaccaci and Sergeant Newland became involved in a dogfight with several Fokker D-7s and Pfalz D-3s. During the fight, three enemy fighters got on the tail of Iaccaci's plane, but Sergeant Newland "fired 150 rounds into one with double guns at about 80 yards range. It went down and was seen to crash and burst into flames on the ground near the main road south of Lesdins." Iaccaci dived on another enemy machine and fired one hundred rounds into it. This enemy aircraft "dived down almost vertically and hit the ground south of Morcourt near the railway." During the air battle, No. 20 Squadron destroyed four enemy planes and drove down three others out of control.[29]

While on a nine-plane offensive patrol at eight A.M. on 16 September near St. Quentin, No. 20 Squadron pilots intercepted some twenty silver-gray Fokker D-7s. In the dogfight that took place, the Bristol Fighters managed to destroy four enemy planes and drove down another three out of control. In the air battle, Sergeant Newland, Capt. August Iaccaci's observer, shot down a Fokker and watched it hit ground west of Lesdin.[30] Later in the day, No. 20 Squadron was moved to the Suzanne Airdrome a few miles closer to the battle front.[31]

On 27 September 1918 Capt. August T. Iaccaci fought his last big battle. His squadron engaged about twenty Fokker D-7s a few miles northeast of St. Quentin at 10:30 A.M. The nine-plane Bristol Fighter formation succeeded in destroying three enemy machines and shooting down a fourth one out of control. In the dogfight, Iaccaci dived on one of the Fokkers and "fired 200 rounds into this E.A. which fell obviously completely out of control and was seen to crash S. of Fontaine." His observer, Newland, fired a drum into a second Fokker and watched it go down out of control.[32] After the air battle, the squadron returned to its new airdrome at Proyart.

Capt. A. T. Iaccaci became ill during the first week of October and, on 4 October, was transferred to a general hospital in the United Kingdom. Both Iaccaci boys had served effectively in one of the top fighter squadrons of the war. According to Bailey and Franks's article, entitled "Combat Log No. 20 Squadron RFC/ RAF," which appeared in *Cross and Cockade Journal*, No. 20 Squadron was credited with the destruction of 315 enemy aircraft and the probable destruction of 295 other enemy planes, as well as flaming three balloons, "giving it a total of 613 victory claims—therefore, making it the highest scoring squadron in the RFC/RAF." On the other hand, the squadron "suffered the loss of some 41 crewmen killed in action or who died of wounds, 65 missing and presumed dead, 61 prisoners of war, 17 killed in accidents or died of injuries, and 64 wounded in action. This gave a total of 248 casualties from a variety of sources listed above."[33]

Both Paul T. and August T. Iaccaci returned to the United States early in 1919. Indeed, they had done well as combat pilots during their tenure with the Royal Air Force. In Bruce Robertson's edited work entitled *Air Aces of the 1914–1918 War*, August T. Iaccaci was credited with eighteen victories, and Paul T. Iaccaci was listed as having eleven kills. These figures are cited in many other articles and books that have been published in recent years.[34] A close study of combat reports and documents in the Public Records Office indicate each of the Iaccaci brothers had only five victories by the pilot and the rest by their very able observers. Certainly, the two Iaccacis were great fliers and managed to maneuver the Bristol Fighter into position to enable the observers to achieve great success. If the Bristol Fighter operation was considered a team performance, then the score listed in Robertson's study is an accurate one.

The Sopwith Dolphin
Courtesy Imperial War Museum

FIFTEEN

Capt. James William Pearson

The flight of No. 23 Squadron's Sopwith Dolphins circled at ten thousand feet over Montdidier-Vignieres-Contoir on an offensive patrol in the late afternoon of 3 June 1918. The weather was fine and the visibility was excellent as the five pursuit pilots scanned the sky for a possible enemy formation. Lt. James William Pearson, flying on the extreme left of the patrol, had been involved in two previous air battles but had had no success in shooting down an enemy machine. Consequently, he was extremely alert in searching for enemy aircraft. He, like most fighter pilots, was a "hunter," not one who tried to avoid combat. Pearson checked the Dolphin's cockpit one more time to ascertain all was in order; suddenly, he spotted a formation of eight Pfalz scouts in the neighborhood of Montdidier. He immediately wagged his Dolphin's wings to attract the No. 23 Squadron patrol's attention. After some preliminary maneuvering, the RAF formation attacked the German planes. Pearson singled out one of the Pfalz scouts and dived, "firing a burst of about 100 rounds, closing the range to about 15 yards." In his words, "I noticed smoke and then flames coming from its fuselage. I then zoomed away and saw [the enemy aircraft] go down vertically well on fire." The No. 23 Squadron formation returned to the Bertangles airdrome, where Maj. C. E. Bryant, the squadron commander, listed Pearson's first victim as shot down in flames.[1]

Lt. James William Pearson, a native of Nutley, New Jersey, had received his preliminary flight training in Canada and was commissioned a second lieutenant in the Royal Flying Corps on 27 November 1917. In late December 1917, he was sent overseas and, on 7 January 1918, arrived in the United Kingdom. After further training in a fighter aircraft, he was, on 6 April 1918, posted to No. 23 Squadron, located at Bertangles (north). This

Squadron, which had been operating over the battle lines since March of 1916, was one of the outstanding pursuit squadrons of the war. According to the squadron's history, it had destroyed 154 (crashed, in flames, or forced to land in our lines) and 93 down out of control. In addition, pilots of No. 23 Squadron had destroyed five kite balloons in flames and forced down forty-three other observation balloons. One of the unit's top aces was another American, Capt. Clive Warman, who had destroyed ten enemy aircraft and two observation balloons before being severely wounded in August 1917. Warman had received the British Distinguished Service order and the Military Cross during his two month service with No. 23 Squadron.[2]

In spite of low clouds and rain, a considerable amount of flying took place on 6 April 1918, the day Pearson reported to No. 23 Squadron.[3] However, the next several days proved to be terrible flying weather, and Lieutenant Pearson saw little activity over the battle front. His first real air-to-air combat occurred on 27 May at 11:25 A.M., while a part of No. 23 Squadron offensive patrol in the Maricourt area. Capt. H. V. Puckridge, his flight leader, observed a German reconnaissance aircraft flying southeast and fired a burst from both guns at a range of thirty yards. Unfortunately, his guns jammed, and he had to pull out to correct the stoppage. Young Pearson then attacked, "getting in a burst of about 50 rounds." The enemy plane suddenly put its nose down, dived east and disappeared "into a thick layer of clouds at about 8000 feet."[4] The combat was judged indecisive, but it did serve to whet Lieutenant Pearson's appetite for more dogfighting.

On a good visibility morning three days later, Lts. H. F. Faulkner and Pearson spotted an Albatros two-seater a little south of the city of Albert at six thousand feet. Both pilots attacked, but Lieutenant Faulkner's guns jammed. Pearson dived on the enemy observation plane and "got in about 100 rounds from under 100 yards. The E.A. there upon made a half roll, stalled and went into a vertical dive. The E.A. was still going down vertically at about 2000 feet from the ground." At this moment, seven German fighters appeared over the Sopwith Dolphin pair, and Faulkner and Pearson had to climb and, therefore, were unable to see what happened to the Albatros observation plane. This dogfight was also labeled as indecisive, even though considerable damage was inflicted on the enemy aircraft.[5]

During the period 3–9 June, the Royal Air Force claimed, officially, fifty-six enemy aircraft brought down and twenty-six others brought down out of control. Twelve RAF Squadron planes were missing. Young Pearson scored his first official kill on 3 June 1918. By and large the weather during the month of June was good, and, as a result, there was considerable air activity. No less than 262 enemy aircraft were listed as shot down by the RAF, and another 106 were considered "down out of control." Ninety-eight Royal Air Force planes were listed as missing.[6]

At 11:30 A.M. on 1 July 1918, Captain Puckridge, Lt. James W. Pearson, and three other Dolphin pilots, while on an offensive patrol at 12,500 feet in the vicinity of Hangest, observed seven green-tailed Albatros scouts. The Germans turned to the northeast, and the No. 23 Squadron pilots

> climbed parallel with them. When we got to their height they turned west. We then attacked. I saw Captain Puckridge go down on an Albatros scout. While he was diving another [German] got on his tail. I then got on the tail of the one attacking Captain Puckridge and fired a good burst into him at close quarters. The [enemy aircraft] broke up in the air.

Puckridge, in the meantime, shot down the first plane. Lieutenant Pearson, a little later, got on the tail of another Albatros scout and fired a burst of fifty rounds at close range. The enemy went down out of control; but due to further combat, Pearson did not see this plane crash. Maj. C. E. Bryant credited Lieutenant Pearson with one "crashed" victim and one "down out of control," giving the American three.[7]

During the week of 29 July–4 August, Royal Air Force squadrons claimed, officially, seventy-three enemy aircraft brought down and nineteen others driven down out of control. Five enemy balloons were destroyed. In addition, two enemy machines were shot down by anti-aircraft guns. Fifteen of the British machines were missing in action. Approximately 134½ tons of bombs were dropped and 9,207 photographic plates were exposed.[8] On 1 August Lt. James William Pearson shot down one German plane to run his offical score to four.[9] The Sopwith Dolphin squadrons, numbers 19, 23, 79 and 87, had now become some of the most effective units in the RAF.

With good visibility on the afternoon of 22 August, Capt. A. J. Brown and Lieutenant Pearson, while on an offensive patrol in the Amiens-Abbeville-Étaples sector, spotted a red-tailed Rumpler observation plane at approximately fifteen thousand feet. In his combat report, Captain Brown stated,

> Lt. Pearson and I climbed, and about 2:00 P.M. I got about 500 feet below the E.A., Lt. Pearson being about 1500 feet lower. The E.A. had by this time climbed to about 20,500 and was going north up the coast. I stalled four times, getting in bursts of about 50 rounds each time. After the last burst the E.A. dived and I lost control and spun for about 500 feet. After getting out of the spin I could not see the E.A. anywhere and as I was running out of petrol I returned to the airdrome. Lt. Pearson fired a drum from his Lewis gun from a range of about 1500 feet, but had to give up the chase before I did owing to engine trouble.

The combat was labeled as indecisive, even though the pair had inflicted some damage on the Rumpler.[10]

On the following afternoon, which was described as fair but cloudy, Lt. James W. Pearson, while leading a No. 23 Squadron patrol in the vicinity of Cappy, observed five Fokkers with silver "vertically striped red fuselage and red tail and elevator" somewhat above the Dolphin formation. "Each time we tried to climb up to them they made off East. Later on they came down to about 1000 feet and I saw them just over some clouds about 5000 below our formation. I attacked one, getting in about 50 rounds at 300 yards, when the [Fokker] spun down through the clouds. . . ." Pearson was unable to see the results of the combat, and the squadron commander declared the drive as "indecisive."[11]

Although the weather during September 1918 was less than perfect, air activity was great. According to RAF communiqués, approximately 425 enemy aircraft were shot down, and another 180 were brought down out of control. The Royal Air Force also listed nearly 250 of their own planes as missing.[12] Lieutenant Pearson was involved in several air duels during the month. On an overcast afternoon on 14 September, Pearson, while leading a flight of three Dolphins, observed a Halberstadt at approximately four thousand feet near the town of Vermand and dived on the German, firing some one hundred rounds into him. "The last seen of [enemy aircraft] it was going east, still losing height. The observer stopped firing after getting off a short burst and never re-opened fire." Once again, the air combat was listed as an indecisive battle.[13]

Four days later on a cloudy afternoon, Lieutenant Pearson and Lt. H. A. White engaged four reddish-brown Fokkers at six thousand feet over Lihaucourt. In Pearson's words,

> I got behind them and climbing into the sun, dived on them. I singled out the leading [Fokker] and fired a burst of about 40 rounds from at the most 75 yards. Black smoke then started to pour from the fuselage and the E.A. at once dived, disappearing into the clouds. I am convinced that the E.A. was on fire, especially as I used Buckingham ammunition, which I had in one of my guns for balloon attack. . . .

This enemy aircraft was listed as a decisive kill, moving Pearson into the ace category.[14]

There was considerable rain and cloudy weather during the month of October; but, according to RAF communiqués, some 225 enemy planes were destroyed and approximately eighty were driven down out of control. The British apparently lost about 150 of their own aircraft during October. The American, J. W. Pearson, now a captain, scored two more victories during this period. At 11:30 A.M. on the misty morning of 28 October, Captain Pearson's formation encountered some twelve gray camouflaged Fokkers with yellow noses over Bois du Nouvion. Six of the Fokkers were four thousand feet below the other six. Pearson attempted to climb to meet the top Fokker flight; suddenly, he half rolled his Dolphin and plunged down on the lower formation. A part of the No. 23 Squadron patrol remained on the same level as the upper Fokker formation in order to protect those battling the lower group. Captain Pearson attacked one of the Fokkers, "getting in a burst of about 50 rounds at close range. The [Fokker] turned over and started to float down in a series of stalls, eventually turning over on its back. I last saw him still going down in this manner about 2000 feet from the ground apparently completely out of control." Then Captain Pearson got in a burst of 150 rounds on a second Fokker at about one hundred yards range. This enemy aircraft went down in "an uncontrolled spin and . . . crashed in the woods" below. No. 23 Squadron scored several kills during the combat, and Capt. J. W. Pearson was credited with two victories.[15]

At high noon on 1 November, a poor visibility day, Captain Pearson and Lts. H. N. Compton and E. J. Taylor caught a DFW two-seater over Petit Beart at two thousand feet. In his combat report, Pearson stated he fired a long burst into the enemy aircraft and the machine "went down in a glide, eventually striking a tree with its left wing and crashing in a field." After strafing German infantry troops on the ground, the three pilots returned to Bertry, their new airdrome. The destruction of the DFW was confirmed in the Royal Air Force Communiqué.[16] According to the No. 23 Squadron history, Capt. J. W. Pearson was credited with ten enemy aircraft victories and, a short time after the war ended on 11 November, he was awarded the British Distinguished Flying Cross, which said that he demonstrated "at all times a fine example of skill and courageous determination."[17]

Captain Pearson was given authority to proceed to Nutley, New Jersey, on a medical leave on 10 March 1919. In September 1919 he resigned from the Royal Air Force and returned to New York.[18]

Fokker D-7
Courtesy U.S. Army Air Forces in National Archives

SIXTEEN

Lt. Bogert Rogers

The weather was beautiful in the late afternoon of 22 July
1918 as a No. 32 Squadron patrol circled over Mont Notre
Dame at twelve thousand feet. Lt. Bogert Rogers, a twenty-one-
year-old Californian flying on the right side of the formation, felt
very comfortable as he manipulated the controls on his highly
stable SE-5A. Up to this point, the No. 32 Squadron offensive patrol had spotted no enemy aircraft and, of course, had not been
engaged in combat on this sunny afternoon. Suddenly, the young
Californian spotted several Fokker D-7s engaged with a flight of
Sopwith Camels a few hundred feet below. Rogers wagged his
wings, hoping his flight would see the action, and dived into the
combat. He immediately picked out a Fokker on the fringe of the
battle and "fired a burst of 75 round at close range. E.A. [enemy
aircraft] pulled up in a slow stall, turned over on its side, and
went down for over 3000 feet out of control." Lieutenant Rogers
was unable to observe the Fokker crash due to the wild dogfight
then going on. "This machine was not seen again during the
fight." Since no other pilot in the swirling engagement actually
saw the German machine crash, Rogers's commanding officer,
Maj. J. C. Russell, "considered this machine was driven down out
of control."[1] Despite the fact Bogert Rogers did not receive credit
for a crashed victim, he was, nonetheless, happy to at least get a
down-out-of-control victory—his first since joining No. 32
Squadron on 2 May 1918.

Bogert Rogers was born 24 June 1898 in Los Angeles, California. He attended Stanford University and enlisted in the Royal
Flying Corps in Canada in September 1917. He completed his
ground school training at the University of Toronto, No. 4 School
of Military Aeronautics, on 25 October 1917. He received his

early flight training in the "Canuck," the Canadian version of the JN-4, during the period 27 October to 19 November 1917. He took further flight training at Taliaferro Fields, Fort Worth, Texas, during the period 25 November to 30 December 1917. He received his wings and second lieutenant's commission in January 1918 and was sent overseas to England, where he did further training in the Avro and the SE-5A, while assigned to No. 93 Squadron. He was posted to No. 32 Squadron, RAF, then based near the battlefront on 2 May 1918. Lieutenant Rogers was, indeed, happy his new squadron was flying the SE-5A; he had fallen in love with that type of fighter during his training period because of its great stability.[2] There were at least six American flyers assigned to No. 32 Squadron, including such aces as Capt. Alvin Andrew Callender, Lt. F. L. "Bud" Hale, and Lt. J. O. Donaldson.

During the latter part of the month of July and the first three days of August, No. 32 Squadron flew out of Touquin in the Marne River area. When the Allied offensive in the Aisne-Marne sector ended on 3 August, the squadron was moved back to the Somme area, on the British front, and stationed at Bellevue, some fifteen miles southwest of Arras. From this airdrome, the squadron was to participate in the British-French Amiens offensive in the Somme sector which began on 8 August 1918. Lieutenant Rogers spent much of the month of August in low-level strafing and bombing attacks on the German ground troops.[3]

Aerial combat became much more intense during the period 2–8 September. According to Royal Air Force Communiqué No. 23, the British "claimed officially 101 E.A. brought down and 51 driven down out of control. Eighteen enemy balloons were destroyed. Sixty-six of our machines are missing."[4] At eleven A.M. on 6 September, Lt. Bogert Rogers, while flying a "special line patrol" at twenty-one thousand feet a little east of Roisel, observed a Rumpler two-seater coming west and slightly below. Rogers "manuevered in position and attacked E.A., firing 100 rounds. E.A. dived and turned East." The California youth

again got into position under the tail of E.A., firing 100 rounds at point blank range. E.A. went into a flat spin which developed into a vertical spin, volumes of white smoke issuing from fuselage of E.A. Pilot followed E.A. down for 5000 feet, where, being attacked by 4 Fokker Biplanes he was compelled to leave the Rumpler.

A little later, Rogers attacked another observation plane, but "owing to gun trouble, was unable to engage him." After returning to his home airfield, Rogers described the combat to Maj. J. C. Russell, his commanding officer. Russell then wrote on the report, "I consider this machine was driven down out of control."[5] Several hours later, Lieutenant Rogers was involved, along with a flight of No. 32 Squadron SE-5As, in a dogfight at fourteen thousand feet over Holmon, a little west of St. Quentin. Six Fokker D-7s were attacking a small group of DH-9s at long range, when the SE-5s entered the battle. Rogers picked out one of the Fokkers and fired one hundred rounds at very close range. The enemy aircraft "was last seen turning over on its back, and going down." Rogers then turned and climbed back to protect the DH-9s.[6]

Air activity was, again, restricted by weather during the week of 9–15 September.[7] The following week, however, the air-to-air combat picked up. Royal Air Force Communiqué No. 25 reported "during the period under review we have claimed officially 105 E.A. brought down and 38 driven down out of control. Fifty five of our machines are missing. Approximately 169 tons of bombs were dropped and 8,411 plates exposed."[8] Once again, the young California man participated in the week's action. At 6:10 P.M. on 16 September, Lieutenant Roger's patrol engaged some nine Fokker D-7s at eight thousand feet over Sancourt. Rogers made a hard left-hand turn and got on the tail of one of the Fokkers attacking a SE-5 fighter. He immediately opened fire with his Vickers and Lewis guns at very close range. The enemy plane "side-slipped, and then went into a slow spin, out of control." Rogers "was unable to observe further, owing to the general engagement." Nonetheless, the squadron considered this enemy machine as driven down out of control. Bogert Rogers was now credited with four kills since he had joined No. 32 Squadron in May.[9]

No. 32 Squadron engaged fifteen Fokker D-7s in a wild dogfight on a cloud-filled sky over Emerchicourt on 27 September. The air battle started at thirteen thousand feet; Lieutenant Rogers selected a Fokker slightly below the rest and dived on it "firing a burst of 50 rounds at medium range, where upon the E.A. half rolled away." Rogers turned to continue his attack when another Fokker "climbed up vertically dead in front almost stalling." Rogers instantly fired both guns and saw tracers entering the cockpit and fuselage of the enemy aircraft. The enemy "fell over in a steep sideslip and at once burst into flames." Rogers was not able to follow the stricken German fighter down, due to the presence of other enemy Fokkers. However, pilots from No. 62 Squadron confirmed his "kill" as crashing in flames.[10] This victory moved Lieutenant Rogers into the ace category, and a few weeks later he was to receive the British Distinguished Flying Cross for his combat performance.

The first two weeks of October 1918 tended to be poor flying weather for Allied and German pursuit squadrons. High altitude patrols were especially a problem. Nonetheless, No. 32 Squadron continued to do considerable low-level strafing and bombing. Lieutenant Rogers, always eager to get in the air, contributed his part in the attacks on German infantry.[11]

On 1 November 1918 Lt. Bogert Rogers fought his last big air battle. At 1:25 P.M., despite poor visibility, his No. 32 Squadron patrol became involved with thirty Fokkers at sixteen thousand feet, some six miles east of Valenciennes. One of the Fokkers, when pulling out of a dive, came directly underneath Rogers, who half rolled and "went down vertically on it, getting in a burst of 50 rounds at point blank range." This enemy aircraft "pulled up, stalled, fell over on its right side and with engine still on went down out of control falling about from side to side." Lieutenant Rogers was able to observe the Fokker for about three thousand feet; but, when attacked by five other German machines, he had to break away from the falling Fokker D-7. Maj. J. C. Russell later wrote on Rogers's combat report "I consider this machine was driven down out of control."[12] This combat marked Lieutenant Rogers's sixth victory, although some reports indicate his late afternoon kill on 6 September was unconfirmed.[13] In addition to Lieutenant Rogers, at least three other Americans became aces in No. 32 Squadron. This group included Capt. A. A. Callender, Lt. John O. Donaldson, and Lt. Frank L. Hale.[14] Callender was killed on 30 October 1918, and Donaldson[15] was shot down and became a prisoner of war in September.

Bogert Rogers was promoted to captain on 20 November 1918, some nine days after the war ended. He remained with No. 32 Squadron until May of 1919, when he was separated from the RAF service and returned to the United States. Documents in the RAF Museum in Hendon (the northern part of London, England) indicate Rogers was indeed born in Los Angeles, California, but lists him as British in nationality. This, no doubt, was typical of many Americans who flew with the RAF, since it was sometimes difficult to regain American citizenship after enlisting with the British forces. In this case, Rogers had no real difficulty in regaining American citizenship. He died on 24 July 1966 and was interred in Forest Lawn Cemetery, Hollywood, California.[16]

Harold A. Kullberg
Courtesy Duerson Knight

SEVENTEEN

Lt. Harold A. Kullberg

Harold Albert Kullberg, son of Charles A. and Hilda (Streed) Kullberg, was born in Somerville, Massachusetts, on 10 September 1896. He attended public schools in Somerville and Concord and the Wentworth Institute in Boston.[1] During his Wentworth Institute days, stories of the air war in Europe and its "knights of the blue," such as Mick Mannock, Manfred von Richthofen, Georges Guynemer, René Fonck, and Oswald Boelcke fired his imagination. Like many other young Americans, he was eager to try his hand in the hostile skies over no man's land.

Shortly after the United States entered the First World War, Kullberg enlisted in the Royal Flying Corps at Toronto, Canada, after having been turned down as too short to pass the requirements of the United States Air Service. He attended the School of Military Aeronautics in Toronto, trained at Deseronto and Camp Borden in Canada, and spent several weeks at Hicks Field, Fort Worth, Texas.[2] Kullberg was commissioned a second lieutenant on 12 December 1917 and sailed for England in January 1918. A few days after his arrival in England, he was assigned to a scout squadron in the Surrey district and stationed at Stockbridge and Tangmere. On 12 April 1918 he was promoted to first lieutenant[3] and, four weeks later, on 10 May 1918, he was posted to No. 1 Squadron, RAF,[4] then located at Clairmarais, a short distance from St. Omer, France.[5]

During the last few weeks before Lieutenant Kullberg's assignment to No. 1 Squadron, the outfit, commanded by Maj. H. Adams, had been fiercely involved, along with other British air units, in the effort to stop the German advance in what later was known as the Battle of Lys. During the middle of April the squadron was forced to evacuate its airdrome at St. Marie Cappel, because of the German advance, and pull back to Clairmarais. Not only was No. 1 Squadron heavily engaged in air-to-air fighting with such crack units as *Jagdgeschwader I*, commanded by the Red Baron, Manfred von Richthofen,[6] but it was also required to participate in strafing and bombing missions against the advancing Hun forces. However, by the beginning of May, the German drive had lost most of its steam, giving the exhausted Allied squadrons an opportunity to rest and organize a concerted effort to achieve aerial superiority.[7]

Fortunately for Kullberg, his arrival at No. 1 Squadron headquarters coincided with the unit's first real lull in the fighting. This break in the combat allowed him time to familiarize himself with the squadron's planes, equipment, and personnel, as well as the geography of the batttle area patrolled by that senior outfit.[8] Consequently, the Massachusetts man was ready for the increased tempo of air activity that prevailed during the last week of May.

Harold Kullberg was involved in his first real aerial battle at two P.M. on 27 May 1918, when his patrol, led by the ace Capt. P. J. Clayson and flying SE-5As, engaged a gray camouflaged Halberstadt two-seater over enemy lines near the town of Bailleul. All five pilots in the patrol managed to fire a burst into the enemy aircraft from close range. The Halberstadt went down out of control and "probably crashed." This conclusion was confirmed by Allied anti-aircraft batteries in the neighborhood.[9]

At seven A.M. on the following morning, young Kullberg's patrol caught a DFW two-seater observation plane at three thousand feet over the battle lines and engaged it at close range. "After a few turns, the enemy aircraft went down out of control in a slow spiral, crashing at [Vieux-Berquin]." Kullberg made a decisive contribution to the destruction of this aircraft, which was confirmed by the patrol.[10]

For No. 1 Squadron, June was "a generally dull month both in weather and action," although the unit's top ace, Capt. P. J. Clayson, did manage to score four kills during that period.[11] Low clouds and periods of rain "kept both sides firmly fixed to their waterlogged airfields for most of the month."[12] Yet, Kullberg, the lad who was too short for the American Air Service, continued to get in his share of licks against the enemy. On 1 June his patrol, in an engagement with eighteen enemy aircraft over Ploegsteert

Woods, watched the wings "fall off of one Pfalz."[13] Eight days later, a No. 1 Squadron patrol of which Kullberg was a part dived on a Fokker triplane forcing it to land, and in the process the enemy plane "turned up on its nose."[14] On 15 June, braving low clouds and a fine mist, Kullberg attacked a German kite balloon, "which caught fire after a few bursts."[15] P. J. Clayson led a patrol on 27 June, which included Lt. Kullberg, who attacked an armored LVG reconnaissance plane and watched it "burst into flames and crash ½ a mile E. of Meteren."[16] In each of these victories Kullberg provided a decisive contribution to the squadron's success.

In July 1918 Harold Kullberg continued his aggressive activities against German aviation. On the first day of the month, he and two other pilots attacked a Halberstadt observation plane at five thousand feet in the locality of Messines. The enemy aircraft "dived vertically, its top plane crumpled up and it burst into flames at about 1,000 feet from the ground."[17] Nine days later at 8:50 P.M., Lieutenant Kullberg, flying alone, attacked a formation of seven Fokker D-7 biplanes. He described the engagement in the following words: "I dived on one enemy aircraft and fired 150 rounds in short bursts at close range. E.A. went down in a slow spiral and crashed just S. of Oostnieuwkerke."[18] On 22 July Lieutenant Kullberg's patrol blasted an enemy kite balloon with seven hundred rounds and the "balloon collapsed."[19] One week later, the Massachusetts boy caught an Albatros two-seater near Steenwerck and fired several short bursts into it. According to his combat report, "the machine dived vertically downward from 3,000 feet and crashed . . . near Steenwerck."[20] At 6:05 P.M. on the last day of July, Kullberg dived on a red-tailed Pfalz scout and forced it to land near Cheluvelt. "The pilot was obviously wounded," according to Kullberg, since "the machine did a slow spiral and the pilot showed no fight at all."[21]

Allied armies that had fallen back under German blows in March and April of 1918 were now, in midsummer, preparing themselves to strike back. More and more American troops were arriving and making their presence felt on the western front. Two American pursuit squadrons, the 17th and 148th, had been attached to RAF headquarters and were making a contribution.[22] In addition, many other American pilots had been posted to individual British squadrons.[23]

Marshal Ferdinand Foch, supreme commander of Allied forces, wanted a British offensive in Flanders in order to liberate important French coal mining areas, but British Field Marshal Sir Douglas Haig objected on the grounds that the terrain was unsuitable and the general area was of less importance than that east of Amiens. Foch not only accepted Haig's preference, but also placed the French First Army under his command for the operation. The actual field command for the Amiens effort would be under British General Sir Henry Rawlinson.[24]

Since German General Erich Ludendorff had predicted that should the Allied armies launch an offensive the attack would concentrate on the Ypres area, German troops in the Amiens area were lax and careless during the first week of August. They were caught off guard by a well-mounted assault secretly prepared.[25] No less than seventeen hundred Allied aircraft were moved into the area to cover the Allied drive planned for 8 August. As a part of the heavy air reinforcement in the Amiens sector, No. 1 Squadron, now commanded by Maj. W. E. Young, was moved up from Clairmarais to Fienvillers on 5 August.[26]

The British offensive began at 4:20 A.M. on 8 August and was launched without preliminary bombardment which might have alerted the enemy. Just before zero hour, approximately four hundred tanks (many of them speedy new Whippets) emerged from their assembly areas, "reaching the front lines as the rolling barrage came down, and the infantry rose and followed. On the right the French—who had only a few tanks—opened a forty-five minute bombardment and then advanced."[27]

At first the attack was severely hampered by a dense ground fog, which blinded the vast aerial forces concentrated to support it. Nonetheless, during the first day the Allied offensive gained approximately nine miles and captured some fifteen thousand prisoners and over four hundred artillery pieces. As the ground fog cleared near midday, the air squadrons were able to strafe and bomb the retreating Germans and inflicted heavy casualties. Late in the afternoon of the first day, the Germans began to bring in air reinforcements of their own.[28]

At 10:25 on the morning of 9 August, Lt. Harold Kullberg caught a Fokker D-7 over Proyart and "fired about 150 rounds at close range and he [the Fokker] burst into flames at 1,000 feet." Moments later, he was attacked by another Fokker but managed to maneuver into position to fire about one hundred rounds into the attacker who "went into a sideslip" and disappeared. The victory over Proyart marked the tenth "kill" Kullberg had participated in since joining No. 1 Squadron three months before.[29]

The second phase of the Allied counteroffensive, sometimes called the Battle of Bapaume, began on 21 August and lasted until 31 August. As the Allied armies moved forward toward Bapaume, Ludendorff ordered a general withdrawal from both the Lys salient in Flanders and from the Amiens area. His plans were disrupted when elements of the British forces penetrated across the Somme River, taking Peronne and threatening St. Quentin. The Canadian Corps shifted to the north flank of the battle lines and broke through near Quéant on 2 September. At this point, the entire German situation deteriorated, necessitating a general retirement to their final position—the Hindenberg Line.[30]

During the last two weeks of August, No. 1 Squadron was heavily engaged in low-level strafing operations but performed occasional escort missions. Late in the afternoon of 30 August, while escorting Royal Air Force DH-9 two-seaters in the Bourlon area, Lieutenant Kullberg's formation of SE-5As was attacked by a large number of Fokker D-7 fighters. Kullberg described the resulting air battle in the following terms:

> Three of them [Fokker D-7s] got on the tail of a straggling DH-9. I dived from behind at one and fired a burst from both guns at close range. [The enemy aircraft] spun and when he pulled out his wing came off. Later two enemy aircraft started to attack a DH-9 from below. It turned and fired at one of them at close range. The E.A. went down out of control and was last seen by Lt. Pegg to crash.[31]

These victories ran Kullberg's score to twelve and certainly established him as one of the top fighter pilots in the outfit.

At 6:20 P.M. on 3 September 1918, Lieutenant Kullberg scored his thirteenth air victory when he shot down a Fokker biplane over Avesnes-Le-Sac. His combat report described the air battle:

> At 6:20 P.M. my formation turned toward Cambrai. I kept on with the Bristol Fighters who were escorting some DH-9's to Valenciennes. On the way back the formation of [enemy aircraft] dived on the DH-9's. I attacked an E.A. and fired about 100 rounds. He dropped into a spin, and I saw him crash near Avesnes-Le-Sac. I saw a burst of smoke where the E.A. crashed.[32]

On the following day, Kullberg was recommended for an award by Maj. W. E. Young, the squadron commander.[33]

In spite of his highly successful tour as a fighter pilot, young Kullberg found himself in some legal difficulty on 5 September 1918. A provost marshal from the Third Army Headquarters reported to Major Young, commanding officer of No. 1 Squadron, that he had reason to believe Kullberg was in possession of a camera, which was in violation of military rules. Kullberg was questioned and admitted to having a camera and was subsequently placed under arrest. Major Young then corresponded with Fifty-first Wing Headquarters with regard to what action should be taken.[34] Apparently Wing Headquarters realized Kullberg's combat experience was needed, for, in his answer to Young, Lt. Col. R. B. Blomfert wrote:

> Lt. H. A. Kullberg is to be released from arrest without prejudice to his again being placed under it. He can continue to fly. Please call upon Lt. H. A. Kullberg to forward without delay, an explanation of why he was in possession of a camera contrary to G.R.O. No. 4775 dated 15/8/18, and also a statement of what subject his films consisted.[35]

In response to Fifty-first Wing Headquarters request, Kullberg, on 7 September, stated:

> I brought the camera with me from America, intent on getting pictures which, when I returned home after the war, would be of interest to my people and help them understand my explanations of the interesting features of this country. I had absolutely no intention of taking pictures that would prove of military value. The pictures I had taken were mostly personal ones, views of the French peasantry, pictures of myself with my machine, and machines lined up outside hangers.[36]

Before the camera controversy could be settled, No. 1 Squadron, escorting a formation of DH-9s from Nos. 98 and 107 Squadrons in a bombing raid on the Valenciennes railroad station on 16 September, became involved in a wild dogfight with enemy pursuit planes. A running battle ensued to the target and back "and most of the SE-5A pilots were engaged with one or other of the enemy machines."[37] In the combat Kullberg observed an SE-5A going down with two enemy scouts on its tail. He drove them off and, getting on the tail of one, followed him down. After a long burst of machine-gun fire, the German "went down in flames." Kullberg then found five Fokkers on his tail and was forced to spin down to ground level and, even though wounded three times in the leg, he was able to "contour chase" at treetop level all the way back to his home field at Fienvillers.[38] He was to spend the next six months in the Prince of Wales Hospital recovering from his wounds.

On 20 September, four days after Harold Kullberg was wounded, his squadron commander wrote the provost marshal of the Third Army stating that the heroic and highly successful American had been sent to an English hospital and asked that his camera "which was confiscated by you on the 5th of September, be returned. . . ."[39] Apparently, the case was dropped.

Lt. Harold A. Kullberg, the holder of the British Distinguished Flying Cross and, according to squadron records, credited with the destruction of fourteen airplanes and two balloons during his four months at the front, was demobilized on 12 July 1919.[40] Canadian records indicate he returned to his home in Somerville, Massachusetts, in the summer of 1919.[41]

Oberleutnant Hermann Göring with several German pilots,
summer 1918.
Courtesy Imperial War Museum

EIGHTEEN

Capt. Alvin Andrew Callender

Alvin Andrew Callender was born in New Orleans, Louisiana, on 4 July 1893 and was educated at Boys High School and Tulane University. He received his degree in architecture from Tulane in 1914 and worked in that field of endeavor for several months. Always interested in adventure and performing in "just causes," young Callender joined the Louisiana National Guard's Washington Artillery and served on the Mexican border during the Pancho Villa disturbances of 1916. On 6 April 1917, a few months after the Villa incident, the United States declared war on Germany. Callender, determined "to see a bit of the scrap," was very interested in joining the American Air Service. However, frustrated by the delays with the United States forces, he crossed the border into Canada and joined the Royal Flying Corps on 19 June 1917.[1]

After three months of flight training at Borden in Canada, Callender won his wings and was commissioned a lieutenant in the Royal Flying Corps. He was a little disappointed that he was not sent overseas immediately. Instead, several of the newly commissioned pilots became instructors flying gunnery training machines in Canada and in Texas. During his service at Camp Hicks, near Ft. Worth, Texas, Lieutenant Callender helped in training several ensigns from a group of U.S. naval officers.[2] One of his students was James Forrestal, who later became the first secretary of defense. In January of 1918 Alvin A. Callender was sent to England to complete his fighter training at the Central Flying School, Upavon, Wiltshire, in Sopwith Pups, Camels, and SE-5As. On 14 May 1918 he was assigned to the No. 32 Squadron then flying SE-5A aircraft out of Beauvois, some twenty-five miles west of Arras.[3]

During the first two weeks with No. 32 Squadron, Lieutenant Callender made several patrols with "C" Flight but saw very few Hun aircraft. On 19 May he wrote his mother and sister, describing one of his first patrols over enemy lines. In his letter he commented, "Had my first trip over the lines last Wednesday, but haven't had a scrap yet. I have made some lucky turns dodging Archie. The only Hun planes I have seen so far wouldn't let me get anywhere near them, so I haven't had a chance to try my guns yet." In the same letter, he mentions being "over Hunland for two hours, a cylinder on my engine cracked and I lost all the water through the exhaust. My engine did not quit until I was about eight miles on this side of the lines though. So instead of spending the night in Germany, I got a brand new engine. . . ."[4]

Lieutenant Callender scored his first aerial victory while flying with a No. 32 Squadron patrol in the Armentières area at 6:45 P.M. on 28 May. The flight, led by Capt. A. Claydon, spotted four Albatros D-5s at eight thousand feet with another nine enemy planes somewhat higher up. Part of the No. 32 Squadron patrol challenged the top group of German planes while Captain Claydon and Lieutenant Callender dived on the four Albatros planes below. Claydon's victim fell out of control and disappeared in the ground mist below. Callender dived on one of the enemy scouts, "coming up underneath the tail of E.A. firing a short burst from very close range." The Albatros turned sharply, but Callender managed to stay in very close range while firing another 175 rounds. "The E.A. disappeared in the mist out of control." This kill was later confirmed by Lt. S. W. Graham, one of the No. 32 Squadron pilots on the patrol.[5]

At the time young Callender joined No. 32 Squadron, it was, indeed, one of the outstanding fighter squadrons in the Royal Air Force. It had been formed on 12 February 1916 as a fighter squadron at Netheravon from surplus personnel of No. 21 Squadron. Equipped with DH-2 single-seat pusher biplanes, No. 32 Squadron proceeded to France on 28 May 1916. The unit spent short periods at airdromes at St. Omer, Auchel, and Treizennes before moving to Vert Galand. The squadron remained at Vert Galand until late October 1916, when it moved to Léalvillers where it was stationed until the summer of 1917. In its early days, the organization was involved in escort patrols, "but as the size of the patrols increased they grew in offensiveness and the radius of action increased until the squadron was operating far behind enemy lines." Maj. L. W. B. Rees, the commanding officer, was involved in a fight with ten enemy aircraft on 1 July 1916 and was badly wounded. Nonetheless, he drove down two enemy planes and was awarded the Victoria Cross on 5 August 1916.[6]

Throughout the Battles of the Somme, the battles of the winter and spring of 1917, the Battle of Arras the squadron maintained its offensive patrols. In May 1917 No. 32 Squadron was equipped with DH-5's with which it intensified operations, including ground strafing sorties, especially during The Third Battle of Ypres.[7]

In July the squadron moved to Droglandt and continued its daily offensive patrols throughout the northern offensive until the end of the year. In January 1918 the squadron was reequipped with SE-5A machines. During the March 1918 German offensive, the squadron was again in operation carrying out offensive sorties from Bailleul, Bellville Farm, and Beauvois. In June 1918 the unit transferred to the French front, flying from Fouquerolles, Ruisseauville and, in July, from Touquin airfields.[8]

Lt. Andrew Callender's second victory occurred at seven P.M. on 6 June 1918 when a No. 32 Squadron patrol became involved in a dogfight with nine Fokker D-7s over Montdidier. Callender attacked one of the Fokkers at eight thousand feet and "fired about 8 bursts at intervals down to 4,000 ft. (300 rounds fired in all) E.A. fell out of control, and was seen still out of control at 2000 ft." At this point, Lieutenant Callender "lost sight of the enemy plane owing to the presence of other E.A." Maj. J. C. Russell, commanding officer of No. 32 Squadron, and the Ninth Wing commander considered "this machine was driven down out of control."[9]

The New Orleans boy, along with other members of No. 32 Squadron, was heavily engaged in ground strafing and low-level bombing during the next several days, due to the German offensive in the Compiègne area. Of the six SE-5 pilots that took off for low-level patrol action at 4:30 A.M. on 9 June, only two managed to return to their home airdrome. Captain Claydon and one other pilot were forced to land at Epineuse because they were out of fuel, and Lieutenant Callender landed at Etanese with a broken propeller.[10] At first the word was out that Callender had been attacked by five Huns and he probably was shot down. Andrew wrote his mother on 12 June 1918 and commented, "I turned up a couple of hours later in a French auto and showed them that reports of my death were slightly exaggerated. I believe I got two of the Huns, but I did not have time to see whether they crashed or not after they went down."[11]

The SE-5As primary characteristic was its high degree—for a single seater—of automatic stability. According to one author, "It came as near to 'flying itself' as could be expected from a small machine with good control. Inevitably its stability diminished its controllability, and it was much less quick than the Camel or, take a more truly comparable type, a Spad." But its top speed was higher than the Sopwith Camel, and those who liked it made "great play with the theory that it provided a steady gun platform and that, in consequence, enemy aeroplanes could be engaged at greater ranges than they could from less stable but more sensitive machines." The SE-5A was powered with the liquid-cooled Hispano-Suiza engine and was capable of 132 miles per hour at sixty-five hundred feet. Its armament included a Vickers gun, synchronized to fire through the propeller, and a Lewis gun mounted on the top wing. Perhaps the SE-5A's greatest weakness was its vulnerability to bullets fired into its radiator.[12] This made ground strafing a dangerous operation. No less than a dozen No. 32 Squadron pilots were killed, wounded, or missing during the months of June and July 1918.[13]

At 8:15 A.M. on 8 July, Lt. Andrew Callender and Captain Claydon dived on a Fokker D-7 over the town of Bauvin. Callender fired some seventy-five rounds into the Fokker from close range and watched the enemy do a half roll and spin. The German plane was still spinning after falling some four thousand feet, but Callender did not continue to watch, for Captain Claydon was now under heavy attack from two enemy aircraft, slanting down on him from above and behind. Callender attempted to get on the tail of the two attacking aircraft but was attacked by an enemy triplane. Fortunately, several Sopwith Camels entered the combat, and the triplane dived to the east and safety. When Lieutenant Callender turned his attention again to Captain Claydon, he observed him "S turning" at about four thousand feet, "apparently without engine, with several E.A. following him." Claydon, one of No. 32 Squadron's top aces, was killed in the dogfight.[14]

The squadron, now operating out of Tonquin some twenty-five

miles southwest of Château-Thierry, continued its fierce aerial and ground combat. Late in the afternoon of 25 July, some ten SE-5As from No. 32 Squadron engaged twenty Fokker D-7s at twelve thousand to fourteen thousand feet near the city of Fismes, some ten miles east of Soissons on the Vesle River. During the dogfight, Andrew Callender saw two SE-5As battle two Fokkers a short distance to the southwest of Fismes. Callender "stalled-turned, and dived vertically onto one of the enemy machines, firing a burst of about 125 rounds at a range of 150 to 50 feet." The Fokker sideslipped and then "fell erratically, being seen to crash about halfway between Fismes and Fere en Tardenois."[15] This kill marked Callender's fifth victory and moved him into the ace category.

After the Allied counteroffensive in the Aisne-Marne sector on 3 August 1918, No. 32 Squadron was shifted back to the Somme area on the British front and stationed at Bellevue some eighteen miles northwest of Bapaume. From this base, the squadron participated in the British-French Amiens offensive, driving the Germans out of the Somme sector. The drive opened on 8 August 1918 with ten British and eight French divisions engaged. From the air forces' point of view, according to one source, the Amiens offensive "was the most complete surprize of the War." Behind the front from Courcelles to Albert the Allies had concentrated something over nineteen hundred planes:

> The German fighters were outnumbered more than six to one and when the thick mist lifted around 9:00 A.M. the greatest armada ever assembled in the war took to the sky. Tremendous confusion within the German lines produced exceptional targets. Transports were blown off the road and horses stampeded. Time and again parties of infantry were scattered in panic by low flying single seaters. Bomb after bomb was showered on demoralized enemy troops in full retreat toward the Somme.[16]

However, the initial Allied air advantage was soon to vanish. Late in the afternoon of the first day of the Amiens offensive, the Germans were able to shift vast aerial reinforcements, including the Richthofen *Jagdgeschwader,* commanded by Hermann Göring, since the baron's death on 21 April 1918, into the Amiens-Somme battle area.[17]

The result of the German air reinforcements was to increase the intensity of the air fighting over the Amiens-Somme front.

During the next several days, No. 32 Squadron pilots scored several aerial victories and Lt. Andrew Callender was to add to his own score. While on an offensive patrol at 11:30 A.M. on 9 August, Lieutenant Callender met a formation of six Fokker D-7s at ten thousand feet and, at the same time, noticed three more Fokkers above at about thirteen thousand feet. Young Callender decided it would be wise to attack the higher formation rather than maneuver over the city of Villers. He was able to get on the tail of the rearmost Fokker "firing 150–200 rounds, at 25 to 50 yards range." The enemy aircraft "went into a fast spin, and was last seen at 8,000 feet, still spinning, when he disappeared into a cloud, having been seen to spin over 5,000 feet." Callender followed the stricken enemy plane until he was "fired on from behind, from the next E.A. which he turned on, and fired 50 rounds into, while approaching each other, head on." The first combat was witnessed by a member of No. 32 Squadron, so Andrew Callender was credited with having shot the enemy Fokker down out of control.[18]

On the following morning, while on an offensive patrol in the Peronne area, Lieutenant Callender's flight was attacked from above by a formation of nine Fokker D-7s. Callender quickly maneuvered his SE-5A into position to challenge one of the Fokkers following one of the No. 32 Squadron planes and "fired 75 rounds, at 50–75 yards range." The enemy aircraft "went down in a slow spin, being last seen, still out of control, 8,000 feet below, when it disappeared into clouds." The Ninth Wing commander stated, "I consider this machine was driven down out of control" for Andrew Callender's seventh air victory.[19]

Aerial fighting on the first three days of the Amiens offensive was extremely heavy. While British losses were severe, German air losses "were irreparable." For example, the Richthofen Circus had been roughly handled. In a brief period, it "was reduced from 50 to 11 aircraft." Although air activity was less intense during late August and early September 1918, No. 32 Squadron did have several lively patrols escorting DH-9s to places such as Marquion and Cambrai. Callender missed much of the action during the last two weeks of August, since he was given a rest leave to tour Scotland during that period. His letter home reflected his excitement on being able to visit such places as Edinburgh, Perth, Aberdeen, Inverness, and the Lake District.[20]

When Capt. H. L. W. Flynn, commander of "C" Flight, failed to return from a combat mission on 3 September, Andrew Callender was promoted to captain and took over the leadership of "C" Flight. Three days later, Captain Callender's flight intercepted six Fokker biplanes in the process of attacking British DH-9 observation planes at fourteen thousand feet over Holnon, a little west of St. Quentin. In the dogfight, Lt. G. E. B. Lawson, a member of Callender's flight, managed to shoot down one of the enemy planes. The Callender patrol was able to drive the Fokkers to the east and rescued the DH-9s.[21]

At 6:10 P.M. on 16 September, Captain Callender's patrol observed nine Fokker D-7s in a dogfight with a formation of Sopwith Camels at eleven thousand feet over Sancourt. Callender dived on the enemy flightleader, who was shooting at the rear Camel, and "fired about 125 rounds, at 50–100 yards range." The Fokker sideslipped and spun out of control. The American followed the enemy aircraft for several thousand feet, then engaged a second German plane without results. The commanding officer of the Ninth Wing, Royal Air Force, wrote on Captain Callender's combat report "I consider this machine was driven down out of control." In No. 32 Squadron records, Callender had achieved his eighth kill of the war. Unfortunately, the Royal Air Force Communiqué does not mention this victory.[22]

Late in the afternoon of 24 September, Captain Callender's offensive patrol, flying in the Cambrai-LeCateau-Bohain area, saw "DH-9's and escort machines in a running fight nearing Cambrai from the East." The New Orleans boy "swung in behind 7 Fokker biplanes which were following the DH-9's, and attacked them from the East with his lower formation." The enemy pilots, taken by surprise, immediately scattered. Callender attacked the leader, who half rolled and attempted to go under Callender, who also half rolled on top of the German and again fired a burst. The enemy aircraft "went up in what appeared to be a climbing turn, but stalled and went down out of control." Callender concluded the Fokker crashed near the northern edge of Bourlon Wood. He then maneuvered on to the tail of a second enemy plane and "fired 100 rounds in several bursts." The enemy aircraft stopped maneuvering and went into a steep spiral—apparently out of control. While reloading his Lewis gun, Callender lost sight of the Fokker in its plunge toward the east near Marquion. Once again the commanding officer of the Ninth Wing, RAF, considered "both these machines were driven down out of control." Although the Royal Air Force Communiqué for 24 September 1918 did not mention Callender's success, No. 32 Squadron now considered him to have achieved his tenth victory.[23]

Although the weather on the western front during the month of October 1918 was frequently cloudy, rainy, and windy, air fighting, ground strafing, and bombing activities increased in violence. Captain Callender's "C" Flight was very active during this period, inflicting much damage on the retreating Germans, but the New Orleans youth was unsuccessful in adding to his victory total. By 25 October, the Allied armies on the British front had advanced far beyond the Somme River. Two days later, No. 32 Squadron shifted its base from Bellevue to Pronville to move close to the front.[24] According to one source, on 30 October the RAF achieved its greatest aerial success. "Sixty-seven enemy planes were downed for a loss of 29 aviators killed or missing and eight more wounded. Four of these casualties were from No. 32 Squadron." Callender's offensive patrol had escorted several DH-9s to La Louvière and Manage, and at 9:20 A.M. the SE-5As broke out of the clouds over Ghislain. Below, the DH-9s were being attacked by eight Fokker D-7s. Callender's "C" Flight dived on the enemy aircraft, forcing the British observation planes to turn back toward their own lines. Suddenly, seventeen additional German fighters plunged into the dogfight. Even though No. 32 Squadron managed to shoot down several of the enemy, they also suffered heavy casualties of their own. Capt. Alvin Andrew Callender, who was shot through the lungs, managed to reach the battle lines north of the city of Valenciennes, where he crashed just inside Allied territory. Canadian soldiers pulled the unconscious American from the wreckage of his plane but, unfortunately, could not save his life. Callender died about one hour after the crash.[25]

In 1926 New Orleans' first municipal airport was named the Alvin Callender Field. Three decades later, a United States Naval Station was completed on the same site and now bears the same name.[26]

Lt. Oren J. Rose
Courtesy Ola Sater

NINETEEN

Capt. Oren J. Rose

A heavy ground mist obscured the battle-scarred landscape in the Arras-Amiens sector in the late afternoon of 30 July 1918. Nonetheless, a five-plane formation from No. 92 Squadron, Royal Air Force, patrolled back and forth at ten thousand feet over no man's land, searching the sky for enemy reconnaissance planes. The patrol, flying SE-5As, was led by the veteran fighter pilot Maj. A. Coningham, who had already earned the Distinguished Service Order and the Military Cross. Flying on the extreme left of the formation was Lt. O. J. Rose, an American and a recent addition to the squadron's roster of fighter pilots. Because of poor visibility, the SE-5A pilots probably did not expect to encounter enemy aircraft, especially observation planes, but they remained alert to any possibility.

As No. 92 Squadron banked to the left to return to their home airdrome at Drionville, France, they were surprised to see seven Fokker D-7s flying in the same direction, but at a slightly lower altitude. On Major Coningham's signal, the SE-5As slanted down toward the German formation. Because of his own position, Lieutenant Rose selected a Fokker on "the extreme left and dived on his tail opening fire at about 75 yards range with a continuous burst." He then pulled up in a right-hand turn to avoid ramming him. The enemy machine went into a spin and appeared to fall out of control. Rose was not able to see the German crash because of the ground mist and the presence of other enemy aircraft in the area. However, the likelihood of the Fokker recovering from the death spin at such a low altitude was extremely slim, and Lieutenant Rose was credited with a victory.[1] Other members of the patrol were heavily engaged but were unsuccessful in knocking down an enemy.[2]

Oren John Rose was born on 23 March 1893 in Platte County, Missouri, and, at the time of his enlistment in the Royal Flying Corps in 1917, lived at 4447 Chestnut Street in Kansas City. After studying military aeronautics at the University of Toronto for four months, he went overseas. His flight training was completed in England and Scotland during the early months of 1918. In June of that year, he was assigned to No. 92 Squadron, then training for combat while flying out of Tangmere near Chichester in Sussex. The squadron had only recently been equipped with the SE-5A fighter and would not proceed to the combat zone until 1 July.[3]

Relatively few of the No. 92 Squadron pilots had had any combat flying experience. Consequently, the first few days of operation from their new airdrome at Bray Dunes were spent in practice patrols. These training flights continued until 12 July when, under the leadership of Major Coningham, the outfit began combat patrols in the vicinity of the front lines. One week later, No. 92 Squadron moved to Drionville where its duties were expanded to include escort work as well as line patrols. The unit scored its first aerial victory on 22 July when Capt. J. M. Robb, a flight commander who had had combat experience with No. 32 Squadron, shot down a Fokker biplane a little south of Bailleul railway station. During the next eight days, pilots of the squadron were to destroy four more enemy aircraft.[4]

At 7:20 P.M. on the last day of July, Lieutenant Rose was to score his second aerial victory. During an offensive patrol over no man's land, ten SE-5As from No. 92 Squadron attacked several enemy aircraft. During the engagement, Rose became separated from the patrol led by Major Coningham. In his effort to rejoin the SE-5A formation, he spotted an enemy two-seater observation plane near Gailly-de-la-Lys. Rose immediately maneuvered his fighter into position on the enemy's tail and "fired four bursts at him at short range." In the words of Lieutenant Rose, the two-seater "dived about 2000 feet and flattened out. The observer started firing at me without any effect. I dived on his tail giving him a good burst of fire. He then spun to the ground and crashed."[5]

On 2 August No. 92 Squadron moved to Serny airdrome, some twenty-five miles west of Armentières, where they would coordinate with No. 46 Squadron (flying Camels) in their patrol activity. During the next several days, these two squadrons were responsible for afternoon patrols, while two Australian fighter squadrons handled morning patrols. It was assumed that the SE-5A pilots would engage the enemy at high altitude while the Camel pilots would pick up enemy aircraft driven down by No. 92 Squadron and any other enemy planes operating at lower levels.[6]

With the opening of the Allied armies' Amiens offensive on 8 August, the air activity increased sharply. At midday on 11 August, twelve SE-5As attacked fourteen Fokker biplanes and three enemy two-seaters over the German airdrome at Nesle. In the ensuing air battle, three enemy aircraft were shot down while No. 92 Squadron lost one. During the hectic battle, Lt. O. J. Rose and two other SE-5A pilots strafed the airdrome but were unable to "set on fire the remaining two hangars which were being dismantled."[7]

Three days after the Nesle Airdrome attack, a patrol from No. 92 Squadron encountered a large formation of Fokker D-7s near the town of Péronne, some twenty-five miles east of Amiens. In his combat report, Lieutenant Rose gave a colorful description of his role in the air battle that took place at fourteen thousand feet:

> While on Offensive patrol at 11.05, Capt. Robb leading, we attacked a large Formation of EA underneath. Capt. Robb and Lieut. O'Shea went down first I followed, on missing my first burst I pulled up and saw two EA on Lieut O'Shea's tail. I went to his assistance at once firing from quite a distance to shake them off but they stuck. I closed down on one firing a good burst from 100 yds. He immediately burst into flames but the other got Lieut. O'Shea and dived East. I then attacked another and got on his tail closing in, firing short bursts. His wing came off and my attention was then necessary to the rear, as I then had two EA on my tail. By their accurate shooting my machine became badly damaged and I was barely able to make my get-away.[8]

These two kills ran Rose's victory score to four and marked him as one of the top pilots in the squadron.

No. 92 Squadron continued its offensive patrol duties during the rest of the month of August, but also participated in heavy raids on the German airdromes at Haubourdin on 16 August and Lomme on 17 August. In both cases, hangars and enemy aircraft were destroyed.[9]

Lieutenant Rose chalked up his fifth victory on 25 August when he intercepted a Fokker biplane over Armentières and sent it down out of control. The enemy machine was last seen in a violent spin very near the ground.[10] During the month of September, Lieutenant Rose continued his aggressive and highly successful combat against the German *Jagdstaffelns* in the Lille-Armentières-Cambrai sector. At eleven A.M. on 4 September, he caught a Halberstadt two-seater over the River Scarpe and sent it crashing to the earth a short distance from the city of Douai.[11] On 15 September a second German observation plane, this time a Hanoveraner, went down under the American pilot's guns and crashed a little west of the city of Lille. He had ambushed the two-seater by plunging out of a nearby cloud and firing a long burst before the German pilot was aware of his presence.[12]

Two weeks later, while on offensive patrol, Rose scored a double victory. At 11:40 A.M. he observed a green-camouflaged Fokker biplane attacking the rear machine of No. 208 Squadron Camel formation and dived to the rescue. The Fokker pilot broke off his attack and turned to the east. After rejoining his own patrol, Rose noticed the same enemy machine again stalking the Camel formation. Rose again faced the enemy to turn east but "could not follow as my Lewis gun blew down on my head." A few minutes later, Rose intercepted the same Fokker at approximately eight thousand feet and "got a perfect shot at him at 75 yards. He started a vertical dive and smoke came from his machine; he burst into flames at about six thousand feet." The enemy crashed on Canal des Torcens just east of Beaurevoir.[13] Some twenty minutes after the encounter with the Fokker, Rose dived and came up under the nose of a Halberstadt two-seater and "fired a good burst." Then he did a quick turn to get on the enemy's tail. As the Halberstadt spun down out of control "his right upper wing came off," and the enemy crashed northeast of the town of Bellicourt.[14]

In late September 1918, Marshal Ferdinand Foch, supreme Allied commander, planned a double penetration of the German lines in two major assaults. One of these was to be the Franco-American drive in the Meuse-Argonne area toward the Mézières, a vital German supply center and railroad junction. The other was to be a British offensive between Péronne and Lens, with the railroad junction of Aulnoye as the main objective. Indeed, the seizure of these vital railroad junctions would jeopardize the entire German logistical situation on the western front. In addition, Foch planned supplemental drives to be made in Flanders by

British, Belgian, and French forces and, between La Fère and Péronne, by another French-British force. The Meuse-Argonne offensive was launched on 26 September with other drives getting underway on the next day.[15]

The British drive in the Péronne-Lens sector got underway on 27 September, causing No. 92 Squadron to move to Proyart South with assigned patrol activity between Cambrai and St. Quentin. Lieutenant Rose was now the top-scoring ace in the squadron and, despite poor weather conditions in October, he added to his rapidly mounting victory list. On 3 October Rose chalked up two kills. The first came at 8:15 A.M. when he shot a green camouflaged Fokker D-7 down in flames a little north of the town of Beaurevoir for victory number ten. The second kill occurred thirty minutes later when he sent a Fokker biplane crashing to earth in the outskirts of Fresnoy.[16] On the following day, Rose and his wing man Lt. J. V. Gascoyne attacked a Hanoveraner two-seater near the city of Malencourt. His first burst with his Lewis and Vickers machine guns apparently killed the observer, but his guns malfunctioned before he could destroy the enemy machine. Instead, Gascoyne was credited with driving the German down out of control.[17]

Rose's twelfth aerial victory came on the afternoon of 8 October when he and seven other pilots from No. 92 Squadron engaged eight Pfalz D-3s and Fokker D-7s in the vicinity of Le Cateau. Rose described the combat: "I climbed up to 14000 feet and one [a Pfalz Scout] came head on and a bit below; I attacked and he turned East. I fired two good bursts, one dead on his tail. He went into a stall and spun down and crashed just north of Le Cateau. The other seven attacked me from above. . . . " Fortunately, Rose escaped without real damage.[18]

In a cloud-filled sky on 9 October, Lieutenant Rose's patrol spotted a Hanoveraner two-seater at low altitude over the city of Montigny. Rose dived out of formation and attacked the two-seater, but, just as he was lining up the target for a close burst of machine-gun fire, he was attacked by a Fokker with a "white tail and green camouflaged wings." Rose did a sharp climbing turn and got on the Fokker's tail. In his combat report, Rose stated, "I fired a long burst from both guns and he went into a vertical dive and crashed." The destruction of the enemy fighter was confirmed by members of Rose's patrol and marked the Kansas City boy's thirteenth kill. His own SE-5A fighter suffered heavy damage from the Hanoveraner as he fought the Fokker.[19] Since No. 92 Squadron headquarters was in the process of moving closer to the battle front on that day, the patrol that had been involved in the Montigny fight landed at its new airdrome located at Estrées-En-Chausée.[20]

Three days after the Montigny battle, young Rose was granted a rest leave and spent some two weeks in England. He did not return to combat flying until the last week of October. During his absence, the squadron became increasingly involved in the highly dangerous ground strafing duty in support of the advancing infantry.[21] Immediately upon his return to No. 92 Squadron, Oren J. Rose began to increase his score of enemy aircraft destroyed. At 10:05 A.M. on 29 October, he, along with Lt. J. V. Gascoyne, attacked a "light green and black camouflaged" DFW observation aircraft and drove it down out of control. This kill was later confirmed as having crashed.[22] On the following morning, Rose saw a DFW "working" along a canal and "dived right on him and fired several good long bursts at about 50 yards range." The enemy machine nose-dived into the ground and burst into flames just west of Noyelles.[23] The destruction of this aircraft ran his victory score to fifteen.

During the next several days, Rose and other members of No. 92 Squadron were heavily engaged in ground strafing and bombing the German gun positions in the Landrecies-Mézières-Catillon area. On one occasion the Missourian engaged "about 100 enemy troops and guns into which he fired 300 rounds from 1500 feet before picking up an RE-8[24] and showing the observer where the group was, no doubt to call up batteries and direct fire on them."[25]

Lt. O. J. Rose, now a flight leader, scored his sixteenth and last victory with No. 92 Squadron when, at 10:45 A.M. on 4 November 1918, he attacked a Fokker D-7 and shot it down near the village of Landrecies. He described the dogfight:

> On going out to strafe the Huns on the ground I was at about 2000 ft and saw one of our balloons in flames. I turned toward it and saw a Fokker coming East. I attacked him head on and evidently missed him as he went past me. I then turned on his tail and he showed fight. We turned around each other several times and finally I got on his tail just west of Landrecies. I took good aim and fired at about 50 yds. He then went down and crashed. . . ."[26]

One week after Rose's 4 November kill, the First World War, perhaps the bloodiest war in all history, came to a close. The Missourian's sixteen victories marked him as the top ace of No. 92 Squadron and one of the most effective American fighter pilots of the first great air war. Of his sixteen kills, no less than fourteen were seen to crash or go down in flames. Only two of his triumphs were listed as down out of control. Certainly, his confirmed kill rate was one of the highest in the war.[27]

In January 1919 Rose was promoted to captain in the Royal Air Force and, a short time later, he journeyed to Russia where he served five months with the North Russian Expeditionary Forces. He then returned to the United States and entered the business world. He would eventually become an executive in the auto parts and sales industry.[28] With the advent of World War II, Rose was appointed captain in the United States Army, effective 1 September 1942. Ordered to extended active duty on 16 September 1942, he attended Officer Training School in Miami, Florida, where he remained through October of that year. From November 1942 through September 1943, he served as Operations and Training Staff Officer with the 57th and 50th Service Groups at Fort Campbell, Kentucky. For service with the 57th Service Group, he received a commendation for "exceptional performance of duties." From October 1943 through February 1944, he served as commanding officer of the Ninth Aviation Squadron, New Orleans Army Base in Louisiana. From March 1944 until his release from active duty on 13 August 1946, Rose served as chief of the Aircraft Assignment Branch, executive officer, operations officer and administrative officer of Squadron T, 4000 Army Air Force Base Unit, Wright Field in Dayton, Ohio. Although he did not fly during the Second World War, his superb experience in combat flying during the First World War enabled him to carry out his duties in a highly effective way. At the time of retirement from his civilian occupation in the 1960s, Oren J. Rose resided at 11633 Gorham Avenue, Los Angeles, California.[29]

Lt. Cleo Francis Pineau
Courtesy Charles A. Pineau

TWENTY

Lt. Cleo Francis Pineau

I t was 6:35 P.M. on 6 September 1918 when Lt. Cleo Francis
Pineau carefully maneuvered his Sopwith Camel fighter into
position on the right wing of Lt. E. Swale, his No. 210 Squadron
patrol leader, as they circled over the Belgian coastal city of Ostend. The three-plane formation, flying at sixty-five hundred
feet, had been dodging scattered cumulus clouds for several
minutes while searching for a possible target. The pilots maintained a sharp-eyed alert, for the cloud-filled sky could also work
to their disadvantage should an enemy patrol spot the Camels
first.

Pineau had joined No. 210 Squadron, Royal Air Force, a little
over three months before,[1] and had, on one or two occasions,
been engaged in air combat, but up to this moment had not
scored a victory over any enemy aircraft. Consequently, he waited
impatiently but with jaunty confidence for something to happen.
Although by no means the fastest or the best climbing fighter of
1918, the Sopwith Camel could out-turn any machine in the
sky—with the possible exception of the Fokker Triplane. The
Sopwith Camel biplane fighter was powered with a 130 horsepower Clerget (or 150 horsepower Bentley) engine and cruised at
approximately 120 miles per hour at ten thousand feet. It was
armed with two machine guns synchronized to fire through the
propeller. Most famous of a long series of Sopwith fighters, the
Camel was the top Allied fighter in the number of enemy aircraft
shot down. The name "Camel" was chosen because of a distinc-
tive humped fairing over the nose guns. Short fuselage, small tail
surfaces, and a rotary engine combined to give it extreme maneuverability. Inexperienced pilots sometimes considered the
Camel tricky and unstable, but veterans generally swore by it.[2]

Indeed, Pineau had no fear of a real dogfight while flying the Sopwith Camel.

Suddenly, a formation of white-tailed Fokker D-7 biplanes broke through the clouds a few hundred feet below the Camel patrol. In succinct terms Pineau's combat report told the story of the next few moments: "patrol dived on 5 Fokker biplanes over Ostend. I fired 150 rounds into one which turned over on its back and went down out of control." This victory, Lieutenant Pineau's first, was confirmed by Lieutenant Swale.[3]

C. F. Pineau was born in Albuquerque, New Mexico, on 23 July 1893 and educated in the public schools of that city. He joined the Royal Flying Corps in Toronto, Canada, and received his primary flight training in the Curtiss JN-4 and the Avro biplane. Commissioned as a second lieutenant on 19 December 1917, he sailed for England from Halifax on 12 January 1918. During the next four months, he polished his flying skills in the Sopwith Pup and the Camel. By the time of his assignment to No. 210 Squadron on 2 June 1918, he had accumulated eighty-seven hours of flight time.[4]

No. 210 Squadron, originally known as No. 10 Squadron Royal Naval Air Service, had achieved considerable success during the summer of 1917 and in the spring of 1918. During the period 25 April 1917 through 3 August 1917, the well-known pilot, Lt. Col. Raymond Collishaw, the winner of the DSO, DSC, and the DFC, had served with this outfit as a flight sublieutenant, flight lieutenant, and flight commander. During the summer months Collishaw "had 25 decisive combats; destroying 11 enemy machines and sending down 14 out of control." No. 10 RNAS became No. 210 Squadron RAF on 1 April 1918. At the time young Pineau joined the unit, it was commanded by the veteran pilot, Maj. B. C. Bell, who also held the DSO and the DSC.[5] From 2 April 1918 until 8 July 1918, 210 Squadron operated out of airdromes at Triezennes, Liettres, St. Omer, and St. Marie-Cappel. On 9 July, the squadron became a part of the Fifth Group, RAF, and continued under that command until 22 October 1918, flying out of airfields located at Teteghem and Eringhem.[6]

On 18 September 1918, Lieutenant Pineau's flight, while on offensive patrol at eighteen thousand feet over Zeebrugge, "was attacked by 15 Fokker biplanes." Pineau turned sharply to the right and "engaged one enemy aircraft, firing 300 rounds. E.A. went down out of control and crashed into the sea 3 miles N.W.

of Zeebrugge." This enemy machine "painted with black and white checks all over" marked the New Mexican's second "kill."[7]

Six days later, a patrol from No. 210 Squadron became involved in a blazing dogfight with sixteen Fokker biplanes over the battle front. Young Pineau singled out one of the black and white checked Fokkers and, using his Sopwith Camel's great turning ability, got "on its tail and fired 80 rounds at point blank range." The stricken Fokker D-7 spun down and crashed a little north of the town of St. Pierre Cappelle for Pineau's third aerial victory.[8] Five minutes later, he maneuvered into position behind another enemy machine and fired sixty rounds at a range of fifty yards. The German aircraft, badly damaged, "turned over on its back and went down in a flat spin," finally disappearing in a cloud near the ground some three miles southeast of the city of Nieuport. This machine was later confirmed as a "down out of control" victory for the American.[9] Indeed, Lt. C. F. Pineau was rapidly establishing himself as one of No. 210 Squadron's most effective fighter pilots.

In a letter written to his mother in Albuquerque, New Mexico, on 30 September 1918, young Pineau discusses his combat actions of recent weeks and goes into considerable detail in describing how he almost lost his life:

Dearest Mother, Thanks very much for your letter of August 29th. Well it has been raining all day very hard and we have done no flying. Suppose you received my letter telling of my success this month—I sure tried hard to get my fifth Hun plane for Sept.—but I could not get another in fact they nearly got me instead. After one fight day before yesterday five "Hun" Scouts chased me back to our lines and yesterday I left my formation and dived down on a two seater Hun plane 5000 ft. below—when suddenly to my surprise I saw 10 Hun Scouts (Fokker Biplanes) right in front of me. Well I believe it was just luck that got me away—for just as they were getting onto me the rest of our formation of scouts which were above came down and 2 Hun planes were shot down in flames 3 more were shot down and seem to crash and 2 went down out of control. I don't believe the Huns saw the machines above. They were too anxious to get me. I of course did not take part in the fight for as soon as I saw the 10 Huns I done a *half roll* and dived away at about 300 miles per hr.—That may seem to you like a lot of speed but I was going straight down with my motor full on—After getting away from that "scrap" quite safely I met 4 more Hun Scouts which followed me back to our lines.[10]

At this point the enemy pilots abandoned the chase and Pineau escaped.

On 1 October 1918 Cleo F. Pineau became an ace when he shot down a gray and black Fokker D-7 a short distance southeast of the town of Roulers. In his combat report, Pineau stated, "In general engagement with 11 Fokker biplanes over Roulers I attacked one and fired 330 rounds at about 25 yards range. E.A. sideslipped a little, turned over and then burst into flames." [11] Like most highly successful fighter pilots, Lieutenant Pineau believed in getting very close to the enemy before firing.

Lt. Cleo Francis Pineau's last flight was on 8 October, just before the Allied armies took the city of Ostend. Fifteen planes from No. 210 Squadron were sent out on an offensive patrol. They were in three layers of five each, and Pineau was in the top formation. At 9:23 A.M., Lieutenant Pineau was seen to attack a Fokker D-7 some four miles east of Roulers and "the enemy machine fell out of control and crashed." [12] When Pineau began to climb back to help his formation in their duel with some fifteen enemy fighters,

> every enemy plane seemed to dive at me at once. One sent a tracer bullet over my shoulder which destroyed my left gun and instrument board. Another hit my right side, breaking my control. One underneath wrecked my motor, and that settled it. I began to fall and lost consciousness. In dropping from such a height, the flyer usually dies of suffocation caused by being unable to inhale air into his lungs, due to the vacuum caused by the increased rapidity of his descent. I don't know what saved me, but when I came to I was uninjured, but a prisoner in the hands of the Huns. [13]

Shortly after C. F. Pineau was taken prisoner, he was sent back to German headquarters at Ghent where his captors attempted to get information from him. In his words,

> I, of course, sat tight. They then took me to a room in a hotel and left me alone with another British airman who also was a prisoner. They thought that when we were left alone together we would naturally spill all the beans, but the British Intelligence Officer was up to all the Hun dodges and had told us that dictagraphs were usually concealed behind the wall paper or some other place in any room where we were liable to be placed.

Consequently, Pineau and the other prisoner divulged no real information. Lieutenant Pineau was shifted to various German prisons until finally released on 18 November some seven days after the end of the war.[14]

Within a few weeks from the time of his release, Lieutenant Pineau returned to the United States where he discovered he had been awarded the Distinguished Flying Cross by King George V of England on 3 December 1918 for his performance in combat. The citation described Pineau as

> an officer of exceptional merit, who sets a very high example of courage and devotion to duty to other pilots. He has destroyed four enemy machines and driven down two out of control. After one of these combats, on 8th October, in which he destroyed a Fokker biplane, he was reported missing. (Air Ministry).[15]

The medal was sent to Cleo F. Pineau's mother in Albuquerque, for at the time of the aerial award it was believed that the young pilot had been killed on 8 October. He had served with one of the top fighter squadrons of the war. During No. 210 Squadron's approximately eighteen months of combat service, its pilots destroyed 148 enemy aircraft and sent down 173 out of control for a total of 321 victories.[16]

After his return to the United States, Lieutenant Pineau was happy to hear that the American manufacturers "were going to restore motorcycle racing to its former high place on the map" and declared he would be back on the track again as he had been before the war. He planned to "rejoin the Miami Cycle & Mfg. Co. as soon as he obtains his discharge."[17]

Maj. Raymond Collishaw at Izel le Hameau on 10 July 1918
Courtesy Imperial War Museum

TWENTY-ONE

Lt. Kenneth R. Unger

Despite the sky filled with cumulus clouds in the late afternoon of 27 September 1918, the visibility was good as Lt. Kenneth R. Unger maneuvered his Sopwith Camel at five thousand feet over Nieuport in an offensive patrol mission.[1] Unger's unit, formerly known as Royal Naval Air Service Number 10 Squadron, was now identified as Royal Air Force Number 210 Squadron. The organization had been equipped with the Bentley-powered Camel for several months. Indeed, the Camel had become famous for its maneuverability and its outstanding combat performance. The rotary-powered biplane would shoot down:

> . . . 1294 enemy aircraft between its entry into combat with the RFC in July 1917 and the Armistice, the highest figure for any World War I scout. The reasons for the Camel's maneuverability were its instability in all three axes, the concentration of weight in the nose and the immense torque of its rotary engine. It differed markedly from the Sopwith Pup and Triplane, which were docile by comparison. However, the qualities which made the Camel outstanding in expert hands could be fatal when flown by novices.[2]

As Lieutenant Unger and his men searched the sky for a possible target, they suddenly spotted anti-aircraft shells bursting around and above the clouds over the town of Nieuport. In Unger's words, "I climbed to top and side of a cloud." Almost immediately, a Halberstadt two-seater came out of a nearby cloud "and I fired two bursts of about 30 rounds each, at a range of 120 yards. The enemy plane side-slipped, rolled over on its back, stalled and flat spun into the ground . . . southeast of Nieuport." The destruction of this German plane was confirmed by "Headquarters, Belgian 2nd Army Division."[3] This "kill" ran Kenneth Unger's victory total to five and gave him the rank of "ace."

Kenneth Russell Unger was born in Newark, New Jersey, on 19 April 1898 and was educated at Montclair Academy.[4] In the Register of Officers in No. 210 Squadron, he was listed as a Methodist, and his next of kin was his mother, Mrs. A. W. Osmun, who then lived in Madison, New Jersey. Apparently, Unger was rejected in the U.S. forces and joined the Royal Flying Corps in Canada in June 1917. The nineteen-year-old youth attended the University of Toronto Ground School, and after completing his flight training, was assigned as a flight instructor at Fort Worth, Texas, in November 1917. As a second lieutenant he went overseas in April 1918. After further flight training in Avros, Sopwith Pups, and Sopwith Camels, he was posted to No. 210 Squadron on 18 June 1918.[5]

No. 210 Squadron had achieved considerable success during the last several months of 1917 and the early part of 1918. One of its top pilots during the summer of 1917 was Raymond Collishaw, who had scored no less than twenty-five victories before transferring to another squadron. At the time Unger joined the organization, Maj. B. C. Bell, holder of the DSO and the DSC, was in command. During the spring and early summer, No. 210 Squadron was based at Triezennes, Liettres, St. Omer, and St. Marie Cappel. On 9 July the squadron was transferred to the Fifth Group, RAF, and continued under that command at Teteghem and Eringhem until 22 October 1918. For its performance during this period, No. 210 Squadron was to receive congratulations messages from His Majesty the King of the Belgians, the Chief of Staff to the Belgian Army, and the Lord Commissioners of the Admiralty.[6]

Lieutenant Unger fell in love with the quick maneuverability of the Camel, and on 26 June he and two other pilots from the No. 210 Squadron shot down a Fokker D-7. On 20 July, during an afternoon marred by heavy thunderstorms, he was able to send a Fokker down out of control. Eleven days later, during another poor visibility day, he again shot a Fokker D-7 down out of control for his third victory since joining No. 210 Squadron.[7]

During the month of August, No. 210 Squadron, like most other pursuit squadrons, was involved in ground strafing, dive-bombing, and dogfighting over the front because of the Allied Amiens offensive. On 24 September a flight from No. 210 Squadron became engaged with some sixteen Fokker D-7s at eight thousand feet in the St. Pierre Cappelle area at 2:40 P.M. Lieutenant Unger observed one enemy fighter "on the tail of one of our machines. I got within 15 yards of the E.A. [enemy aircraft] and opened fire." The enemy fighter "went straight up, stalled and spun down. Last seen spinning into a cloud." There was little doubt the enemy machine crashed, but since no one was able to confirm its destruction Lieutenant Unger was credited with having sent the plane "down out of control."[8] This combat marked Unger's fourth victory. No less than seven German aircraft were destroyed during the midafternoon combat.

Lieutenant Unger's fifth victory took place on 27 September and, on the following day, despite low clouds and rain, he flew an offensive patrol and a bombing mission in the Dixmude area. While on this patrol in the late afternoon, he spotted a Fokker biplane that had become detached from its formation. Unger made a quick right turn with his Sopwith Camel and attacked the enemy head on. In his report he stated the enemy machine "dived under me and I did a half roll. I came out 20 yards from his tail and fired 50 rounds. E.A. went down in an erratic side-slip out of control and disappeared in a cloud." Even though the German plane was not observed to have crashed, Lieutenant Unger was given credit for a down-out-of-control victory.[9]

The weather on 1 October was described in the Royal Air Force Communiqué as "fine, with some clouds." At 9:45 A.M. Kenneth R. Unger and his Camel flight were engaged in an offensive patrol a few miles northeast of Ypres at twelve thousand feet. Unger became separated from his patrol and was startled to see a combat between "8 Spads, 6 Hanriots and about 15 E.A. [enemy aircraft]." He quickly dived and attacked one German machine, probably a Fokker, firing one hundred rounds at a "range of 30–10 yards. E.A. emitted a large cloud of smoke and went down in a side-slip. The smoke increased as E.A. went down and the machine was evidently on fire." The German was considered to have gone down in flames and the New Jersey boy was given credit for his seventh kill, making him one of the leading aces in No. 210 Squadron.[10]

Bad weather prevailed for most of the week of 7–13 October, and, on the whole, there was relatively little air-to-air combat. Nonetheless, the pilots of No. 210 Squadron managed to get in some strafing and low bombing operations. The weather on 14 October was described as "fair but cloudy." While dodging the cumulus clouds at thirteen thousand feet a little south of Lichtervelde, Lieutenant Unger was attacked by an all black Fokker Triplane. After making a hard right turn the American managed to fire approximately 100 rounds into the Fokker Triplane from a "range of 75 to 50 yards. E.A. stalled and went out of control, probably crashed." The squadron commander credited Unger with a down-out-of-control kill for his eighth victory since the middle of June.[11]

According to RAF Communiqué No. 30, covering the period 21–27 October, British air squadrons "claimed officially 45 E.A. brought down, and 26 driven down out of control. In addition, one E.A. was brought down by A.A. Forty-one of our machines are missing. Aproximately, 53½ tons of bombs were dropped and 3,954 plates exposed."[12] Lt. K. R. Unger helped the RAF score when at 10:30 A.M. on 27 October, while circling over Locquiqnol, he got on the tail of a dark green, while-tailed Fokker D-7 and fired "200 rounds at a range of 60 to 20 yards." The enemy Fokker dived vertically and crashed into Mormal Forest northeast of Locquiqnol. This victory, number nine for Unger, was confirmed by a Captain Joseph and a Lieutenant Buchanan.[13]

According to the RAF Communiqué, the week of 28 October–3 November was an even more successful period than the previous week. No less than 138 enemy planes were brought down, and 42 were driven down out of control. In addition, two enemy aircraft were shot down by anti-aircraft fire. Fifty RAF planes were missing. Approximately 102 tons of bombs were dropped and 8,042 photograph plates were exposed. During the same week, Maj. W. G. Barker, flying a Sopwith Snipe, fought a heroic battle against some forty enemy aircraft and won the Victoria Cross.[14] No. 210 Squadron scored three confirmed victories. Lieutenant Unger described his own victory on 30 October: "I was about 1000 feet below my formation when the patrol engaged Fokker biplanes. One dived on my tail. I did a right hand turn and got on his tail and fired two bursts at a range of 30 yards. E.A. went down almost vertically, smoking and crashed about 200 yards east of Rombie." This kill, confirmed by the whole patrol and the Royal Air Force Communiqué No. 31, placed Unger's total victories at ten.[15] Two days later, while on a special mission in the Estreux area, Lieutenant Unger spotted a German kite balloon painted bright yellow with "one big black cross on each side" and immediately attacked it at thirty-five hundred feet. He fired some 150 rounds at very close range and watched the observer parachute out. The balloon burst into flames, and its destruction was confirmed by a No. 210 Squadron patrol.[16] The observation balloon kill ran Lt. Kenneth R. Unger's victory score to eleven and moved him into the top twenty American aces category. On 9 November two days before the end of the war, Lieutenant Unger "fired 700 rounds into enemy troops who were in a quarry and saw them run into a woods; he then dropped a message giving this information to our infantry who occupied the quarry and then advanced upon the wood."[17] Shortly after the Armistice, Lt. Kenneth R. Unger was to receive the British Distinguished Flying Cross for his five months of combat with No. 210 Squadron.

Lieutenant Unger remained with No. 210 Squadron until 2 February 1919 and returned to the United States on 20 February. After the war, he became a pilot for the original Air Mail Service between Salt Lake City, Utah, and Oakland, California. He joined the U.S. Navy in World War II and flew cargo planes and retired as a lieutenant commander. Unger died on 6 January 1979 at Pompano Beach, Florida, at the age of eighty.[18]

Lt. Norman Cooper (left)
Courtesy Ola Sater

TWENTY-TWO

Lt. Norman Cooper

Norman Cooper of Schenectady, New York, whose real name was E. S. Tooker,[1] enlisted in the Royal Flying Corps in Canada and, on completion of pilot training, was posted overseas. On 28 June 1918 he was assigned to No. 73 Squadron,[2] flying Sopwith Camels out of Planques in the Noyon-Montdidier sector on the French end of the battle front. During this period, a large German offensive was underway, and No. 73 Squadron was engaged in many strafing missions in an effort to stop the German drive. In addition, the squadron was heavily involved in offensive patrols.[3]

Although a new member of the squadron, Lieutenant Cooper flew several strafing missions during the first two weeks of his assignment. During the nine days of the German drive, No. 73 Squadron destroyed or drove down out of control no less than twenty-four enemy aircraft and fired some thirty-five thousand rounds of machine-gun bullets at ground targets.[4] No. 73 Squadron moved back to the British front for a few days, where it flew several offensive patrols and escort missions, but, with the German drive underway in the Château-Thierry-Reims sector, the unit moved back to Touquin on the French front. From 14 July until 3 August, the squadron participated in stopping the German offensive and assisting the French counteroffensive.[5]

During the French-American push in the Château-Thierry-Soissons area in late July, Lieutenant Cooper was to participate in shooting down his first enemy aircraft. At 7:45 P.M. on 25 July, Lts. W. S. Stephenson and Cooper caught a German LVG two-seater at five thousand feet over Cohan. Both Camel pilots fired long bursts into the enemy aircraft and watched it "flatten out slightly when near the ground, and crashed."[6]

Four days later, Lts. E. J. Lussier, A. McConnell-Wood, and

Norman Cooper, while escorting Allied planes at a low altitude, intercepted a yellow camouflaged LVG a little north of Vezilly. The combat report signed by all three of the Camel pilots stated, "he immediately started north with his nose down, and we all dived on him several times. When at about 200 feet he went into a steep side-slip and crashed into the ground. The observer must have been wounded after the first couple of dives, as he did not fire after that." This kill was a shared success.[7]

On 3 August 1918 No. 73 Squadron shifted back to the Bellevue airdrome, some ten miles southwest of Arras, where it participated in the British Fourth Army offensive on the Amiens front and the Third Army's push on the Bapaume front. During this period in August, No. 73 Squadron was heavily involved in offensive patrols and low bombing attacks on the retreating German forces. From this time onward the squadron was attached to the Tank Corps and, in strafing of anti-tank guns, provided real help.[8]

During the Amiens drive, Lieutenant Cooper was involved in several aerial dogfights. At 8:10 A.M. on the cloudy morning of 19 August, Lieutenants Baldwin and Cooper were attacked by eight Fokker D-7s a few miles southeast of Combles. Cooper made a hard right-hand turn with his Camel, got on the tail of one of the Fokkers, and "fired a long burst into him at close range. He went into a vertical nose-dive, and crashed S.E. of Combles."[9] Certainly, by this stage in combat, Cooper had learned the Sopwith Camel's advantages and disadvantages. The Camel, once mastered, was a good fighting machine, but pilots with faint heart needed extra care. To the novice it was difficult to fly since engine, guns, and the pilot's cockpit were "all concentrated within the first seven feet of the aeroplane's fuselage. This helped to give the Camel, with the rotary engine's torque, turning capabilities not previously seen in a fighter." Of course, the experienced pilot welcomed this response and maneuverability, but the inexperienced flier frequently ended up in disaster.[10]

Some six days later, on 25 August 1918, Lts. Norman Cooper and E. J. Lussier, a young man from Chicago, Illinois, observed some five Fokker D-7s "painted a dark gray" at eight thousand feet a little northeast of Bapaume. The No. 73 Squadron pair immediately turned sharply to the right and got on the tail of the Fokkers. Lussier sent one of the enemy machines crashing to the earth while Lieutenant Cooper "fired a burst of about 100 rounds into one who burst into flames."[11]

On 15 September, a beautiful clear day, Lt. Norman Cooper and a formation of Sopwith Camels led by Captain Baldwin encountered a flight of Fokker D-7s over Cambrai at four thousand feet. Once again, the highly maneuverable Camels were able to get in position to attack the enemy machines. Cooper was able to fire a burst of two hundred rounds into one of the Fokkers "and the machine went spinning down out of control into a cloud." Although Cooper was not able to actually see the enemy plane crash, he was given credit for the "kill."[12] Several hours later, at 6:15 P.M., Norman Cooper was to score his second victory of the day in the vicinity of Cambrai. In his combat report, the Schenectady, New York, boy wrote "I fired several short bursts into E.A. who went into a vertical nose-dive, and crashed in the ground N.E. of Bourlon Wood."[13]

On 16 September No. 73 Squadron moved its base to Foucaucourt, a few miles east of Amiens and much closer to the battle lines. From this airdrome, the squadron continued its strafing and low-level bombing of the German infantry and artillery forces. A second move was made on 23 September when No. 73 Squadron was relocated at Estrées-en-Chaussée.[14]

The Sopwith Camel pilots continued to strafe and bomb the retreating German forces during the last six weeks of the war. On 3 October Lt. Norman Cooper observed British troops being held up east of Gouy by several trenches full of enemy infantry. He immediately "dived on these trenches, and raked them with machine gun fire." The Allied troops took the opportunity to advance, and the Germans ran from their trenches. Then Cooper signaled another Camel pilot nearby and the two "flew along in front of [the British] infantry, spraying the retreating enemy with machine gun fire." A little later on the same day, Lieutenant Cooper found another trench full of German troops and repeatedly dived on them, going down as low as one hundred feet from the ground and "machine-gunned them until they waved a white flag and gave themselves up to [British infantry]."[15] For this courageous performance, Lieutenant Cooper was awarded the Distinguished Flying Cross.[16]

No. 73 Squadron continued its low-level operation against the enemy ground forces until the end of the war. As the German troops continued to retreat, the squadron moved its base almost weekly, and at the time of the Armistice it was stationed at Malincourt. During the several months on the various battle fronts,

No. 73 Squadron had destroyed eighty-one enemy aircraft and sent another fifty-one down out of control for a total of 132 victories. Because many of its combat missions were at a very low altitude, the squadron suffered some forty-eight casualties of its own.

During the final weeks of the bloody struggle, Cooper led many patrols and was promoted to captain on 18 November 1918.[17] In the 4½ months of his assignment to No. 73 Squadron, Cooper destroyed three enemy aircraft and brought down two out of control. He also assisted in the destruction of two other enemy machines.[18]

Cooper, apparently fearing the possibility of losing American citizenship, listed his nationality as British.[19] He returned to Home Establishment on 11 January 1919,[20] and on 15 March 1919 he was transferred to the unemployed list.[21] Shortly thereafter, he returned to the United States.

Lt. Louis Bennett
Courtesy West Virginia Library

TWENTY-THREE

Lt. Louis Bennett

L ouis Bennett, Jr., the only son of Louis Bennett and Sallie Maxwell Bennett, was born in Weston, West Virginia, on 22 September 1894. He and his older sister, Agra, were children of wealthy and prominent parents. Their paternal grandfather, Jonathan McCauley Bennett, was an attorney, railroad entrepreneur, banker, and large landowner. Louis Bennett, their father, was an attorney and a school teacher and had extensive land holdings. In fact, he was the Democratic nominee for governor of West Virginia in 1908. Young Bennett's mother also came from a wealthy and prominent family. James Maxwell, her father, was a banker and businessman in Wheeling, West Virginia. Young Louis has been described as "a bright, likeable child but with a headstrong inclination to have his own way. He had noticeable mechanical interests and abilities and had his own automobile and motorcycle at the tender age of 12 years." [1]

Louis Bennett attended Cutler and St. Luke's preparatory schools in Pennsylvania and, in 1913, enrolled in Yale University. Not only was young Bennett a fine student, he also participated in lacrosse, wrestling, track, and rowing. In addition, he had a real interest in aviation. In the summer of 1916, "already a member of the Aero Club of America, he enrolled in the pilot training of the Burgess Company at Marblehead, Massachusetts, but was called away to join the Yale Battery at Tobyhanna, Pennsylvania. However, his interest in aviation did not lag." In early 1917 he pushed the idea of creating an aviation corps to be trained in West Virginia, "later to be accepted into the United States Air Service as a unit based on the concept of the *Escadrille* Lafayette." [2] The governor of West Virginia helped finance the project, and Bennett purchased a Curtiss JN-4D biplane for training purposes. In addition, young Bennett hired Capt. E. A. Kelly, an RFC pilot, to do the instructing of those young men that might join the organization known as the West Virginia Flying Corps. Kelly was injured in a flying accident and was replaced by William Fry.[3]

Even though several young Americans joined the flight program in West Virginia, the program was never really accepted by the United States Army.[4] A few of those cadets who had joined the West Virginia Flying Corps later finished their pilot training at other flight schools in the United States. Louis Bennett, however, decided "the quickest and most direct route was through the British Royal Flying Corps." In early October 1917, he traveled to Toronto, Canada, and enlisted in the RFC. He was posted to the RFC Cadet Wing at Camp Borden, Long Branch, Ontario. Despite having several hours of flight training before his enlistment, he spent over three months in the pilot programs in Canada and the various Taliaferro fields at Ft. Worth, Texas. Bennett was commissioned on 21 January 1918 and, shortly thereafter, sailed for England. On arriving in London, he was posted to the Central Flying School at Upavon. After graduation on 6 March 1918, he was promoted to full lieutenant. On 12 May, he was assigned to the No. 90 Squadron flying Sopwith Dolphins out of Shotwick. This outfit, formed on 8 October 1917, was assigned to the duty of home defense. Since No. 90 Squadron was involved in relatively little action, the aggressive Louis Bennett almost immediately sought assignment to one of the pursuit squadrons fighting in France.[5] The twenty-three-year-old Bennett's efforts finally paid off, and on 21 July 1918 he was posted to the No. 40 Squadron, flying SE-5As out of Bryas, four miles northwest of St. Pol on the British front. He was assigned to "C" Flight, commanded by Capt. G. E. H. McElroy, one of the top RAF fighter aces.[6]

Needless to say, Lt. Louis Bennett was pleased to be assigned to No. 40 Squadron since it had an outstanding record. The squadron had, for the most part, been employed on offensive patrols and as escort to bombing formations. During the summer of 1917, No. 40 Squadron "took part in a number of organized balloon attacks." In addition, low flying attacks on enemy ground targets were first carried out by No. 40 Squadron, during the battle on the Cambrai front in November of 1917. The squadron was again involved in ground strafing during the big German drive on the British Third and Fifth Army fronts in March 1918, during the April fighting in the Lys Valley, and during the last few months of the war in the Arras area. Several outstanding pilots had served with No. 40 Squadron. Maj. R. S. Dallas, a thirty-nine-victory ace, took command of the outfit on 15 March 1918 and was to lead the squadron effectively until his death on 19 June 1918.[7] Edward "Mick" Mannock, who would eventually become the top RAF ace of the war with seventy-three kills, joined the squadron in April 1917. Subsequently, he served with No. 74 Squadron and finally commanded No. 85 Squadron. By the end of the war, No. 40 Squadron, one of the outstanding RAF units, had destroyed 130 enemy aircraft, sent 144 planes down out of control, destroyed 30 balloons, and drove 10 balloons down in a damaged state.[8]

Although Bennett became a member of No. 40 Squadron on 21 July, his first offensive patrol mission, made with Captain McElroy, did not take place until 30 July. On the next day he flew his second offensive patrol, but it was a disaster. McElroy, his flight commander, was shot down and killed by ground fire. The tragedy was, indeed, a blow to young Bennett, for he and McElroy were very much alike in their aggressiveness: "Both were fearless, reckless and expert marksmen. McElroy's flight was always noted for its great determination, reckless bravery and abandonment. Bennett's temperament and tendencies dovetailed nicely with this setting." For the next six weeks, "C" Flight was led by Capt. George C. Dixon, a seven-victory Canadian, who had only recently transferred from Mannock's No. 85 Squadron.[9]

During the next two weeks, Lieutenant Bennett participated in several offensive patrols with "C" Flight, but combat action was fairly light.[10] Like most fledgling pilots, Bennett had difficulty seeing other aircraft in the air. He did, however, on one occasion engage an enemy two-seater, but his guns jammed. Within a few days, he began to spot German observation balloons and took pot shots at them on two or three occasions. Since his guns were not loaded with Buckingham ammunition, he was unsuccessful. This would soon be corrected, for on 14 August young Bennett was to acquire a SE-5A of his own.[11] After this point he was able to dictate the type of machine-gun ammunition he preferred.

On the bright sunny day of 15 August, Lieutenant Bennett launched his brilliant, but brief, career as a fighter pilot. "While on offensive patrol near Brebieres at 12 noon," Bennett saw 5 Fokker D-7s flying east. He quickly maneuvered his SE-5A into position behind one of the enemy aircraft "and fired about 40 rounds closing to very close range. E.A. fell out of control but could not be watched to the ground, owing to clouds (confirmed by another pilot)."[12] In his combat report, Bennett stated he had fired, "about 40 rounds at a range of from 80 yards down to a few feet."[13] Certainly, the aggressive West Virginian believed in getting close to his victim before pressing the triggers.

On 16 August, another "fair weather" day, Bennett flew two offensive patrols, one at dawn and the second in mid-afternoon. Much to his disappointment, he did not spot an enemy plane or observation balloon. His mother addressed a letter to him on the same day, advising him of his father's death. Destiny was to deny young Bennett the "receipt of that letter,"[14] for he too would pass on to Valhalla very soon.

The next day dawned fair in the morning but became overcast in the afternoon. Louis Bennett, Lt. F. H. Knobel, and a third SE-5A pilot took off on an offensive patrol early in the day. At 7:40 A.M., Lieutenants Knobel and Bennett "attacked an L.V.G. two-seater and fired many bursts into E.A. which went down and crashed south of Henin Lietard." This "kill" was confirmed by ground anti-aircraft observers. The victory was shared by Bennett and Lieutenant Knobel.[15]

Lieutenant Bennett immediately returned to his airdrome at Bryas where he armed his Vickers and Lewis machine guns with Buckingham ammunition and then took off with Lt. L. H. Sutton. Apparently, Bennett had seen an observation balloon at the town of Merville a little north of Lens. At approximately eight A.M., he spotted the kite balloon again and dived and attacked it "firing about ¾ of a drum of flat nosed Buckingham and finishing at very close range. One observer made a parachute descent and the balloon burst into flames almost instantaneously."[16] The two No. 40 Squadron pilots returned to their home base but Bennett's SE-5A ran out of fuel and he had to make a forced landing a short distance from Bryas.[17]

In the words of one author, "fighter pilots were among the most isolated of fighting men, and necessarily so. Bound to a round-the-clock routine of patrol work, they could very seldom enjoy those longer periods of 'rest' between periods of front-line service which were part of the infantryman's war."[18] Without a doubt, Lieutenant Bennett fit this description of the fighter pilot of World War I. He now had a severe case of "balloon fever." His main objective of the moment was to attempt to shoot down the entire German balloon line. This was, indeed, a very dangerous task, for the protective anti-aircraft fire surrounding the observation balloons could throw up a terrific amount of lead and "flaming onions." In addition, the balloons were also frequently covered by friendly fighters.

The sky on 19 August was filled with clouds, but the visiblity was relatively good. Young Bennett was scheduled for a midmorning patrol along with several other No. 40 Squadron pilots. Much to his disgust, oil troubles with his SE-5A caused a considerable delay, and he was not able to take off with his comrades. The problem was finally solved several minutes after his patrol had departed and he immediately took to the air in a try to catch up with his patrol. Unfortunately, he was unable to catch up or locate his teammates. At ten A.M., however, Bennett "saw a series of hostile balloons up, all along the line, and chose the most easterly one of a group well east of Merville." He dived from eleven thousand feet and "fired about ¾ drum of flat nosed Buckingham into the balloon which burst into flames, one observer making a parachute descent." Some ten minutes later he selected a second balloon a little east of Merville and much closer to the trench lines. Once again dodging the heavy ground fire, he attacked the observation balloon and fired the rest of the drum of Buckingham at very close range. The balloon "burst into flames almost instantaneously," and one observer descended by parachute. Both victories were confirmed by Allied anti-aircraft batteries in the neighborhood.[19]

Shortly after returning to No. 40 Squadron's home field, Bennett's plane was refueled and rearmed. The impatient American took off alone and headed back to the German balloon line east of Merville. At 1:40 P.M. the eagle-eyed Bennett spotted another hostile observation balloon at two thousand feet just east of the town of Merville. Diving through the broken cloud layer, he was able to get in close and fired one half of a drum of Buckingham ammunition at the unsuspecting victim. The German observer immediately bailed out, and the kite balloon burst into flames. Bennett banked his fighter to the left and attacked a second balloon "as it was being hauled down at 500 feet and fired a ½ of a drum of flat nosed Buckingham at very close range when the gun jammed. The balloon was seen to be on fire on the ground." This balloon was "confirmed by 'A' Battery as seen in flames."[20] Bennett now returned to Bryas Airdrome in an excited state of mind. In a little less than four hours, the West Virginian had performed the unbelieveable feat of shooting down four enemy balloons and had run his victory score to seven in only four days.[21]

Despite "mist, low clouds and some rain" on 20 August, Lieutenant Bennett flew two offensive patrols and, on the following day, engaged in two more patrols. There was little activity on either day—much to Bennett's disappointment.

On 22 August, however, combat activity increased dramatically. Numbers 208 and 40 Squadrons, escorted by No. 22 Squadron flying Bristol F2B fighters, carried out an early morning bombing raid on German-held Gondecourt Airdrome: "Seventy-five 25 pound bombs were dropped from below 1000 feet and a direct hit was made upon a hanger which caught fire. A large number of rounds were fired into hangers, machine gun emplacements, a locomotive and a train in the railroad station."[22] On the way home, No. 40 Squadron pilots spotted several hostile observation balloons a little east of La Bassée. Two of the balloons were shot down by Louis Bennett, who had, in the last few days, acquired a reputation as a "balloon buster." His combat report described his brilliant performance on that sunny clear morning: "Whilst returning from bomb raid on Gondecourt Airdrome. B. E. observed a balloon east of the village, apparently near Don. S.E.-5a attacked and fired ¼ of a drum of flat nosed Buckingham at close range. Balloon caught on fire and went down in flames, observer descended by parachute." A few moments later, Bennett saw two balloons together further north and attacked the higher one. This one was shot "down in flames." The second balloon was apparently hauled down, and Bennett was unable to find it after getting the first. Both of Bennett's balloon victims were "seen in flames by several pilots of the same patrol."[23] This combat pushed Bennett's victory total to nine and established him as one of the hottest fighter pilots on the British front in August 1918.

The aggressive and tireless Bennett participated in three offensive patrols on 23 August. The dawn patrol was quite productive. At 7:15 A.M. "C" Flight, led by Captain Dixon, sighted three LVG two-seaters near the battle lines. The patrol dived upon the enemy aircraft. At six thousand feet, Lieutenant Bennett banked his SE-5A to the east, cutting off one of the fleeing two-seaters. He fired a short burst from the front then maneuvered to a position under the LVG's tail and out of the range of the observer's rear gun. From this point, he "fired 300 rounds following E.A. from 3000 feet to 500 feet. The cockpit was observed to be full of smoke and the observer had disappeared." The hostile aircraft "continued straight down and crashed" just south of Quiery La Motte for Bennett's tenth kill since 15 August 1918.[24]

Low clouds marked the morning hours of 24 August 1918, the final day of Lt. Louis Bennett's life. Indeed, the intrepid West Virginian's luck ran out, but not without real cost to the Germans. At approximately noon, Bennett and Lt. Reed G. Landis, who during the last weeks of the war would command the U.S. 25th Squadron,[25] volunteered for an offensive patrol between Lens and La Bassée. Unfortunately, Landis had to return to his home airdrome because of engine trouble. Bennett, however, continued on alone to the vicinity of Haisnes, where he spotted a German observation balloon. According to the First Brigade summary, Bennett attacked the hostile balloon "near Annay at about 12:40 P.M. on the 24th instant. This pilot did not return from the flight, but from information received from A.A. observers there is no doubt that a hostile balloon was brought down in flames by this pilot."[26] What really transpired is described by an eye-witness account of Mademoiselle Planey, a member of a prominent family in Don, located three miles north of Provin. She wrote in a letter to Mrs. Louis Bennett, Sr., which is quoted in George H. Williams's article on young Bennett as follows:

> We all remember August 24, 1918 because it was my father's birthday. About one o'clock an aeroplane came directly over the British lines and immediately attacked a German observation balloon stationed over Provin. The anti-aircraft guns, which always protected them, at once trained on him but not withstanding, he succeeded in sending down that balloon in flames, although the two occupants escaped in parachutes. Then, not satisfied with this victory, he cooly and courageously flew off toward Hantay (three miles to the northwest and one mile southwest of Don). Here the Germans were frantically pulling down the second balloon. Regardless of the easy target he presented to the anti-aircraft guns, he followed it, pouring in bullets until it fell. His own petrol tank must have been hit, for then near the ground his machine burst into flames before he could fly away. It fell near the station at Marquillas (1½ miles north of Hantay and two miles west of Don). The Germans so admired the courage of this pilot that they burned

their hands to extricate him alive from the burning machine. His leg was broken and he was badly burned. He was carried to Wavrin, which was further back from the front.

Planey did not see Bennett's attack on still a third balloon, but the balloon observer, Emil Merkelbach, later commented to Mrs. Bennett,

> I noticed that the enemy pilot was approaching my balloon with great speed, although our heavy machine guns and anti-aircraft batteries were firing at him all the time. The aviator paid no attention, but continued to follow me. From a height of 50 meters he opened fire on my balloon. Fortunately, I was not hit but the enemy aviator had been set afire through the attack of our machine guns. He attempted to rescue himself by jumping from the burning machine before it struck the earth.[27]

Lieutenant Bennett was buried in the Wavrin German Military Cemetery with full military honors. Maj. Robert J. O. Compston, the new commanding officer of No. 40 Squadron, recommended Bennett for the Distinguished Flying Cross and wrote his mother, "Never have I seen such sterling work done in so short a time." The brave young American had amassed a score of three aircraft and nine balloons in ten days. He was over the lines twenty-two times, totaling forty-one hours of flying—undoubtedly, one of the most brilliant records of the first air war.[28]

Lt. Frank Lucien Hale
Courtesy Stewart K. Taylor

TWENTY-FOUR

Lt. Frank Lucien Hale

Frank Lucien Hale was born in Syracuse, New York, on 6 August 1895 and grew up in Fayetteville, a small town on the eastern outskirts of that city. Frank, or "Bud" as he was usually known, was always an "adventuresome type, in love with speed, machinery and guns."[1] When he was thirteen, an automobile owned by a neighbor broke down near the Hale home, and the owner pushed it into their yard and left it. Young Frank at once went to work on the automobile, found and fixed the trouble, and drove the car around the neighborhood even though he had never touched a car before.

Hale's rugged individualism may have caused an unscheduled departure from Fayetteville High School when he refused to apologize to one of his teachers for a disciplinary problem he had created. Consequently, he dropped out of school and never received his high school diploma.[2]

The restless Hale joined the Fourth Cavalry, New York National Guard unit in 1914 and, two years later during the Pancho Villa crisis, he was sent to the Mexican border. While serving with the U.S. Cavalry unit in 1916, he had his first airplane ride in a Curtiss Jenny. This undoubtedly influenced his decision to join the aviation service. Unfortunately, he was rejected by the American Air Service for the lack of a high school diploma and because of the fact he got dizzy in the old "spinning chair" test. The dizziness problem was attributed to a childhood accident in which a horse fractured his skull. Despite this handicap, he journeyed to Toronto, Canada, where he joined the Royal Flying Corps.[3] After completing flight training at Deseronto Field, he was retained as a flight instructor. A short time later, he was transferred to Texas where he instructed American cadets in the Jenny aircraft.[4] Although not wildly enthusiastic about instructional duties, he nonetheless proved effective in this assignment. It was in Texas where he had his only serious crash when the engine on his Jenny quit on take-off. After spending several weeks in the hospital, he returned to Toronto, and in the late spring of 1918 was sent overseas. On 10 August he was posted to the Royal Air Force No. 32 Squadron, then flying the SE-5As[5] based at Bellevue on the Arras-Doullens Road.

No. 32 Squadron, commanded by Maj. J. C. Russell, had just returned, on 3 August, from Touquin, where it had fought in the Aisne-Marne counteroffensive. From Bellevue airdrome the squadron participated in the British-French Amiens offensive, driving the Germans out of the Somme sector. This drive opened on 8 August with ten British and eight French divisions engaged. In the opening hours of the offensive, Allied aircraft outnumbered the German air forces by "more than six to one," and the tremendous confusion within the enemy's lines produced exceptional targets.[6] However, the initial Allied air advantage was soon to vanish. Late in the afternoon of the first day of the drive, the Germans were able to shift vast aerial reinforcements, including the Richthofen *Jagdgeschwader,* now commanded by Hermann Göring, into the Amiens-Somme battle area.[7]

Apparently, young Hale was thrown into action immediately, "as in a letter dated August 13, to his parents, he mentions having been assigned a new machine all his own . . . and having been over the lines in it several times." In the letter, he states that on his first mission, while escorting Allied bombers, he fired "about 50 rounds at one 'Hun Scout,' that the German plane went into a spin but that at this point another plane attacked . . . and he saw nothing more of his target."[8]

The German air reinforcement increased the intensity of the air fighting. During the last two weeks of August, No. 32 Squadron pilots scored several aerial victories. At seven P.M. on 25 August, "Bud" Hale chalked up his first official kill of the war when, as a part of a SE-5A patrol, he shot down a Fokker biplane near the town of Hancourt. Hale's combat report described the action:

> Pilot accompanying patrol over Hancourt, at 17000 feet, observed
> 4 Fokker biplanes about 1500 feet below, and to the East. Pilot
> dived and attacked one E.A. firing 100 rounds into it at very close
> range. E.A. immediately turned over on its back, and went down
> in a spiral dive. Pilot followed it down, observing it to crash about 2
> miles East of an aerodrome, on side of road at Hancourt.

The victory was confirmed by Lts. Bogert Rogers, G. E. B. Lawson, and E. L. Zink.[9]

Nine days after the Hancourt fight, young Hale, while flying on an offensive patrol, became involved in an air duel with several Fokker D-7s a few miles north of Cambrai. At 9:45 A.M. he spotted two enemy aircraft flying at some thirty-five hundred feet. He quickly banked to the left and dove on one of the Fokkers "firing a burst of 80 rounds" and watched the enemy aircraft stall, "burst into flames," and crash. Hale observed a second Fokker a little southeast of Arras. He promptly maneuvered his SE-5A into a position on the enemy's tail and fired a burst of approximately one hundred rounds into him at close range. The Fokker went into a vertical dive and appeared out of control. Other air activity in the area prevented Hale from witnessing the actual crash of the second victim. Nonetheless, the commanding officer of the Ninth Wing, RAF, considered the Fokker "driven down out of control" for Hale's third aerial victory.[10]

On 6 September Bud Hale was a part of a six-plane patrol attacking seven Fokker D-7s at fourteen thousand feet over St. Quentin. Hale isolated one of the enemy aircraft and fired some fifty rounds into it from a range of seventy-five yards. The Fokker "stalled to the right, and was last seen spinning about 800 feet below." Hale lost sight of his victim as he turned to assist a nearby flight of Royal Air Force DH-9s, then under heavy attack from enemy fighters. Consequently, he was unable to make a positive victory claim.[11]

Ten days later, at 6:10 P.M., Lieutenant Hale's SE-5A patrol, while flying at fourteen thousand feet, spotted nine Fokker biplanes attacking a formation of Sopwith Camels in the vicinity of Brunemont. Hale picked out one enemy aircraft and fired a burst of fifty rounds into him without results. The American turned and attacked a second hostile aircraft firing approximately one hundred rounds at point blank range into it during a series of violent turns from eight thousand feet down to two thousand feet. The Fokker went down out of control and crashed in a small lake at Brunemont for Lieutenant Hale's fourth official kill.[12]

Perhaps Frank Lucien Hale's most successful day as a pursuit pilot occurred on 27 September 1918. While on an offensive patrol in the vicintiy of Cambrai, he spotted ten Fokker D-7s attacking several DH-9s from No. 27 Squadron. Diving from fourteen thousand feet, Hale managed to get on the tail of one of the enemy aircraft and fired some twenty-five rounds at very close range. The Fokker "fell over on its right wing, and continued down completely out of control into clouds, 4000 feet below." Then Lieutenant Hale was attacked by an enemy Fokker that fired a long burst into his SE-5A. With a climbing turn and a half roll, the American came out on his attacker's tail firing a long burst of 150 rounds from less than fifty yards. According to Hale's combat report, "This E.A. turned over on its back, fell, and was observed to be still falling 2000 feet below, on its back and quite out of control, sideslipping and spiralling." At this point another enemy fighter attacked Hale "who put his machine into a spin and went down into clouds at 5000 feet," came out underneath them and flew west. Then he saw a Fokker below and turned toward it only to have the enemy fire a burst into his radiator. Hale held his fire until "within 50 yards then fired both guns (about 75 rounds) seeing all tracers entering E.A." The enemy aircraft "dived, then zoomed to stalling point, fell on its back and went down, first on one wing and then on the other, helplessly out of control." From this attack, Frank Hale climbed into the clouds to avoid heavy anti-aircraft fire and managed to reach his home base at Bellevue on the Arras-Doullens Road. A few days later, the Ninth Wing commander certified that the "three machines were driven down out of control." [13] For his performance on 27 September, Frank Hale was awarded the Distinguished Flying Cross. [14]

During the next several weeks, pilots of No. 32 Squadron were heavily engaged in low-level strafing and dive bombing work:

> It was during this critical period that the strain told most severely on both planes and men. Although muscular exertion was relatively small, huge amounts of nervous energy were expended. Frequent steep dives into the teeth of machine gun fire, the concussion from the detonation of high explosives, exposure to attack from above and hazards like balloon cables, church spires and smoke stacks made ground strafing universally detested. [15]

Young Hale managed to survive these last weeks of the war but achieved no further aerial victories. [16]

Frank Hale remained on active duty for several months after the war ended. He stayed with No. 32 Squadron until 8 March 1919, when he joined No. 22 Squadron, remaining with that unit until 27 May. He was assigned to No. 79 Squadron until 14 July, when he was transferred to No. 70 Squadron. On leaving the service on 22 July 1919, he was promoted to captain. At that time, he had logged some twelve hundred hours in the air.[17]

Shortly after his resignation from the Royal Air Force, Hale returned to Fayetteville, New York. During the next two decades he worked at many different jobs. As one historical source has stated, "simply as a man he merits attention, despite periodic fights with the bottle and a life that some might consider at least 'unconventional' as a character study of the 'pre-organization man.'"[18] According to this source, Hale's nephew, George Gregory, whom Bud Hale raised along with his own son, described him as

> a man who always started at the top and worked down! For example, he was an executive with the Johnson Outboard Motor firm when he took his son, nephew, and various other young relatives on a two week vacation on a Canadian Island. He and the kids were having such a good time that he couldn't bear to leave after the allotted two weeks, so stayed for nine. He did not consider it in any way important to notify his employer of this decision, and so found himself unemployed upon emerging from the woods.[19]

This apparently did not bother him at all and in this way he worked for a startling number of companies. Shortly before entering World War II service, he was reduced to working for himself—as a Pontiac automobile dealer.[20]

During the 1930s, Hale was unable to qualify for a pilot's license because of a heart condition.

> Nonetheless, he managed always to have an airplane available by writing to manufacturers that he would like to try out their product. In every case they put a brand new plane at his disposal for a trial period, and he managed to stagger these periods so as to always have something in which to take his family and neighborhood urchins for a ride.[21]

Before the Japanese attack on Pearl Harbor, in December 1941, the forty-five-year-old Hale conned his way into the Army Air Corps as a pilot. His sister, Clara H. Gregory, a medical doctor who knew about his heart condition, asked him, "Did you make it by hook or crook, Bud?" To which he replied, briefly, "By crook."[22]

Hale served in various non-combat flying roles during the early months of the war. Finally in 1943, while he was attached to the Eighth Air Force in England, his heart problem was discovered, and he was grounded. A short time later, he was discharged and returned to the United States. Shortly after his return home he secured a job with Bell Aircraft Company in Buffalo, New York. He was found dead in his home on 7 June 1944—one day after D-Day. According to one historical source, "Quite possibly his old soldier's heart couldn't stand the thought of this tremendous battle going on without him. In any case, here ended the career of a real Tiger."[23]

Lt. William L. Dougan
Courtesy Mrs. W. L. Dougan

TWENTY-FIVE

American Air Aces
Who Flew with No. 29 Squadron

N o. 29 Squadron, one of the top fighter units of World War I, was organized at Gosport in September 1915 and entered the combat zone on 17 March 1916. Equipped with DH-2s and commanded by Maj. L. Dawes, the squadron was first stationed at Rouen. In April of 1916, the single-seater outfit moved to St. Omer and, a few weeks later, was transferred to Aberle. In October, No. 29 Squadron was based at Izel le Hameau near the city of Arras, where it remained until April 1917 when it was transferred to the airdrome at Poperinghe. The squadron flew Nieuport 17 Scouts from March 1917 until March 1918, when it was equipped with SE-5A pursuit planes and was led by Maj. C. H. Dixon. During February of 1918, the unit was moved to La Lovie and in March was located at Teteghem and a few days later was transferred to St. Omer.[1]

According to several sources, there were at least a dozen Americans who flew with No. 29 Squadron during the last few months of the First World War. The list included such individuals as Lts. Sydney M. Brown, Frank C. Corbin, Charles Davidson, William L. Dougan, D'Arcy Fowles Hilton, Roderick S. G. Maclean, Joseph Patrick Murphy, Douglas Morrison Murray, David A. O'Leary, F. A. Robertson, R. G. Robertson, and W. D. Wiseman, in addition to Aubrey Diamond and Willard Lauer of the U.S. Air Service.[2] Hilton, Brown, Murray, and Dougan were all listed as aces in various accounts.[3]

Lt. Sydney MacGillivary Brown listed his home as 168 Stirling Place, Brooklyn, New York, and was a student at Princeton University when he joined the Royal Flying Corps. After preliminary flight training in Canada, he was sent overseas, where he spent several months polishing his flying skills in various single-seater pursuit planes. On 3 July 1918 he was posted to No. 29 Squadron, then flying out of St. Omer.[4] He was assigned to "B" Flight, led by Capt. C. H. R. Lagesse, and, four days later on 7 July, he flew his first operational mission.

Lt. Douglas Morrison Murray, whose home was listed at 527 Seminole Avenue, Detroit, Michigan, joined the Royal Flying Corps in Toronto, Canada, in the autumn of 1917, where he did the first part of his flight training. As a second lieutenant, he sailed from Halifax on 12 January 1918.[5] After several months of training on the SE-5A, he was assigned to No. 29 Squadron in the summer of 1918.

Lt. William Lee Dougan, born in Salem, Missouri, and later moved to Neosho, Missouri, joined the British Army in Windsor, Canada, in 1915. He trained first with the Thirty-third Infantry Battalion then transferred to the Motor Transport Division, with which he went to France. Later he served with an ambulance corps. In 1917, Dougan applied for and was granted a transfer to the Royal Flying Corps. He did his flight training in England, and in January 1918 he was injured in an airplane crash. In a letter written from London to his mother, Ida Dougan, he commented on the accident:

> I finished my work [with a training squadron] on Monday and nearly finished myself also. They sent me up in a dud machine. After I was up I knew I was going to have trouble. A wind came up and my engine was missing. I landed or rather crashed with the wind. I went thru the wind screen and landed about 20 ft away on my head & right arm. They are a little sore but not much. Of the machine nothing was left. Even the motor was broken into several pieces. Nobody expected to find me alive but I got up with a smile on my face.[6]

A few weeks later, he was posted to No. 29 Squadron, then operating on the British end of the battle lines. The Americans who were posted to No. 29 Squadron were quite pleased with their assignment to the unit because of its great record. Indeed, No. 29 Squadron had had, at one time or another, some of the best pilots of the war. James B. McCudden, a fifty-seven victory ace who served with the squadron for several months during 1916, had won the Victoria Cross. Others included Capt. A. S. Shepherd, Capt. E. W. Molesworth, Capt. J. Brearley, Maj. C. H. Bowman, and Capt. C. H. R. Lagesse.[7] By the end of the war, No. 29 Squadron had achieved 379 victories.[8]

During the months of June and July, Lieutenant Dougan flew

Lt. Sydney MacGillivary Brown
Courtesy Jack Eder

more than a score of operational missions and was involved in several dogfights with German aircraft. Although he was not successful in shooting down an enemy machine, he managed to polish his air combat skills. His "C" Flight commander, Capt. C. J. Venter, a South African, scored several of his victories during this period.

At the end of July, No. 29 Squadron was transferred from St. Omer to the Hoog Huis Airdrome. The month of August turned out to be the squadron's most successful period of "their whole war." At Hoog Huis the unit came "under the control of the 11th

Army Wing and was up to its full establishment of twenty-four SE-5As."[9] Captain Lagasse shot down a German DFW on 4 August and, four days later, the squadron "had a field day." The SE-5A outfit managed to destroy an observation balloon, an LVG two-seater, and six Albatros pursuit planes. One of the Albatros planes was knocked down by Lt. D. A. O'Leary, one of the Americans. On 9 August, the No. 29 Squadron pilots shot down five enemy planes.[10] On the following day, Lt. William L. Dougan fired three hundred rounds into a hostile kite balloon and watched it go down in flames for his first air victory.[11]

The "Glorious Twelfth" of August "proved to be the finest days' shooting in 29's history to date when a total of eleven victories were claimed and confirmed."[12] Bill Dougan, "at 9:20 A.M., shot a Fokker off Capt. Davies' tail, and the left hand top plane of E.A. broke off. E.A. fell to the ground."[13] The German machine crashed near Comines for young Dougan's second kill of the war.

Late in the afternoon of 12 August, Captain Lagasse, leading a patrol of No. 29 Squadron pilots, spotted four Fokker D-7s and promptly attacked the enemy leader and shot him down. Capt. C. J. Venter fired a long burst into a second Fokker and watched the German pilot bail out while the plane went down in flames. Lt. E. O. Amm destroyed the third enemy machine while the American, Sydney M. Brown, blasted the fourth Fokker. Brown's victim's "wings folded up" and crashed. This was the New York lad's first victory since joining No. 29 Squadron. That evening, the No. 29 Squadron pilots "celebrated with high spirits, inviting the members of all nearby units to join them."[14]

During the next week, No. 29 Squadron pilots destroyed some sixteen enemy aircraft. On a cloudy 19 August at 11:15 A.M., Lieutenant Brown "fired 150 rounds at a DFW and drove it down eastward until [the enemy aircraft] crashed into trees on the Bailleul-Nippe Road." This marked Brown's second kill.[15]

Ten more air victories were scored by No. 29 Squadron pilots during the last week of the month of August. At 7:10 P.M. on 24 August, a formation led by Capt. E. O. Hoy attacked two formations of Fokker D-7s a short distance southeast of Comines. The RAF patrol managed to destroy four enemy planes and one observation balloon. Lt. William L. Dougan dived on three "green fuselage, red tail, silver wing Fokkers" at eight thousand feet and chased them east. "Picking out the rear one, he fired 300 rounds, and followed it down to 4,000 feet, crashed it S.E. of Comines close to a canal." This victory by the Missouri man was confirmed by Captain Hoy.[16] In a letter to his sister Kathleen, written on the next day, Dougan indicated he had great difficulty in getting back to his home airdrome: "Twenty miles over Hunland and under 4000 ft. How I got back I don't know. Archie had me going in every direction. Knowing Hun scouts were above me I had a bad time until I got back to our side. The rest were surprised to see me back. They thought I was gone."[17]

The month of August had, indeed, been a good time for No. 29 Squadron. The unit claimed fifty-nine enemy aircraft destroyed or out of control for the loss of only two pilots (both prisoners of war) and one pilot injured in a flying accident.[18]

In September 1918 No. 29 Squadron was moved to La Lovie for a few days and then was returned to Hoog Huis.[19] Not content to rest on their fantastic August record, the organization "continued their run of destruction." Not only were the pilots involved in air combat but carried out several strafing and bombing raids. On 2 September, No. 29 Squadron along with No. 74 Squadron, No. 41 Squadron, and No. 70 Squadron staged a massive raid on the German airfield at Linselles. No. 29 Squadron made the first attack on the airdrome, dropping a total of fifty-one twenty-five–pound Cooper bombs from two thousand feet on the German hangars. They then climbed to a top cover position while the other three squadrons flew low to release their bomb loads and strafe the airfield. Several of the hangars were seen to be on fire and others badly damaged. All the participating aircraft returned safely.[20]

During the next two weeks, No. 29 Squadron scored some ten air victories. On 16 September, a bright sunny day, at approximately nine A.M., a patrol led by Captain Lagesse engaged some fourteen Fokker D-7s and three Fokker Triplanes in the vicinity of Armentières and Lille. In the fierce dogfight which took place between seven thousand feet and one thousand five hundred feet, no less than seven enemy planes and one balloon were destroyed. Lt. William L. Dougan, who was only 5'5" tall, fought one of the Fokker D-7s down to three thousand feet, firing two hundred rounds at close range, and the Fokker crashed south of the town of Wervicq. This victory was confirmed by Captain Hoy and marked Bill Dougan's fourth kill since joining the squadron.[21] During the air battle, No. 29 Squadron lost Lt. P. G. A. Fleming, who became a prisoner of war.[22]

Lieutenant Dougan, on several occasions during September, led No. 29 Squadron patrols. Between 16 September and 25 September, he was involved in several strafing and bombing missions. On 25 September the entire squadron was moved to La Lovie airfield "but little time was wasted in settling in and the fighting continued." Two days after the move, Capt. C. W. Wareing shot down a balloon in flames and Capt. E. C. Hoy blasted the tail off a Fokker D-7.[23]

On 28 September, three days after the move to La Lovie, some sixteen No. 29 Squadron pilots braved heavy rain and poor visibility in a bombing and strafing raid in the Moorsledge–Houthulst Forest–Roulers area. In the battle, the squadron received its biggest setback in months when four of its "doughiest fighters were lost." Capt, E. C. Hoy, Lt. B. R. Rolfe, Lt. D. A. O'Leary, and the American, Lt. Bill Dougan, were shot down and became prisoners of war.[24] In a letter written to his mother from Hospital St. Elizabeth in Antwerp on 1 December 1918, Bill Dougan stated, "I am getting along fine. The doctor says I can get up in a couple of weeks." He indicated that he had "been a long time in bed" and described the disaster:

I was shot down on the morning of Sept. 28, the day the big push started. Our Commanding Officer told us the night before that a big push was to start from the sea to the other end of the line to bring about peace by Xmas and that we had to knock all the Huns out of the sky. Well I guess I did my share. I had the greatest half hour I ever had in my life. I got four balloons in flames and a two-seater. Balloons count the same as an aeroplane. They should count more as they are harder to get. The fifth balloon caused my downfall. It was pulled down very low and two machine guns on the ground made it very warm for me. I was hit six or seven times in the left leg but could have got back to our lines if I hadn't got hit in the chest. It just touched the lung and I could only gasp. I knew I was about to faint so shut off my engine and adjusted the tail plane and started to glide into a field. I never got there. Fainted on the way and my bus crashed through a house. It went through the roof and attic where I left my wings and half way through the next floor. I hit my head on the dash and woke up undid my belt and got out. The Huns put a ladder up and got me down. The officer of the balloon took me over to their mess. They bound up my wounds, gave me a drink and took my picture. They were good fellows. They sent for an ambulance which took me to a dressing station where they dressed my wounds. They didn't think I would live and they put me in a room with three Huns who were about to cork out. A padre came in and gave them the last sacrament. He asked me my religion but didn't seem to care much for me. They found I was still alive in the afternoon so sent me to another hospital. They operated on me and took a lot of lead out of me.[25]

After four days, the Germans sent Lieutenant Dougan to another hospital on a Red Cross train. Dougan spent several weeks in bed and was finally transferred to a Belgian Red Cross station on 15 November, some four days after the Armistice.[26]

In the late afternoon on the day Dougan, Hoy, Rolfe, and O'Leary were shot down, No. 29 Squadron pilots destroyed three Fokker D-7s. At 4:30 P.M., Lt. S. M. Brown, while on an offensive patrol, dived his SE-5A "on one of nine Fokker biplanes at 12000 feet, over Menin. He fired 100 rounds. E.A. turned over on its back, went out of control and crashed." This victory, Brown's third, was confirmed by two other No. 29 Squadron pilots.[27]

With the big Allied Meuse-Argonne and the British offensive underway, No. 29 Squadron "maintained their ceaseless search for enemy aircraft." The German *Jagdstaffeln,* however, continued to fight fiercely. The No. 29 Squadron scored several victories during the first week of October. On 5 October the unit moved to Hoog Huis again to keep up with the retreating Germans.[28] Early in the morning of that day, the American, Lt. Douglas M. Murray, scored his first air victory when he attacked a hostile observation balloon a little to the northeast of Menin. The "balloon disappeared and was seen by ground observers to burst into flames."[29] Two other balloons and a Fokker triplane were shot down by No. 29 Squadron on the same mission.[30] On 8 October Lieutenant Murray along with Lts. E. C. Amm, D. M. Layton, and J. P. Murphy forced a Fokker D-7 to land in Allied territory. According to the combat report, the kill was "given to Murray." This marked his second victory.[31]

During the next several days, No. 29 Squadron fighter pilots chalked up several more victories but lost three of their own, including Capt. C. W. Wareing, who had eight kills to his credit. On 27 October at 9:20 A.M., four No. 29 Squadron pilots destroyed two Fokkers, sent a third down out of control and flamed an observation balloon. According to the combat report, Lt. Sydney M. Brown "fired 100 rounds at close range, the HKB [hostile kite balloon] burst into flames" for his fourth victory.[32] Late in the afternoon on the following day, four No. 29 Squadron pilots de-

Lt. Douglas M. Murray
Courtesy Ola Sater

stroyed three Fokker D-7s. Lieutenant Brown came down on the Fokker formation and "firing 100 rounds at one—sent it down out of control and saw it crash in a field southeast of Avelohen."[33] This victory put Lt. Sydney M. Brown in the ace category, and a few weeks later he was awarded the Distinguished Flying Cross.[34] Brown made his last operational flight on 3 November and, on the following day, proceeded to the United Kingdom on a rest leave. He returned to No. 29 Squadron then stationed at Bickendorf, Germany, during the early months of 1919.[35]

Despite the fact the war was coming to a close, the German air forces continued to battle in the sky. During the first eleven days of November, No. 29 Squadron, now based at Courtrai, engaged the enemy almost daily. On 9 November the squadron shot down some fourteen German aircraft.[36] At 9:45 A.M., Lt. D. M. Murray, a member of "B" Flight, attacked some six Fokkers at eleven thousand feet and drove one down out of control, and it was confirmed as having crashed near Audenarde. Some forty-five minutes later, he sent "another one out of control near Minte, and then pulled out owing to lack of ammunition."[37]

On the day before the end of the war, No. 29 Squadron pilots engaged a large formation of Fokker D-7s and shot down five of them. These were "the final combat claims for 29 Squadron" and pushed the unit's total to 379 victories. Of these victories, 187 were enemy scout planes, 104 were C-Types (two-seaters), 48 were unidentified, and 40 were observation balloons. During the last four months of the war, No. 29 Squadron was one of the most effective pursuit organizations of the Allied air units. Of the Americans assigned to No. 29 Squadron, Lt. D. F. Hilton, who flew with the unit from June to November 1917, became an ace. Lt. S. M. Brown scored his fifth kill on 28 October 1918, and Lt. D. M. Murray was credited with five victories in several sources. Lt. W. L. Dougan had four victories confirmed but scored five more on the day he was wounded and crashed on the German side of the battle lines.[38] Consequently, Dougan was considered to have destroyed five observation balloons and four aircraft. On Christmas day, Dougan was transferred to the Prince of Wales Hospital in London, and a few days later he received a personal letter from King George V congratulating him on his performance as a pursuit pilot.

In March 1919 Dougan got out of the hospital and was soon back in the flying service on active duty. In October 1919 he was discharged from the Royal Air Force. The Missouri man was much respected by his squadron mates. Maj. C. H. Droan, in a letter to Dougan's mother, stated,

> I am asked by both officers and men of the squadron to tell you how much we mourn his loss. He was always so keen and cheerful. His gallantry in the air and his cheery and unselfish disposition endeared him to us all. His Flight Commander, who unfortunately is also missing, used to say that there was no one he preferred to have behind him in a scrap than Dougan.[39]

Bill Dougan returned to Neosho, Missouri, and married Helen North. They had two sons, young William, who became a fighter pilot in World War II, and Michael, who was born in 1944 and is presently a history professor at Arkansas State University. During the 1920s Dougan, the World War I ace, participated in barnstorming and crop dusting activities and in World War II, he worked as a test pilot for Lockheed Aircraft Company. Dougan died in Neosho, Missouri, in 1968.[40]

*Lt. Harold A. Kullberg (front left) with members of No. 1
Squadron RAF.*

TWENTY-SIX

Summary and Conclusion

O f the several hundred Americans who joined the Royal Flying Corps, which became the Royal Air Force on 1 April 1918, most of them hoped to help the British win the First World War. Only a few merely wanted to fly. Some twenty-eight of the Americans who joined the Royal Air Corps and the Royal Air Force became aces during the first great air war. Many others scored victories against the Germans but did not reach the ace level. Almost all of the Americans who joined the British air units enlisted through Canada and did part of their air training there or at Fort Worth, Texas. They were required to do further training in England or Scotland before being assigned to British pursuit squadrons on the western front. A few were posted to reconnaissance and bombardment squadrons.

Only a few Americans participated in the great Somme battle that lasted from 1 July 1916 to 15 November 1916. During this campaign the German losses were 500,000, and the German morale was lowered, but the Allies were no better off. British losses were 400,000, and the French lost 200,000.[1] During the summer and early autumn of 1916 Lt. Frederick Libby, the Colorado cowboy, served as an observer with No. 23 Squadron and No. 11 Squadron, managed to shoot down some ten enemy aircraft, and was awarded the Military Cross. In November 1916 Libby returned to England and took pilot training during the next several months. In April 1917 he was posted to No. 43 Squadron, then flying Sopwith two-seaters, and in July he was promoted to captain. In August 1917 he was transferred to the DH-4 – flying No. 25 Squadron. While flying with these two squadrons he scored some fourteen victories. Despite flying aircraft that was not as maneuverable as the German Fokkers and Albatroses, his excellent eyesight was effective. In September of that year he was

DeHavilland 2
Courtesy Imperial War Museum

asked by Gen. William "Billy" Mitchell to return to the United States and participate in the training of other Americans who would be flying with the United States Air Service.[2]

Capt. Clive W. Warman, who had served with a Canadian regiment in 1915, was wounded and recovered in an English hospital. After he regained his health he was given permission to train as a pilot in the fall and winter of 1916. In June 1917 he was posted to No. 23 Squadron, then flying Spad-7s. During the next two months he scored some fifteen victories.[3] On August 1917 he was badly wounded but managed to land on the English side of the battle front. Because of his excellent eyesight and his thorough flight training he became one of the top American aces of the war.

During the late fall of 1917 Lts. D'Arcy Fowles Hilton, Jens Frederick Larson, Francis Peabody Magoun, and Oliver C. LeBoutillier participated in the Cambrai offensive. Their training program in Canada and the United Kingdom helped them a great deal. LeBoutillier, flying the Sopwith Camel, and Larson, piloting the SE-5, had a real advantage over most German aircraft. In addition, Larson had an expert commanding officer, Maj. Sholto Douglas, who no doubt assisted him greatly.[4]

During the first six months of 1918, the Germans launched five great offensives against the Allied forces. On 21 March 1918 they began the big Somme campaign, which lasted until 4 April. Lts. George W. Bulmer flying Bristol Fighters, William C. Lambert, John Griffith, Francis P. Magoun, and John F. Larson flying SE-5s, Emile John Lussier flying Sopwith Camels, Francis W. Gillet flying Sopwith Dolphins, and Eugene S. Coler flying Bristol Fighters were all involved in the Somme campaign. These American aces were flying outstanding aircraft, and because they had had good flight training they played a significant role in bringing the German drive to a halt. Lieutenant Griffith, then flying with No. 60 Squadron, had excellent advice from Maj. J. T. B. McCudden, who was very skilled in leading fighters over the front.[5] Capt. G. E. H. McElroy, then flying with No. 24 Squadron, helped Lt. William C. Lambert a great deal.[6]

The German Lys offensive, which opened on 9 April and ended on 29 April, saw the same American pilots involved in air combat. Capt. Oliver C. LeBoutillier was also engaged in this campaign. While flying the highly maneuverable Sopwith Camel, LeBoutillier witnessed the shooting down of the top German ace, Manfred von Richthofen, on 21 April by Capt. Roy Brown of No. 209 Squadron.[7]

Relatively few Americans flying with the Royal Air Force were engaged in the German Aisne drive toward Paris which took place on 27 May 1918. The French air units were heavily involved in this operation, which came to a halt on 6 June.[8] According to *War in an Open Cockpit,* No. 32 Squadron was engaged on the northwest flank of the operation. Lts. Alvin Andrew Callender and Bogert Rogers, who later became American aces, were engaged in this drive flying SE-5s.[9]

The fourth German offensive opened on 9 June 1918 in the Noyon-Montdidier area. The No. 73 Squadron, flying Sopwith Camels, moved south into the French front and were heavily engaged in strafing and air combat. Lts. Norman Cooper and Emile John Lussier were very active in this drive. A few other Royal Air Force squadrons were in combat on the northwest flank. On 12 June this operation ended.[10]

Bristol F2B Fighter
Courtesy U.S. Army Air Forces in National Archives

The German Champagne-Marne offensive opened on 15 July, and No. 23 Squadron again moved to the French front and were hotly engaged. Much of this squadron's activity was strafing of the German troops on the ground. As a result, the German attack made negligible gains. Only in one region, west of Reims, did they make a serious threat, crossing the Marne River for the last time in the war. Not only were the French air squadrons involved, but the United States Air Service squadrons were also in combat. By 17 July the fifth German offensive—sometimes called the Second Battle of the Marne—had come to an end.[11]

On 8 August 1918 the British Fourth and the French First armies began their offensive at Amiens with four hundred tanks and several hundred aircraft. The German front collapsed completely, and Gen. Erich von Ludendorff called this offensive the "Black Day of the German Army" and pulled his troops back several miles. On 21 August Field Marshal Douglas Haig shifted his forces to the north and attacked near Arras. The RAF air squadrons played a major role in the Amiens-Arras drive.[12] Most of the American aces who were assigned to RAF squadrons suc-

Fokker D-7
Courtesy U.S. Army Air Forces in National Archives

ceeded in shooting down many of the German planes. In September the Allied armies and air units began their drive in the Somme-Flanders sector and continued their combat until the Armistice. Most of the Americans flying Sopwith Camels, Sopwith Dolphins, Bristol Fighters, and SE-5 pursuit planes were highly successful. Certainly these planes were equal or superior to the German air squadrons.

During the First World War over three hundred Americans served with the British. Some fifty-one were killed in combat, thirty-two were wounded, thirty-two were prisoners of war, and eight were listed as missing. The twenty-eight American aces who flew with the British scored some 294 victories, and only two, Alvin Andrew Callender and Louis Bennett, were killed in air combat. Eight were wounded in battle, and two were prisoners of war. There is no question but these aces were well trained, had excellent eyesight, and had muscular coordination. The planes they flew, such as the Camel, SE-5, Bristol Fighter, and the Sopwith Dolphin, were excellent. Of the top twenty-nine American aces who flew with the United States Air Service and the Royal Air Force, seventeen flew only with the British.

Unfortunately, those American aces who flew only with the British in World War I are little known by the American public. It is for this reason that this book has been written. Certainly individuals such as William C. Lambert, Francis W. Gillet, O. J. Rose, Harold Kullberg, and Clive Warman should catch the attention of those American "buffs" and scholars of military aviation.

American Pilots Who Flew Combat Only with the RFC/RNAS/RAF During World War I

This information was taken from various documents in the Directorate of History in the National Defence Department Headquarters, Ottawa, Canada. In addition to the name and rank of the individual, the date of entry and exit from the numbered squadrons is listed, as well as casualties. In some cases, service with a squadron is vague, and only the year is recorded.

NAME	RANK	DATE OF SERVICE	CASUALTIES
Number 1 Squadron, RAF			
H. B. Bradley	Lt.	30 Mar 1918–25 June 1918	missing
D. W. Hughes	Lt.	11 Apr 1918–3 May 1918	wounded
E. L. Humphrey	2nd Lt.	Nov 1918–6 Dec 1918	
H. A. Kullberg	Lt.	10 May 1918–16 Sept 1918	wounded
F. P. Magoun	Lt.	14 Nov 1917–10 April 1918	wounded
		9 Oct 1918–6 Jan 1919	
W. C. Taylor	2nd Lt.	1918	
Number 3 Squadron, RAF			
D. D. Ashley	2nd Lt.	4 Sept 1918–10 Dec 1918	
G. Goad	2nd Lt.	31 Jan 1919	
T. R. Hosterrer	Lt.	19 Sept 1918–27 Sept 1918	killed
M. C. Kinney	Lt.	11 Mar 1918–16 Aug 1918	wounded
R. L. McCleod	2nd Lt.	21 Dec 1918–30 Jan 1918	
		21 Aug 1918–28 Sept 1918	wounded
A. E. McManus	2nd Lt.	2 June 1918–5 Nov 1918	
J. E. Mutty	2nd Lt.	28 Oct 1918–30 Jan 1919	
L. W. Prescott	Lt.	22 Apr 1918	killed

NAME	RANK	DATE OF SERVICE	CASUALTIES

Number 4 Squadron, RAF

R. Moore	Lt.	11 May 1918–3 Nov 1918	
G. H. Olney	2nd Lt.	29 Dec 1917–8 June 1918	
E. M. Roberts	2nd Lt.	30 Apr 1916–2 July 1916	wounded

Number 6 Squadron, RAF

F. M. Stieber	2nd Lt.	10 Feb 1919–Mar 1919	

Number 7 Squadron, RAF

F. S. McClurg	Capt.	28 July 1917–8 June 1918	
R. C. Murray	2nd Lt.	6 Mar 1919–13 Apr 1919	

Number 8 Squadron, RAF

C. W. Appley	2nd Lt.	1918–2 Sept 1918	killed
J. M. Brown	2nd Lt.	30 Mar 1918–13 Apr 1918	
E. C. Goldsworthy	Lt.	Feb 1919	

Number 9 Squadron, RAF

H. W. Brighton	Lt.	1 Dec 1917–16 Dec 1917	
H. S. Fey	Lt.	28 Jan 1919–18 Mar 1919	
R. E. White	2nd Lt.	27 May 1918–17 July 1918	POW

Number 10 Squadron, RAF

F. A. Green	Lt.	2 Feb 1919–7 Feb 1919	
D. A. McKenzie	Lt.	12 July 1918–28 Oct 1918	killed

Number 11 Squadron, RAF

E. S. Coler	Capt.	12 Mar 1918–16 Sept 1918	wounded
D. A. Curtis	2nd Lt.	31 Oct 1918–28 Mar 1919	
F. Libby	Capt.	July 1916–8 Nov 1916	

Number 13 Squadron, RAF

M. P. LaFleur	2nd Lt.	2 Oct 1918–10 Jan 1919	
H. B. Lilley	Lt.	11 June 1917–18 Dec 1917	
E. G. Plum	Lt.	13 May 1918–28 Jan 1919	
T. L. Tibbs	Capt.	25 Mar 1917–10 July 1917	

Number 15 Squadron, RAF

C. N. F. Jeffery	Lt.	26 June 1917–22 July 1917	
		8 Aug 1917–7 May 1918	

NAME	RANK	DATE OF SERVICE	CASUALTIES
Number 16 Squadron, RAF			
E. M. Chant	Lt.	21 Jan 1918–25 Mar 1918	killed
W. M. Clayton	2nd Lt.	20 Dec 1918–1 Jan 1919	
H. S. Fey	Lt.	31 May 1918–27 Jan 1919	
Number 18 Squadron, RAF			
B. K. Adams	2nd Lt.	27 Feb 1918–14 Mar 1918	killed
F. R. Knapp	Lt.	29 Mar 1918–16 Apr 1918	POW
R. B. Smith	2nd Lt.	2 Mar 1918–27 Mar 1918	POW
Number 19 Squadron, RAF			
E. G. Boyle	2nd Lt.	2 Nov 1918–29 Mar 1919	
J. W. Crane	Lt.	7 June 1918–30 Oct 1918	missing
C. M. DeVitalis	Lt.	17 Mar 1918–1 July 1918	
R. W. Duff	2nd Lt.	13 Aug 1918–18 Nov 1918	
R. S. V. Elliott	Lt.	2 Nov 1918	
W. F. Leach	Lt.	28 May 1918–17 June 1918	wounded
M. E. Miller	2nd Lt.	11 Aug 1918–9 Dec 1918	
J. A. Mitchell	2nd Lt.	31 Oct 1918–16 Dec 1918	
G. W. Northridge	Lt.	17 May 1918–9 Aug 1918	wounded
R. Watts	Lt.	22 Oct 1916	POW
Number 20 Squadron, RAF			
E. Bryant	2nd Lt.	29 Apr 1919	
D. G. Campbell	Lt.	11 Dec 1917–19 Feb 1918	killed
A. T. Iaccaci	Capt.	24 Apr 1918–5 Oct 1918	
P. T. Iaccaci	Capt.	25 Apr 1918–8 Sept 1918	
G. W. Schermerhorn	2nd Lt.	1 Feb 1919–10 Mar 1919	
Number 21 Squadron, RAF			
C. R. Benedict	2nd Lt.	7 Nov 1918	
A. R. Evers	2nd Lt.	7 Mar 1918–17 June 1918	injured
J. V. Flanagan	2nd Lt.		
M. L. Howard	Lt.	23 Feb 1917–24 Jan 1918	
J. G. Newton	2nd Lt.	7 Sept 1918–6 Feb 1919	
J. Pollins	2nd Lt.	21 Sept 1918–28 Sept 1918	killed
G. H. Snow	Lt.	5 Mar 1918–27 June 1918	wounded

NAME	RANK	DATE OF SERVICE	CASUALTIES

Number 22 Squadron, RAF

G. W. Bulmer	Capt.	29 Dec 1917	
		25 May 1918–20 Aug 1918	
W. M. Clayton	Lt.	1 Jan 1919–6 Mar 1919	
M. Goldsmith	Lt.	18 Aug 1918–7 Nov 1918	
F. L. Hale	Lt.	8 Mar 1919–27 May 1919	

Number 23 Squadron, RAF

B. M. F. Albanese	Lt.	9 Aug 1918–11 Aug 1918	wounded
J. W. Pearson	Capt.	6 Apr 1918–18 Jan 1919	
R. G. Searson	2nd Lt.	9 Aug 1918–10 Oct 1918	
C. E. Thomas	2nd Lt.	6 Aug 1918–1 Feb 1919	
A. O. B. Turner	Lt.	11 Nov 1918	
H. Walten	2nd Lt.	Feb 1919	
C. E. Walton	Lt.	9 May 1918–22 July 1918	
C. W. Warman	Capt.	16 June 1917–20 Aug 1917	wounded

Number 24 Squadron, RAF

M. L. Howard	Lt.	24 Jan 1918–23 Feb 1918	
T. M. Harries	2nd Lt.	19 Aug 1918	
W. C. Lambert	Lt.	20 Mar 1918–20 Aug 1918	
E. P. Larrabee	2nd Lt.	28 Aug 1918–20 Sept 1918	POW

Number 25 Squadron, RAF

F. Libby	Capt.	1917	

Number 27 Squadron, RAF

J. H. Bauer	2nd Lt.	2 Nov 1918–10 July 1919	
T. A. Dickinson	2nd Lt.	8 July 1918–11 Apr 1919	
A. W. Greene	2nd Lt.	7 Feb 1918–17 Feb 1918	killed

Number 28 Squadron, RAF

C. W. Lingham	Lt.	23 Aug 1917–7 Sept 1917	
P. G. Ratliff	2nd Lt.	13 Feb 1918–29 Mar 1918	
B. H. Redner	2nd Lt.	23 Oct 1918–4 Dec 1918	

Number 29 Squadron, RAF

S. M. G. Brown	Lt.	3 July 1918–Nov 1918	
F. Corbin	2nd Lt.	Feb 1919	

NAME	RANK	DATE OF SERVICE	CASUALTIES
W. L. Dougan	2nd Lt.	4 June 1918	wounded & POW on 28 Sept 1918
W. P. Murphy	Lt.	30 Sept 1918–14 Oct 1918	wounded
T. Stead	2nd Lt.	18 Oct 1918–29 Oct 1918	wounded
D. F. Hilton	Lt.	7 June 1917–Nov 1917	wounded
D. M. Murray	Lt.		

Number 32 Squadron, RAF

G. H. Bonnell	Major	5 July 1916	
A. A. Callender	Capt.	16 May 1918–30 Oct 1918	killed
M. E. Dezee	Lt.	18 May 1918–13 June 1918	
H. McK. Gordon	2nd Lt.	3 Nov 1918–17 Mar 1919	
F. L. Hale	Lt.	10 Aug 1918–8 Mar 1919	
B. Rogers	2nd Lt.	23 Sept 1918	
C. A. Sperry	Lt.	6 July 1918–28 Sept 1918	
M. A. Tancock	Lt.	10 Aug 1918–4 Mar 1919	
W. Amory	Lt.	5 Sept 1918–30 Oct 1918	POW
W. A. Anderson	Lt.	24 June 1918–18 July 1918	killed

Number 33 Squadron, RAF

Clyde Frey	Lt.	21 Mar 1918–28 Mar 1918	

Number 34 Squadron, RAF

F. B. Farquharson	2nd Lt.	1917	
P. G. Ratliff	2nd Lt.	30 Mar 1918–24 Apr 1918	POW
W. C. Simon	2nd Lt.	23 June 1918–3 July 1918	

Number 35 Squadron, RAF

C. T. Bremicker	Lt.	28 Mar 1918–23 Apr 1918	
J. M. Brown	2nd Lt.	13 Apr 1918–3 Oct 1918	killed

Number 36 Squadron, RAF

S. G. Kulp	Cadet	7 Mar 1919–12 Apr 1919	

Number 38 Squadron, RAF

C. Frey	Lt.	31 May 1918	

Number 40 Squadron, RAF

Louis B. Bennett	Lt.	21 July 1918–24 Aug 1918	killed
R. A. Anderson	Lt.	23 July 1918–28 Aug 1918	POW

NAME	RANK	DATE OF SERVICE	CASUALTIES
W. D. Archer	Lt.	21 Sept 1918–9 Oct 1918	wounded
R. J. Donaldson	Lt.	2 June 1918–28 Jan 1919	
A. B. Dunn	Lt.	17 Oct 1918–24 Feb 1919	
R. R. Spafford	Lt.	9 Aug 1918–7 Nov 1918	

Number 41 Squadron, RAF

G. T. Collinson	2nd Lt.	4 Sept 1918–18 Feb 1919	
G. J. Farnsworth	Lt.	21 Aug 1918–25 Mar 1919	
J. P. McCone	Lt.	7 Dec 1917–24 Mar 1918	missing
H. J. G. Rudolph	Lt.	18 Aug 1918–6 Feb 1919	

Number 42 Squadron, RAF

J. M. P. O'Keefe	2nd Lt.	9 July 1918–11 Nov 1918	

Number 43 Squadron, RAF

T. E. Babbitt	2nd Lt.	18 June 1918–17 July 1918	missing
C. R. Borkland	Lt.	19 June 1918–3 Aug 1918	
D. R. Day	Lt.	2 July 1918–30 July 1918	
Vrsvt Irvine	Lt.	May 1918–19 July 1918	missing
Frederick Libby	Capt.	1917	
A. H. Pannill	Lt.	17 July 1917–1 Sept 1917	wounded
H. McD. Starke	2nd Lt.	27 Sept. 1917–27 Oct 1917	wounded
C. R. F. Wickenden	2nd Lt.	27 Sept 1917–27 Oct 1917	wounded
C. G. Catto	Lt.	24 Mar 1918–3 Nov 1918	
G. B. Craig	2nd Lt.	9 Sept 1917–3 Oct 1917	
Max Gibson	Lt.	12 June 1918–12 Sept 1918	
J. R. O'Connell	Lt.	6 Aug 1918–2 Jan 1919	

Number 46 Squadron, RAF

A. A. Allen	2nd Lt.	19 Sept 1917–11 Oct 1917	killed
H. F. Cullen	2nd Lt.	31 Aug 1918	
Raymond Moore	Lt.	28 July 1918–12 Aug 1918	killed
J. O'Donoghue	2nd Lt.	21 Sept 1918–4 Nov 1918	missing
R. Viall	Lt.	July 1918–Nov 1918	

Number 48 Squadron, RAF

N. Goldsmith	Lt.	29 July 1918–17 Aug 1918 29 Jan 1919	
P. T. Iaccaci	Capt.	8 Sept 1918–4 Oct 1918	

NAME	RANK	DATE OF SERVICE	CASUALTIES
E. R. Stock	Lt.	Jan 1918–19 May 1918	wounded
S. H. Whipple	2nd Lt.	7 Aug 1918–24 Aug 1918	wounded

Number 49 Squadron, RAF

F. B. Denison	2nd Lt.	12 May 1918–10 June 1918	wounded
R. A. Dickenson	2nd Lt.	11 July 1919	
B. Truscott		22 Jan 1918	

Number 51 Squadron, RAF

F. B. Stark	Lt.	22 Mar 1919–24 Mar 1919	

Number 52 Squadron, RAF

F. E. Robinson	2nd Lt.	27 Mar 1918–1 Apr 1918	

Number 53 Squadron, RAF

F. A. Lewis	2nd Lt.	17 Oct 1917–5 Feb 1918	killed
R. C. Murray	Lt.	22 Sept 1918–6 Mar 1919	

Number 54 Squadron, RAF

C. R. Borkland	Lt.	19 Apr 1918–11 May 1918	
R. M. Charley	Capt.	24 Dec 1916–Sept 1917	
F. M. Clark	2nd Lt.	18 July 1918–12 Aug 1918	
H. C. Deeks	2nd Lt.	27 Feb 1918–27 Mar 1918	wounded
W. H. Gibson	2nd Lt.	18 July 1918	
S. Haydis	Lt.	29 June 1918–9 Aug 1918	
T. R. Hostetter	Lt.	5 Apr 1918–11 Apr 1918	killed
W. A. Hunter	2nd Lt.	18 Apr 1918–3 June 1918	wounded
M. B. Lewis	2nd Lt.	19 Apr 1918–15 July 1918	killed
F. J. Martel	Lt.	6 Apr 1917–3 May 1917	
F. M. Ohrt	Lt.	19 Nov 1917–19 Jan 1918	POW
H. J. Richardson	2nd Lt.	23 Feb 1918–25 Mar 1918	wounded
A. H. Santa-Maria	Lt.	1918	

Number 56 Squadron, RAF

H. Allen	Lt.	28 June 1918–10 Aug 1918	killed
J. K. Blair	Lt.	3 July 1918–5 Oct 1918	hospitalized
L. G. Bowen	Lt.	14 Aug 1918–15 Sept 1918	killed
C. F. Frasier	Lt.	27 Oct 1918–16 Jan 1919	
O. C. Holleran	Capt	12 Apr 1918–15 Sept 1918	wounded

NAME	RANK	DATE OF SERVICE	CASUALTIES
K. P. McGowan	2nd Lt.	22 Oct 1918–28 Jan 1919	
J. C. Speaks	Capt.	16 Aug 1918–4 Apr 1919	wounded 28 Sept 1918
F. C. Tarbutt	Lt.	12 Mar 1918–16 June 1918	killed
B. Truscott	Lt.	9 Nov 1917–21 Jan 1918	
W. H. Winkler	Lt.	16 Sept 1918–21 Oct 1918	POW

Number 57 Squadron, RAF

C. W. Peckham	Lt.	10 May 1918–23 June 1918	POW
W. H. Townsend	Lt.	1 Apr 1918–23 Apr 1918	killed
R. Willey	2nd Lt.	1 Apr 1918–20 May 1918	killed

Number 58 Squadron, RAF

C. A. Dixon	2nd Lt.	11 Mar 1919–3 May 1919	
J. H. Gower	Lt.	10 Feb 1919–21 Mar 1919	
E. M. Roberts	2nd Lt.	23 Nov 1916–7 Apr 1917	
F. H. Sullivan	2nd Lt.	29 Mar 1919	killed

Number 59 Squadron, RAF

F. E. Robinson	2nd Lt.	13 Apr 1918–15 Dec 1918	

Number 60 Squadron, RAF

G. B. Craig	2nd Lt.	3 Oct 1917–21 Feb 1918	
J. S. Griffith	Lt.	14 Feb 1918–3 Aug 1918	wounded 18 July 1918
J. G. Hall	Lt.	11 June 1918–8 Aug 1918	killed
W. F. McCarthy	2nd Lt.	3 May 1918–9 Nov 1918	wounded
F. E. Goodrich	Capt.	12 Sept. 1911	killed

Number 62 Squadron, RAF

D. R. Eccles	2nd Lt.	30 Oct 1917–5 Dec 1917	killed
R. W. Murray	2nd Lt.	28 Sept 1918–6 Mar 1919	
J. P. Skrdlant	2nd Lt.	1918	
W. P. Taltavall	2nd Lt.	6 Nov 1918–12 Dec 1918	

Number 63 Squadron, RAF

E. C. Goldsworthy	Lt.	August 1917	

Number 64 Squadron, RAF

C. A. Bissonette	Lt.	21 Nov 1917–24 June 1918	
H. C. Hayes	Lt.	8 Sept 1918–19 Jan 1919	

NAME	RANK	DATE OF SERVICE	CASUALTIES
M. L. Howard	Lt.	24 Apr 1918–25 July 1918	killed
G. T. Olmstead	2nd Lt.	26 July 1918–1 Aug 1918	killed
G. W. Schermerhorn	Lt.	12 June 1918–11 Aug 1918	
C. A. Sperry	Lt.	28 Sept 1918–16 Oct 1918	

Number 65 Squadron, RAF

NAME	RANK	DATE OF SERVICE	CASUALTIES
W. R. Allison	Lt.	18 Oct 1918–14 Dec 1918	
A. R. Bolay	2nd Lt.	26 May 1918–27 May 1918	killed
H. A. Boyle	2nd Lt.	24 Apr 1918–26 May 1918	
J. H. J. Butler	2nd Lt.	1918	
C. R. Campbell	Lt.	1 July 1918–16 Nov 1918	
A. J. Cleare	2nd Lt.	10 Aug 1918	
W. L. Dean	2nd Lt.	6 Nov 1918–17 Mar 1919	
F. Edsted	2nd Lt.	14 July 1918–28 Sept 1918	POW
F. A. Green	2nd Lt.	25 Dec 1918–1 Feb 1919	
H. J. Leavitt	Lt.	3 May 1918–17 May 1918	POW
J. D. H. Lewis	2nd Lt.	29 Oct 1918	
F. R. Pemberton	2nd Lt.	3 Aug 1918–4 Nov 1918	wounded
B. H. Travis	2nd Lt.	1918	

Number 66 Squadron, RAF

NAME	RANK	DATE OF SERVICE	CASUALTIES
J. W. Bishop	2nd Lt.	15 Aug 1918–13 Mar 1919	
H. K. Boysen	Lt.	22 Aug 1917–28 Jan 1918 15 Apr 1918–21 June 1918	wounded
O. W. Lingham	Lt.	8 Apr 1918–7 May 1918	
P. A. O'Brien	2nd Lt.	Aug 1917–17 Aug 1917	POW
C. O. Robinson	Lt.	13 Oct 1917–7 June 1918	
H. A. Smeeton	Lt.	29 Sept 1917–5 Oct 1917	hospitalized

Number 70 Squadron, RAF

NAME	RANK	DATE OF SERVICE	CASUALTIES
B. M. F. Albanese	Lt.	14 Feb 1919–2 Sept 1919	
L. E. Barry	Capt.	17 Apr 1917–Aug 1917	
R. R. Beebe	2nd Lt.	20 Feb 1919	
O. S. Clefstad	2nd Lt.	31 Aug 1918–3 Feb 1919	
F. E. McMacy	Lt.	14 July 1919–22 July 1919	
D. Miller	2nd Lt.	28 June 1918–30 June 1918	killed
W. E. Taylor	2nd Lt.	9 May 1918–31 May 1918	killed

NAME	RANK	DATE OF SERVICE	CASUALTIES

Number 72 Squadron, RAF

O. W. Lingham	Lt.	8 June 1917–Aug 1917	

Number 73 Squadron, RAF

Norman Cooper	Capt.	29 June 1918–11 Jan 1919	
R. D. Doane	2nd Lt.	18 May 1918–19 June 1918	
G. Goad	2nd Lt.	18 Oct 1918–30 June 1919	
C. J. Hall	Lt.	11 Dec 1917	
H. C. Hayes	Lt.	17 May 1918–13 June 1918	
M. F. Korslund	Lt.	7 Apr 1918–12 Apr 1918	killed
E. J. Lussier (born in USA?)	Capt.	24 Mar 1918–29 Dec 1918	
F. M. Stieber	2nd Lt.	July 1918	

Number 74 Squadron, RAF

J. E. Ferrand	Lt.	14 Aug 1918	
L. A. Richardson	Lt.	23 Mar 1918–19 July 1918	wounded
E. W. Roesch	2nd Lt.	5 Oct 1918–27 Dec 1918	
C. E. L. Skedden	Lt.	26 Dec 1917–8 May 1918	killed
T. L. Tibbs	Capt.		

Number 75 Squadron, RAF

T. H. Blatchford	2nd Lt.	8 July 1918	

Number 78 Squadron, RAF

F. B. Stark		26 May 1919	

Number 79 Squadron, RAF

B. M. F. Albanese	Lt.	9 Oct 1918–14 July 1919	
E. A. Coapman	Lt.	29 Dec 1917–28 July 1918	
H. G. Dugan	2nd Lt.	23 Nov 1917–6 Apr 1918	POW
F. W. Gillet	Capt.	29 Mar 1918–29 Nov 1918	
F. L. Hale	Lt.	27 May 1919–14 July 1919	
G. H. Harding	Lt.	4 Mar 1918–27 Mar 1918	killed
N. D. K. Kennedy	Lt.	14 Mar 1918–2 July 1918	wounded
F. I. Lord	Capt.	20 Jan 1918–19 Nov 1918	wounded 17 Oct 1918
F. E. M. Macy	Lt.	24 Nov 1917–18 April 1918 27 Apr 1919–14 July 1919	
D. A. Martin	2nd Lt.	27 Aug 1918–1 Sept 1918	POW

NAME	RANK	DATE OF SERVICE	CASUALTIES
H. A. Miller	2nd Lt.	30 May 1918–20 May 1918	
J. A. Mitchell	2nd Lt.	8 Aug 1918–31 Aug 1918	wounded
R. J. Morgan	2nd Lt.	25 Aug 1918–28 Sept 1918	POW
N. Munden	Lt.	2 June 1918	
H. M. S. Parsons	2nd Lt.	5 Aug 1918–4 Oct 1918	wounded
B. R. Redman	Lt.	27 Sept 1918–25 Jan 1919	
J. D. Thomas	2nd Lt.	13 Dec 1917–20 Mar 1918	killed

Number 80 Squadron, RAF

R. S. Bowen	2nd Lt.	12 Mar 1919	
F. M. Clark	Lt.	18 July 1918	
H. J. Fitzgibbon	Lt.	22 Apr 1918–2 July 1918	
		6 Aug 1918–3 Sept 1918	
W. A. Hallgren	Lt.	26 May 1918–25 July 1918	wounded
S. C. Leware	Lt.	20 Mar 1919–27 May 1919	
J. I. Maitland	Lt.	12 Aug 1918–15 Sept 1918	hospitalized
G. P. McCraig	2nd Lt.	16 Sept 1918–26 Oct 1918	
J. J. Meredith	Lt.	27 Mar 1918–1 Apr 1918	POW
J. R. Robbins	Lt.	27 Oct 1918	POW
T. Whitman	2nd Lt.	9 Sept 1918–4 Oct 1918	killed

Number 81 Squadron, RAF

B. Truscott	Lt.	1919	
C. W. Warman	Capt.	18 Nov 1918–12 Jan 1919	killed

Number 82 Squadron, RAF

R. Andrews	Lt.	27 Aug 1918–22 Feb 1919	
L. K. W. Barrett	Lt.	26 Mar 1918–24 Apr 1918	killed
A. B. Carmody	2nd Lt.	19 Nov 1917–4 Sept 1918	
G. H. Harding	Lt.	14 Sept 1917–2 Oct 1917	
W. Pendleton	2nd Lt.	1918	

Number 84 Squadron, RAF

E. Bryant	2nd Lt.	29 Mar 1918–17 Apr 1918	
F. R. Christiani	Lt.	26 Aug 1918–29 Sept 1918	killed
D. C. Henderson	Lt.	2 June 1918–14 June 1918	
J. F. Larson	Lt.	23 Sept 1917–11 Apr 1918	
J. E. Robbins	2nd Lt.	18 Aug 1918–19 Aug 1918	
A. M. Rosenbleet	Lt.	31 Oct 1918–10 Nov 1918	POW

NAME	RANK	DATE OF SERVICE	CASUALTIES
		Number 85 Squadron, RAF	
W. D. Archer	Lt.	3 Apr 1918–22 May 1918	
W. Brechenridge	Lt.	12 Apr 1918–25 May 1918	
		Number 87 Squadron, RAF	
F. W. Barker	2nd Lt.	21 Oct 1918–	
H. H. Blanchard	2nd Lt.	1918	
G. S. Harvery	2nd Lt.	6 June 1918–10 Aug 1918	POW
D. C. Mangen	2nd Lt.	1 July 1918–20 Oct 1918	
W. J. Penningroth	2nd Lt.	Sept 1918	
H. C. Thomas	Lt.	⸺	
H. Walden	2nd Lt.	⸺	
C. R. Wrede	2nd Lt.	1 Oct 1918–31 Oct 1918	injured
		Number 88 Squadron, RAF	
E. A. Chapin	Lt.	6 Apr 1918–26 Apr 1918	
J. H. Thompson	Lt.	3 Apr 1918	
J. P. West	2nd Lt.	30 Apr 1918–28 June 1918	killed
		Number 89 Squadron, RAF	
G. Stephenson	Lt.	18 Apr 1918–20 April 1918	
		Number 90 Squadron, RAF	
W. D. Archer	Lt.	22 May 1918–Sept 1918	
Louis Bennett	Lt.	31 May 1918–20 July 1918	
M. C. Brown	Lt.	8 June 1918–23 July 1918	killed
R. W. Duff	Lt.	June 1918–Aug 1918	
J. L. Hill	2nd Lt.	31 May 1918	
W. F. Leach	Lt.	24 Dec 1917–May 1918	
M. E. Miller	2nd Lt.	4 July 1918–Aug 1918	
C. M. D. L. Morgan	Lt.	2 Feb 1918–30 Sept 1918	
F. B. Stark	Lt.	1918	
		Number 91 Squadron, RAF	
W. M. Crofton	2nd Lt.	24 Apr 1918	
M. L. Dunham	2nd Lt.	7 Jan 1918–26 June 1918	killed
N. D. K. Kennedy	Lt.	13 Dec 1917–Mar 1918	
H. A. Kullberg	Lt.	16 Jan 1918–Apr 1918	
N. T. May	2nd Lt.	1918	

NAME	RANK	DATE OF SERVICE	CASUALTIES
W. Pendleton	Lt.	1918	
J. E. Robbins	2nd Lt.	1918	
F. B. Stark	Lt.	1918	
C. R. Wreded	2nd Lt.	16 Feb 1918–1918	

Number 92 Squadron, RAF

E. A. Coapman	Lt.	Nov 1917–Dec 1917	
C. J. Hall	Lt.	19 Oct 1917–11 Dec 1917	
J. G. Hall	Lt.	15 Mar 1918–6 June 1918	
C. M. Holbrook	Lt.	12 May 1918–18 Sept 1918	POW
E. V. Holland	Lt.	1 July 1918–5 Sept 1918	
W. H. Leaf	2nd Lt.	23 Oct 1918–30 Oct 1918	killed
E. J. Madill	2nd Lt.	15 Aug 1918–31 Oct 1918	
O. J. Rose	Capt.	14 Feb 1918–Apr 1919	
G. W. Schermerhorn	Lt.	16 Feb 1918–12 June 1918	
E. Shapard	Lt.	26 June 1918–Nov 1918	
C. A. Sperry	Lt.	16 Feb 1918–22 June 1918	

Number 93 Squadron, RAF

H. B. Bradley	Lt.	13 Dec 1917–2 Apr 1918	
J. W. Crane	Capt.	14 Nov 1917–June 1918	
H. C. Dean	2nd Lt.	16 Jan 1918–	
W. C. Lambert	Lt.	15 Dec 1917–9 Mar 1918	
J. I. Maitland	Lt.	17 May 1918–10 July 1918	
W. F. McCarthy	2nd Lt.	16 Jan 1918–16 Apr 1918	
G. Norris	2nd Lt.	9 Mar 1918–	
L. A. Richardson	Lt.	13 Dec 1917–23 Mar 1918	
R. G. Searson	Lt.	16 Feb 1918–Aug 1918	
R. R. Spafford	Lt.	16 Feb 1918–July 1918	
H. L. Yates	Lt.	21 Feb 1918–16 Mar 1918	

Number 95 Squadron, RAF

G. S. Harvey	2nd Lt.	15 Apr 1918–May 1918	
L. W. Mason	Lt.	1 Oct 1918–	
J. J. Miller	2nd Lt.	1918–25 Apr 1918	killed
F. R. Pemberton	2nd Lt.	23 Mar 1918–June 1918	
J. T. Rogerson	Lt.	1918	

Number 96 Squadron, RAF

F. P. Little	Lt.	10 Mar 1918–	

Number 97 Squadron, RAF

J. H. E. Gower	Lt.		

Number 98 Squadron, RAF

A. W. Greene	2nd Lt.		
I. A. Peers	Lt.	1 Apr 1918–1 June 1918	

Number 99 Squadron, RAF

E. A. Chapin	Lt.	Apr 1918–27 June 1918	killed
W. J. Garrity	Lt.	27 Apr 1918–31 July 1918	POW
C. S. Johnson	Lt.	1918	
J. H. Thompson	Lt.	1918	

Number 100 Squadron, RAF

L. E. Berry	2nd Lt.	18 Sept 1917–24 Oct 1917	POW
V. R. Brown	Lt.	8 Mar 1918–28 May 1918	POW
J. H. E. Gower	Lt.	20 July 1918–22 Jan 1919	
J. G. Lethbridge	2nd Lt.		
R. H. Reece	2nd Lt.	8 Aug 1917–14 Nov 1917	
F. B. Shaw	2nd Lt.	1918	

Number 101 Squadron, RAF

A. B. Mason	Major	29 Dec 1917–10 July 1918	

Number 102 Squadron, RAF

C. C. Caldwell	Lt.	9 Oct 1917–	
G. E. Reynolds	Lt.	14 May 1918–27 June 1918	killed

Number 103 Squadron, RAF

C. M. Arias	2nd Lt.	26 Feb 1919–	
R. E. Dodds	Capt.	26 May 1918–23 Mar 1919	
H. D. Preston	2nd Lt.	7 Jan 1918–14 May 1918	killed

Number 104 Squadron, RAF

B. K. Adams	2nd Lt.	7 Jan 1918–12 Feb 1918	
F. H. Beaufort	2nd Lt.	7 Jan 1918–13 Aug 1918	killed
O. J. Lange	Lt.	17 May 1918–30 June 1918	wounded

NAME	RANK	DATE OF SERVICE	CASUALTIES
T. L. McConchie	2nd Lt.	19 May 1918–1 July 1918	
R. B. Smith	2nd Lt.	12 Nov 1917–Feb. 1918	
J. R. Tansey	Lt.	1918–Jan 1919	
W. C. Whitthorne	2nd Lt.	4 Feb 1918–13 Apr 1918	
D. F. Taber	Lt.	1918–May 1918	

Number 105 Squadron, RAF

J. B. Fitzgerald	Lt.	6 Jan 1919–	
I. A. Peers	Lt.	13 Dec 1917–4 Mar 1918	
J. H. Thompson	Lt.	1918	

Number 106 Squadron, RAF

R. H. Gast	Lt.	11 Feb 1918–	
M. Goldsmith	2nd Lt.	16 Mar 1918–July 1918	
W. C. Whitthorne	2nd Lt.	13 Apr 1918–23 Apr 1918	

Number 107 Squadron, RAF

P. J. Carr	2nd Lt.	21 Aug 1918–3 Dec 1918	
W. F. Long	Lt.	1918–Feb 1919	
A. M. Rosenbleet	Lt.	6 June 1918–11 Aug 1918	
D. F. Taber	Lt.	6 June 1918–16 July 1918	wounded

Number 108 Squadron, RAF

G. T. Collinson	2nd Lt.	8 Feb 1918–4 Sept 1918	
J. C. M. Enslen	2nd Lt.	27 June 1918–	
H. M. Frederick	Lt.	14 June 1918	
F. A. Green	2nd Lt.	8 Feb 1919–4 Mar 1919	
D. F. Taber	Lt.	29 Sept 1918–1 Oct 1918	
G. W. Welch	Lt.	14 Mar 1918–June 1918	

Number 109 Squadron, RAF

J. P. Murray	Lt.	13 Dec 1917–Mar 1918	
G. W. Welch	Lt.	16 June 1918–14 Aug 1918	

Number 110 Squadron, RAF

J. P. Murray	Lt.	Apr 1919–Sept 1919	
W. J. Sanderson	2nd Lt.	17 Oct 1918–	

Number 112 Squadron, RAF

E. Hazell	2nd Lt.	11 Oct 1918–	

NAME	RANK	DATE OF SERVICE	CASUALTIES
	Number 120 Squadron, RAF		
M. G. Horkins	2nd Lt.	8 April 1919–	
	Number 121 Squadron, RAF		
L. F. Callaway	2nd Lt.	1918	
	Number 123 Squadron, RAF		
R. H. Schroeder	Lt.	1919	
	Number 124 Squadron, RAF		
W. J. Sanderson	Lt.	16 June 1918–16 Oct 1918	
	Number 138 Squadron, RAF		
J. D. Davis	Lt.	30 Sept 1918–	
D. R. Day	2nd Lt.	Aug 1918–	
Frank A. Flynn	Lt.	30 Nov 1918–	
	Number 139 Squadron, RAF		
W. C. Simon	2nd Lt.	3 July 1918–15 Nov 1918	
	Number 158 Squadron, RAF		
C. G. Rich	2nd Lt.	——	
	Number 201 Squadron, RAF		
M. I. Ashley	2nd Lt.	21 Aug 1918–2 Feb 1919	
T. B. Burns	Lt.	22 June 1918–2 Feb 1919	
S. Campan	2 Lt.	7 Sept 1918–17 Feb 1919	
H. J. Ewan	T/2nd Lt.	21 Oct 1918	
C. Murray	Lt.	10 May 1918–26 June 1918	
W. P. Wemple	2nd Lt.	1918	
C. L. Wood	2nd Lt.	11 May 1918–10 Aug 1918	POW, died 17 August 1918
	Number 203 Squadron, RAF		
J. W. Crane	Capt.	1 June 1918–7 June 1918	
T. Nolan	2nd Lt.	11 Aug 1918–1 Sept 1918	wounded
R. B. Wiggins	2nd Lt.	23 Sept 1918–11 Dec 1918	
O. C. LeBoutillier	Capt.	Apr 1917–July 1917	

NAME	RANK	DATE OF SERVICE	CASUALTIES

Number 204 Squadron, RAF

NAME	RANK	DATE OF SERVICE	CASUALTIES
H. H. Blanchard	2nd Lt.	1918	
G. Sutcliffe	2nd Lt.	22 Sept 1918–23 Oct 1918	killed

Number 205 Squadron, RAF

| W. E. Taylor | 2nd Lt. | 27 Apr 1918–9 May 1918 | |
| J. C. Wilson | Lt. | 8 Apr 1918–19 July 1918 | wounded |

Number 206 Squadron, RAF

C. S. Johnson	Lt.	9 July 1918–13 Aug 1918	missing
O. C. LeBoutillier	Capt.	July 1917–	
G. W. Welch	Lt.	15 Aug 1918–27 July 1919	

Number 207 Squadron, RAF

| P. S. Crovat | 2nd Lt. | 10 Oct 1918–24 Oct 1918 | |
| J. H. Lethbridge | 2nd Lt. | 24 Jan 1919–11 Feb 1919 | |

Number 208 Squadron, RAF

W. R. Allison	Lt.	25 June 1918–18 Oct 1918	
G. J. Farnworth	2nd Lt.	26 Mar 1919–9 Apr 1919	
J. P. Lloyde	2nd lt.	26 July 1918–10 Sept 1918	POW
T. F. McGuire	2nd Lt.	28 Sept 1918–21 Dec 1918	killed
W. D. Skall	Lt.	26 July 1918–25 Dec 1918	

Number 209 Squadron, RAF

R. R. Beebe	2nd Lt.	1 Sept 1918–20 Feb 1919	
C. R. Campbell	2nd Lt.	16 Nov 1918–5 Jan 1919	
C. A. Denzell	2nd Lt.	10 Jan 1919–	
O. C. LeBoutillier	Capt.	July 1917–9 July 1918	wounded 14 June 1918
B. F. McDonald	Lt.	15 Apr 1918–31 Oct 1918	
J. G. Osborne	2nd Lt.	9 Oct 1918–8 Nov 1918	
A. L. Porter	Lt.	27 June 1918–26 July 1918	wounded
J. O. Taylor	2nd Lt.	9 July 1918–9 Aug 1918	
E. T. Wales	Lt.	29 Oct 1918–14 Nov 1918	

Number 210 Squadron, RAF

| K. W. Akers | 2nd Lt. | 10 Oct 1918–2 Feb 1919 | |
| H. F. Banks | 2nd Lt. | 4 Oct 1918–2 Feb 1919 | |

NAME	RANK	DATE OF SERVICE	CASUALTIES
J. E. Berry	2nd Lt.	25 Sept 1918–2 Feb 1919	
W. Breckenridge	2nd Lt.	25 May 1918–9 June 1918	POW
A. Buchanan	Lt.	June 1918–29 Sept 1918	POW
H. W. Gill	2nd Lt.	Oct 1918	
G. W. Hopkins	2nd Lt.	29 Aug 1918–2 Feb 1919	
R. W. Johnson	2nd Lt.	25 Sept 1918–2 Oct 1918	wounded
G. E. McManus	Lt.	Oct 1918	
C. F. Pineau	Lt.	2 June 1918–8 Oct 1918	POW
J. F. Stafford	2nd Lt.	21 Sept 1918–29 Sept 1918	missing
K. R. Unger	Lt.	18 June 1918–2 Feb 1919	
L. Yerex	Lt.	11 June 1918	

Number 211 Squadron, RAF

D. F. Taber	Lt.	1 Oct 1918–23 Feb 1919	

Number 212 Squadron, RAF

M. G. Horkins	2nd Lt.	Aug 1918–Mar 1919	

Number 216 Squadron, RAF

R. H. Reece	2nd Lt.	15 Nov 1917–11 Jan 1918	
O. B. Santa-Maria	2nd Lt.	14 Nov 1918–	

Number 218 Squadron, RAF

C. M. Arias	2nd Lt.	2 Oct 1918–25 Feb 1919	
J. R. A. Barnes	2nd Lt.	July 1918–11 Nov 1918	

Number 230 Squadron, RAF

Walter R. Godard	2nd Lt.	1918	

Number 231 Squadron, RAF

Walter R. Godard	2nd Lt.	1918	
W. P. Loomis	2nd Lt.	1918	
T. E. Snelgrove	2nd Lt.	10 Mar 1919–24 Mar 1919	

Number 232 Squadron, RAF

S. E. V. Hiscot	Lt.	10 Aug 1918–	
R. T. Ivorton	2nd Lt.	10 Aug 1918–	
W. Pendleton	2nd Lt.	Sept 1918–2 Oct 1918	Int Neth
J. C. Stockman	Lt.	1918–2 Oct 1918	Int Neth

Number 234 Squadron, RAF

C. R. Borkland   Lt.   13 Apr 1918–19 Apr 1918

Number 241 Squadron, RAF

W. T. Brewster   2nd Lt.   1918

Number 242 Squadron, RAF

J. E. Sewell   2nd Lt.   29 Nov 1918–9 May 1919
H. McD. Starke   2nd Lt.   1918–29 Nov 1918

Number 244 Squadron, RAF

S. S. Rackowe   2nd Lt.   1918

Number 251 Squadron, RAF

D. Miller   2nd Lt.   27 May 1918–26 June 1918
C. D. Stephenson   2nd Lt.   11 May 1918–
A. W. Young   Lt.   27 May 1918–7 Jan 1919   hospitalized

Number 253 Squadron, RAF

H. A. Nester   2nd Lt.   14 Oct 1918–24 Feb 1919
H. McD. Starke   2nd Lt.   1918

Number 284 Squadron, RAF

W. M. Russell   2nd Lt.   1918

Notes

ONE   Capt. Frederick Libby

1. Frederick Libby Biographical File, Directorate of History, Department of National Defence, Ottawa, Canada.
2. Toliver and Constable, *Fighter Aces*, 41; Valencia, *Fred Libby*, 13.
3. Whitehouse, *Heroes of the Sunlit Sky*, 61. The Royal Aircraft Factory FE-2B British bomber was powered by a 120 horsepower Beardmore engine and was capable of seventy-two miles per hour at ten thousand feet. The FE initials mean "Fighting Experimental." Various FE-2 models served throughout the war, earning great fame as night bombers.
4. Toliver and Constable, *Fighter Aces*, 41–42.
5. Toliver and Constable, *Fighter Aces*, 41–43. See also Dennis Connell's list of air victories for Frederick Libby.
6. Libby Biographical File.
7. Whitehouse, *Heroes of the Sunlit Sky*, 62. See also "Records of Officers Service, 1916–1918, 43 Squadron," Air 1 Collection, box 1424/204/30, in Public Records Office, London.
8. Toliver and Constable, *Fighter Aces*, 43.
9. Combat Report, 14 September 1916, Air 1, box 2246, Public Records Office, Other No. 11 Squadron combat reports for August, September, and October are also contained in this source.
10. Combat Report, 10 October 1916; Royal Flying Corps Report No. 57.
11. Combat Report, 17 October 1916; RFC Report No. 58.
12. Combat Report, 20 October 1916.
13. Letter, E. B. Haslam to Dr. S. F. Wise, Directorate of History, 5 February 1973.
14. Ibid.
15. Libby Biographical File. The Sopwith 1½ Strutter two-seater had a wing span of thirty-three feet six inches and a fuselage length of twenty-five feet three inches. It was powered by a 130 horsepower Clerget engine, which gave it a speed of one hundred miles per hour and a service ceiling of 15,500 feet.
16. William Robert Dunn, "Frederick Libby, The First American Ace," 7, Air Force Museum, Dayton, Ohio.
17. Combat Report, 6 May 1917. This kill was confirmed by ground observers. Also see RFC Report No. 87.

18. Combat Report, 23 July 1917. Also see RFC Report No. 98.
19. Libby Biographical File.
20. Dennis Connell list. See also RFC Report No. 100.
21. Combat Report, 14 August 1917. See also Dennis Connell list. Another source for this action is to be found in RFC Report No. 101.
22. Combat Report, 15 August 1917.
23. Combat Report, 15 August 1917. This was the second combat report written on 15 August.
24. Combat Report, 17 August 1917.
25. Combat Report, 18 August 1917.
26. Toliver and Constable, *Fighter Aces*, 44.
27. Ibid. See also letter, N. G. Hoskins, Air Historical Branch, Ministry of Defence, London, to Royal D. Frey, curator, Air Force Museum, Dayton, Ohio, 15 June 1973.
28. Dunn, "Frederick Libby, The First American Ace," 8.
29. Whitehouse, *Heroes of the Sunlit Sky*, 61; Toliver and Constable, *Fighter Aces*, 44.
30. Robertson, *Air Aces of the 1914–1918 War*, 44. See also Dennis Connell list.

TWO   Capt. Clive W. Warman

1. Warman Biographical File, Directorate of History.
2. Ibid.
3. Allied preparations for a second coordinated offensive in the Ypres area were spoiled by a German attack preceded by heavy clouds of chlorine gas emitted from several hundred cylinders. This was the first real use of poison gas on this part of the western front. Two German corps smashed through two French infantry divisions and cut deeply into the British lines creating a wide gap. Local counter attacks by the British Second Army finally stemmed the German drive after bitter fighting. In this battle the Germans lost approximately thirty-five thousand men while the British and French forces suffered seventy thousand casualties.
4. Warman Biographical File. After years of violence and unrest in Ireland, armed rebellion broke out in Dublin on Easter Monday (24 April 1916), inspired in part by Sir Roger Casement, Irish Nationalist leader, who landed on the Irish coast by German submarine. By 1 May 1916 the uprising had been put down.
5. Warman Biographical File.
6. Ibid.
7. "History of Number 23 Squadron, RAF," Air 1, box 1595, Public Records Office.
8. Although Maj. Alan M. Wilkinson is listed in Toliver and Constable's *Fighter Aces* as an American, most sources indicate that he was English.
9. "History of Number 23 Squadron."

10. Combat Report, 2 July 1917, Air 1, box 2220, Public Records Office. Other combat reports cited are to be found in the same source.
11. Combat Report, 6 July 1917. Also recorded in Royal Flying Corps War Diary No. 95.
12. Combat Report, 7 July 1917.
13. Combat Report, 11 July 1917.
14. Combat Report, 14 July 1917. Clive Wilson Warman was awarded the British Military Cross on 14 July 1917.
15. Combat Report, 22 July 1917.
16. Combat Report, 23 July 1917.
17. Combat Report, 27 July 1917; See also RFC War Diary No. 99.
18. Combat Report, 31 July 1917; RFC War Diary No. 99.
19. Combat Report, 8 August 1917.
20. Combat Report, 12 August 1917; RFC War Diary No. 101.
21. Ibid.
22. Combat Report, 15 August 1917. This engagement occurred at 7:40–8:30 A.M. Also see RFC War Diary No. 101.
23. Combat Report, 15 August 1917. This report was for the late afternoon operation. Also see Sir O'Moore Creagh and E. M. Humphries, *The Distinguished Service Order, 1886–1923* (1978), 75.
24. Combat Report, 17 August 1917.
25. Combat Report, 18 August 1917. His DSO, awarded on 17 September 1917, described Warman's efforts during this period:

> For conspicuous gallantry and devotion to duty. During two days, whilst operating under difficult conditions in high wind and against strong opposition, he destroyed three enemy machines and a balloon. He displayed the greatest dash and fearlessness in attacking an enemy airdrome, and on one occasion, when separated from his patrol, and surrounded by twenty machines, he fought his way through, although his machine gun was useless, by attacking with his Very pistol; eventually regaining his own airdrome with his machine much shot about. His wonderful coolness and courage have on all occasions been beyond praise.

26. Combat Report, 20 August 1917.
27. Warman Biographical File.
28. "History of Number 23 Squadron, RAF." Most World War I "ace lists" such as Toliver and Constable's *Fighter Aces* and Bruce Robertson's *Air Aces of the 1914–1918 War,* credit Warman with fifteen air victories.
29. Warman Biographical File.
30. See obituary in Warman Biographical File.

THREE   Lt. D'Arcy Fowles Hilton

1. Letter, Stewart K. Taylor to James J. Hudson, 24 July 1985. According to Taylor, the son was killed in action while flying with the RCAF in England on 3 August 1940.
2. Ibid.

3. Letter, Stewart K. Taylor to James J. Hudson, 24 July 1985.
4. Combat Report, 27 June 1917, Air 1, box 1863, Public Records Office.
5. Letter, Stewart K. Taylor to James J. Hudson, 24 July 1985. Captain Chapman a few weeks later became squadron commander, and Capt. J. D. Atkinson became "C" Flight leader. Before Hilton left No. 29 Squadron, Capt. A. G. Jones-Williams was made "C" Flight commander.
6. "Operations Record Book for No. 29 Squadron," Air 27, box 341, Public Records Office.
7. "Operations Record Book for No. 29 Squadron." Also see "Award Recommendation for Lt. D. F. Hilton," Air 1, box 1863, Public Records Office.
8. Combat Report, 9 August 1917, Air 1, box 1221, Public Records Office. Other No. 29 Squadron combat reports for August, September, October, and November are in the same box. This combat was also reported in "Award Recommendation for Lt. D. F. Hilton."
9. Combat Report, 11 August 1917. See also "Award Recommendation for Lt. D. F. Hilton."
10. Combat Report, 13 August 1917.
11. Combat Report, 14 August 1917.
12. Combat Report, 16 August 1917; "Award Recommendation for Lt. D. F. Hilton."
13. Combat Report, 22 August 1917.
14. "Award Recommendation for Lt. D. F. Hilton," 2 November 1917.
15. Richardson's victim was considered out of control, but Hilton's target was marked indecisive in the Combat Report, 30 October 1917. However, the squadron commander in his "Award Recommendation for Lt. D. F. Hilton" listed Hilton as having driven one enemy down and one down out of control.
16. Combat Report, 13 November 1917.
17. "Award Recommendation for Lt. D. F. Hilton."
18. Robertson, *Air Aces of the 1914–1918 War,* 46.
19. Letter, Stewart K. Taylor to James J. Hudson, 24 July 1985.

FOUR   Capt. Oliver C. LeBoutillier

1. Letter, Ola A. Sater to James J. Hudson, 12 January 1986. See also J. J. Smith Collection, World War I Aviation Museum, Parker, Colorado.
2. Oral interview, Oliver C. LeBoutillier by William D. Madsen of the United States Air Force Academy, 7 January 1976, Special Collection Branch, USAF Academy Library, 2.
3. LeBoutillier interview, 3–4.
4. LeBoutillier interview, 4–7.
5. Ibid, 11–12.
6. LeBoutillier interview, 12.

7. No. 9 RNAS commanding officer report, Air 1, box 284, Public Records Office.
8. LeBoutillier interview, 14–15.
9. LeBoutillier interview, 18.
10. Ibid, 21. This kill also is listed in RNAS Number 9 Squadron History.
11. RNAS Number 9 Squadron History, Air 1, Public Records Office.
12. RNAS Number 9 Squadron History.
13. RFC Communiqué No. 99.
14. LeBoutillier interview, 30–31.
15. Ibid, 33–36. Also see Wise, *Canadian Airmen and the First World War*, Vol. 1, 514–515.
16. LeBoutillier interview, 38–39.
17. Ibid, 39–40. See also May, "Lieut. Wilfred 'Wop' May's Account," 111–112.
18. LeBoutillier interview, 40–41.
19. Ibid, 42–43.
20. Connell, "The Richthofen Controversy: 1963–1965, Part III," 171.
21. LeBoutillier interview, 43–44.
22. Ibid, 45. Also see LeBoutillier's Combat Report, 21 April 1918, Air 1, box 1228, Public Records Office. Other LeBoutillier combat reports are located in this box.
23. May, "Account," 112. In addition, the Brown victory is cited in "Material on Brown for Gibbon's Richthofen Story," Air 1, box 262, Public Records Office.
24. According to the RAF salvage crew, the German machine was completely smashed and nothing could be saved. See also Royal Air Force Communiqué No. 4.
25. Royal Air Force Communiqué No. 6; Combat Report, 9 May 1918.
26. Royal Air Force Communiqué No. 7; Combat Report, 16 May 1918.
27. Letter, Ola A. Sater to James J. Hudson, 12 January 1986. In the LeBoutillier interview he indicated he had eight victories.
28. Casualty Return for the Month of June (209 Squadron), Air 1, box 1857, Public Records Office.
29. Letter, C. R. Gamage of RAF Ministry of Defense to Wing Commander F. F. Lambert, 11 June 1985.
30. Oliver C. "Boots" LeBoutillier obituary, *Cross and Cockade Journal* (Autumn 1983), 285.
31. Letter, Ola A. Sater to James J. Hudson, 12 January 1986.

FIVE   Lt. Jens Frederick "Swede" Larson

1. "Lt. J. F. Larson Biographical sheet," Air 1, box 1796, Public Records Office.
2. Letter, Stewart K. Taylor to James J. Hudson, 24 July 1985. The Biographical File on J. F. Larson in the Directorate of History lists Larson as having joined No. 84 Squadron on 30 July 1917.
3. Douglas, *Years of Combat*, 214–220.

4. Combat Report, 26 November 1917, Air 1, box 1227, Public Records Office.
5. "Number 84 Squadron Operations Record Book," Air 27, box 694, Public Records Office.
6. Combat Report, 3 January 1918. Lt. A. W. Beauchamp Proctor would eventually shoot down fifty-four enemy planes during the war.
7. "Number 84 Squadron Operations Record Book."
8. Combat Report, 16 February 1918. Maj. Sholto Douglas signed the combat report.
9. Letter, Stewart K. Taylor to James J. Hudson, 24 July 1985.
10. Combat Report, 18 February 1918.
11. Combat Report, 15 March 1918.
12. Combat Report, 18 March 1918.
13. Combat Report, 1 April 1918.
14. Combat Report, 3 April 1918. Also see Royal Air Force Communiqué No. 1.
15. Combat Report, 6 April 1918.
16. Letter, Stewart K. Taylor to James J. Hudson, 24 July 1985.
17. Letter, Stewart K. Taylor to James J. Hudson, 24 July 1985.

SIX   Lt. Francis Peabody Magoun

1. *New England Aviators, 1914–1918*, Vol. 2, 120.
2. Magoun Biographical File, Directorate of History.
3. *New England Aviators, 1914–1918*, Vol. 2, 120.
4. Magoun Biographical File. No. 1 Squadron before the war had been a balloon and airship unit but in 1914 had relinquished its balloon equipment to the Royal Navy and became a specialized scout unit. Flying Nieuports and later SE-5As, it fought with distinction in Flanders.
5. Shaw, *Twice Vertical*, 54.
6. Captain Hazell was to go on to become one of the top British aces with forty-one victories.
7. Shaw, *Twice Vertical*, 54. The Nieuport 17 was powered by a 110 horsepower LeRhone engine and was capable of approximately 110 miles per hour. Unfortunately, the aircraft had a habit of losing a wing in violent maneuvers.
8. Shaw, *Twice Vertical*, 54–55. Also see Winter, *The First of the Few*, 41–42.
9. Shaw, *Twice Vertical*, 55.
10. Combat Report, 28 February 1918, Air 1, box 2231, Public Records Office. Also see "Personnel of No. 1 Squadron Record of Machines and Balloons Brought Down 1917 and 1918," Air 1, box 1339, Public Records Office.
11. Combat Report, 10 March 1918.
12. Combat Report, 15 March 1918.
13. Shaw, *Twice Vertical*, 55.

14. Memorandum, Maj. H. Adams to Headquarters Tenth Wing, RFC, 31 March 1918, Air 1, box 1339, Public Records Office.
15. Magoun Biographical File. The award was published in the *London Gazette* on 22 June 1918 but was announced in Royal Air Force Communiqué No. 2, 10 April 1918.
16. Combat Report, 28 March 1918. Also see "Personnel of No. 1 Squadron Record of Machines and Balloons Brought Down, 1917–1918."
17. Shaw, *Twice Vertical*, 56.
18. Ibid.
19. See Casualty Card, Royal Air Force Museum, Hendon, England. According to this document Magoun was wounded in the arm.
20. V Brigade War Diary, Air 1, box 2225, Public Records Office.
21. *New England Aviators, 1914–1918,* Vol. 2, 120.
22. *Who's Who in America* (Chicago: Marquis Who's Who, 40th Edition, 1978), 2053. See also letter, Margaret B. Magoun to James J. Hudson, 3 June 1984. Magoun was married to Margaret Boyden on 30 June 1926. From this union four children, Francis Peabody III, William Boyden, Margaret Boyden, and Jean Bartholow were born.
23. Letter, Margaret B. Magoun to James J. Hudson, 3 June, 1984.

SEVEN   Capt. George W. Bulmer

1. Letter, O. A. Sater to James J. Hudson, 12 January 1986. Sater acquired much of his information on George Bulmer from Stewart K. Taylor, a Canadian who knew Bulmer personally.
2. George W. Bulmer Biographical Note Card, Directorate of History.
3. Franks, *Aircraft Versus Aircraft*, 55.
4. Robinson, *Flying the World's Great Aircraft*, 67–70. Introduction by Jeffrey Quill.
5. Combat Report, 6 March 1918, Air 1, box 1220, Public Office. Other combat reports are in the same box.
6. Combat Report, 16 March 1918.
7. Combat Report, 23 March 1918.
8. Cole, *Royal Air Force, 1918*, 63.
9. Combat Report, 6 May 1918. Also see Royal Air Force Communiqué No. 6.
10. Combat Report, 8 May 1918. This victory was also listed in Royal Air Force Communiqué No. 6.
11. Royal Air Force Communiqué No. 7.
12. Combat Report, 16 May 1918.
13. Cole, *Royal Air Force, 1918*, 85.
14. Combat Report, 17 May 1918. This victory was also recorded in Royal Air Force Communiqué No. 7.
15. Combat Report, 9 July 1918. This kill was written up in Royal Air Force Communiqué No. 15.
16. *London Gazette*, 16 September 1918.
17. Bulmer Biographical Card, Directorate of History.

18. Letter, C. R. Gamage to Wing Commander F. F. Lambert, 11 June 1985.
19. Letter, O. A. Sater to James J. Hudson, 12 June 1986.

EIGHT   Lt. John Sharpe Griffith

1. "History of No. 60 Squadron," Air 1, box 173, Public Records Office; John Sharpe Griffith Biographical Note Card, Directorate of History; John S. Griffith obituary, *Long Island Press,* Jamaica, New York, 18 October 1974.
2. "History of No. 60 Squadron," 3.
3. "Correspondence Regarding Recommendation, Promotion of Officers and Monthly Returns of Officers, No. 60 Squadron RFC/RAF, From 23 January 1918 to 28 January 1919," Air 1, box 1555, Public Records Office. Also see "2/Lt. J. S. Griffith Record Sheet," Air 1, box 1554, Public Records Office.
4. Ibid.
5. "History of No. 60 Squadron," 3.
6. Combat Report, 30 March 1918, Air 1, box 2242, Public Records Office. Other combat reports through the month of May 1918 are to be found in this same box.
7. Combat Report, 2 April, 1918.
8. Cole, *Royal Air Force, 1918,* 23. This is an account of the Royal Air Force Communiqués.
9. Combat Report, 6 April 1918.
10. "History of No. 60 Squadron," 3.
11. Royal Air Force Communiqué No. 6.
12. Combat Report, 6 May 1918. This victory also was confirmed in Royal Air Force Communiqué No. 6.
13. Combat Report, 13 May 1918.
14. Combat Report, 14 May 1918. The "J. S. Griffith Record Sheet" also merely listed as an engagement with no results.
15. Combat Report, 15 May 1918.
16. Combat Report, 16 May 1918. Also see Royal Air Force Communiqué No. 7 and Joe Warne, "Number 60 Squadron," *Cross and Cockade Journal* (Great Britain) (Vol. 12, No. 4), 183.
17. Combat Report, 5 June 1918. This combat report and others for June and July are to be found in Air 1, box 2243, Public Records Office. This victory was also listed in "Monthly Return of Officers of 60 Squadron" and the "J. S. Griffith Record Sheet."
18. See "Lt. J. S. Griffith Record Sheet" and Combat Reports for 17 and 30 June.
19. Combat Report, 1 July 1918; Royal Air Force Communiqué No. 14; "Monthly Return of Officers of 60 Squadron"; Warne, "Number 60 Squadron."
20. Combat Report, 2 July 1918. This was the first of two reports on that day.

21. "Lt. J. S. Griffith Record Sheet."
22. Combat Report, 4 July 1918. Also see "Lt. J. S. Griffith Record Sheet," Public Records Office.
23. Combat Report, 7 July 1918; See also Royal Air Force Communiqué No. 14 and "Monthly Return of Officers of 60 Squadron."
24. See Combat Reports for 10 July, 11 July, and 14 July.
25. "Monthly Return of Officers of No. 60 Squadron."
26. Royal Air Force Communiqué No. 16.
27. "Lt. J. S. Griffith Record Sheet." See also RAF Biographical Note Card on John Sharpe Griffith in the Directorate of History, Department of National Defence, Ottawa, Canada.
28. Griffith Biographical Note in Directorate of History, Department of National Defence, Ottawa, Canada; John S. Griffith obituary in Long Island *Press*, 18 October 1974.
29. Griffith obituary.
30. Griffith obituary.
31. *Cross and Cockade Journal* (Spring 1975), 94.
32. Griffith Biographical Note, Directorate of History; *Cross and Cockade Journal* (Spring, 1975), 94; Robertson, *Air Aces of the 1914–1918 War*, 45.

NINE   Capt. Eugene Seeley Coler

1. E. S. Coler Biographical Card, J. J. Smith files, World War I Aviation Museum, Parker, Colorado.
2. E. S. Coler Biographical Note Card, Directorate of History.
3. "History of No. 11 Squadron, Royal Air Force," Air 1, box 166, Public Records Office.
4. Robertson, *Air Aces of the 1914–1918 War*, 43. Also see "History of No. 11 Squadron, Royal Air Force."
5. "History of No. 11 Squadron, Royal Air Force."
6. Ibid.
7. Combat Report, 9 May 1918, Air 1, box 2242, Public Records Office. See also Cole, *Royal Air Force, 1918,* 73.
8. Combat Report, 7 June 1918, Air 1, box 2243, Public Records Office.
9. "History of No. 11 Squadron, Royal Air Force."
10. Combat Report, 13 August 1918, Air 1, box 2243, Public Records Office. This tremendous air victory was also listed in Royal Air Force Communiqué No. 20 and in Cole, *Royal Air Force, 1918,* 160.
11. Ibid.
12. Combat Report, 30 August 1918. This combat along with the 13 August battle was listed in No. 11 Squadron commander's recommendation for Lt. E. S. Coler to the Headquarters, Thirteenth Wing, RAF. The document is to be found in Air 1, box 2011, Public Records Office.
13. Combat Report, 6 September 1918, Air 1, box 2244. This victory was also recorded in Royal Air Force Communiqué No. 23.

14. Royal Air Force Communiqué No. 24.
15. Combat Report, 16 September 1918; Royal Air Force Communiqué No. 25.
16. Capt. E. S. Coler biographical card, Directorate of History.
17. Royal Air Force Communiqué No. 25.

TEN   Lt. William Carpenter Lambert

1. "Lt. Col. William Lambert, 87, War I Ace Downed 22 Planes," *Cross and Cockade Journal* (Summer 1982), 72; Frey, "Forgotten Ace of World War I," 20.
2. Peyton, "The Forgotten Ace of W.W. I," 28. See also Frey, "Forgotten Ace," 20. Also see Air Force Logistics Command oral history interviews of Lt. Col. William C. Lambert by Robert J. Smith.
3. Frey, "Forgotten Ace," 20.
4. Frey, "Forgotten Ace," 20; Glasebrook, *American Aviators in the Great War, 1914–1918,* 66.
5. Peyton, "The Forgotten Ace of World War I," 28; Frey, "Forgotten Ace," 20; Lambert, "A Very Strange Story," 48.
6. Frey, "Forgotten Ace," 21; Peyton, "The Forgotten Ace of World War I," 28.
7. Lambert, *Combat Report,* 38–39. See also Lt. Col. William C. Lambert, oral history interview by Robert J. Smith and Glasebrook, *American Aviators in the Great War, 1914–1918,* 66.
8. Lambert, *Combat Report,* 39.
9. Robertson, *Air Aces of the 1914–1918 War,* 30–31.
10. Peyton, "The Forgotten Ace," 28–29; Saunders, *Per Ardua,* 84–85.
11. Lambert, *Combat Report,* 39–43; Frey, "Forgotten Ace," 21.
12. Lambert, *Combat Report,* 43–44. The creation of the Royal Air Force was due to the farsightedness of a famous South African, Gen. Jan Christian Smuts.
13. Ibid., 45.
14. Ibid., 45–47.
15. Frey, "Forgotten Ace," 21.
16. Lambert, *Combat Report,* 50.
17. Oral history interview of Lt. Col. William C. Lambert by Robert J. Smith.
18. Royal Air Force Communiqué No. 2; Lambert, *Combat Report,* 53.
19. Lambert, *Combat Report,* 53.
20. Lambert, *Combat Report,* 53–56.
21. See chapter 4.
22. This balloon victim was listed in "No. 24 Squadron Record Book," Air 1, box 172, Public Records Office.
23. Lambert, *Combat Report,* 56–57.
24. Lambert, *Combat Report,* 58–59.
25. Peyton, "The Forgotten Ace," 29.
26. Combat Record, 4 May 1918, Air 1, box 2223, Public Records Office. Also see "No. 24 Squadron Record Book," Air 1, box 172, Public Rec-

ords Office. According to No. 24 Squadron Record Book, Lambert shared this kill.

27. Combat Report, 9 May 1918. The kill was shared by Lts. Hellett and Lambert and was confirmed by Royal Air Force Communiqué No. 6.
28. Combat Report, 16 May 1918; 24 Squadron Record Book" in Public Records Office. This action was also described in Lambert, *Combat Report*, 66–67.
29. Lambert, *Combat Report*, 68–69.
30. Combat Report, 19 May 1918.
31. Combat Report, 20 May 1918.
32. Combat Report, 21 May 1918; No. 24 Squadron Record Book, Public Records Office.
33. Combat Report, 21 May 1918; No. 24 Squadron Record Book, Public Records Office.
34. Combat Report, 31 May 1918.
35. Combat Report, 1 June 1918. This report dealt only with the early morning attack.
36. Combat Report, 1 June 1918. This report was written late in the afternoon. See also "No. 24 Squadron History, 1915–1919," Air 1, box 168, Public Records Office.
37. Combat Report, 2 June 86; Royal Air Force Communiqué No. 9. Captain MacDonald was to score a total of twenty victories before the war was over.
38. No. 24 Squadron Record Book.
39. Combat Report, 2 June 1918.
40. Lambert, *Combat Report*, 93–94.
41. Combat Report, 5 June 1918.
42. Combat Report, 15 June 1918; Also see No. 24 Squadron Record Book.
43. Combat Report, 16 June 1918.
44. Combat Report, 17 June 1918; Royal Air Force Communiqué No. 12. In addition, see No. 24 Squadron Record Book. This battle took place over Villers-Bretonneux.
45. Combat Report, 25 June 1918.
46. Letter, W. J. Taunton, Ministry of Defence, London, to Royal Frey, Air Force Museum, Wright Patterson Air Force Base, 3 January 1968.
47. Combat Report, 27 June 1918; "No. 24 Squadron History, 1915–1919," Public Records Office. Also see Lambert, *Combat Report*, 119–121.
48. Combat Report, 29 June 1918; Royal Air Force Communiqué No. 13.
49. Lambert, *Combat Report*, 122–124.
50. Royal Air Force Communiqué, No. 14. See also Combat Report, 4 July 1918.
51. Lambert, *Combat Report*, 160–176.
52. Frey, "Forgotten Ace," 22.
53. Lambert, *Combat Report*, 178.
54. Robertson, *Air Aces of the 1914–1918 War*, 22–31.
55. Combat Report, 1 August 1918.
56. Combat Report, 4 August 1918; Royal Air Force Communiqué No. 18.

57. Combat Report, 7 August 1918.
58. Combat Report, 8 August 1918. See also Saunders, *Per Ardua,* 269–273.
59. Frey "Forgotten Ace," 21; Peyton, "Forgotten Ace of World War I," 29; Lambert, *Combat Report,* 195–197.
60. Combat Report, 9 August 1918; No. 24 Squadron Book, Public Records Office.
61. Combat Report, 10 August 1918.
62. No. 24 Squadron Record Book, Public Records Office.
63. Lambert, *Combat Report,* 210–211.
64. Frey, "Forgotten Ace," 21–22; oral history interview of Lambert by Robert J. Smith.
65. Ibid., 22.
66. Oral history interview of Lambert by Robert J. Smith.
67. Frey, "Forgotten Ace," 22. Lambert in his later years wrote two books: *Combat Report,* and *Barnstorming and Girls* (Manhattan, Kansas: Sunflower University Press, 1980).

ELEVEN   Capt. Frederick Ives Lord

1. The Sopwith Dolphin biplane fighter was powered by a geared Hispano-Suiza engine and had a top speed of 130 miles per hour. Its armament consisted of twin Vickers machine guns on the cowl and twin Lewis guns suspended above the cockpit. Many pilots considered the Lewis guns more of a hazard than a help and removed them. Lord retained one of the Lewis guns, thus making his plane a three-gun fighter. The pilot's head on the Dolphin projected above the top wing to give him better visibility, but this also made him vulnerable should the plane turn over on its back when on the ground. As a result some Dolphins were fitted with a "rolling hoop," which went over the pilot's cockpit, and although it slightly impaired his upward view it gave him an added sense of security, for he felt that the airplane could turn over on the ground without his neck getting broken.
2. See F.1. Lord Combat Report, 28 May 1918, Air 1, box 2232, Public Records Office. All combat reports mentioned are from this source.
3. According to the casualty records in the Royal Air Force Museum, Lord listed his birthdate as 18 April 1896.
4. Lord Biographical File, Directorate of History.
5. "History of No. 79 Squadron," Air 1, box 176, Public Records Office.
6. Lord Biographical File.
7. Combat Report, 7 June 1918. The Albatros D-V biplane was powered by a 180 horsepower Mercedes engine and had a top speed of one hundred miles per hour.
8. The British-built Bristol Fighter was a tough two-seater powered by a 275 horsepower Rolls Royce engine with a top speed of 122 miles per hour and a service ceiling of twenty thousand ft.
9. Combat Report, 27 June 1918. The Fokker Dr-1 Triplane was powered by a 110 horsepower Oberursel rotary engine and had a top

speed of 115 miles per hour. It was a highly maneuverable aircraft. The Pfalz D-3 biplane was equipped with two machine guns and a 160 horsepower Mercedes engine. Its maximum speed was 110 miles per hour.

10. Royal Air Force Communiqué No. 13, listed in Cole, *Royal Air Force, 1918.*
11. Royal Air Force Communiqué No. 22.
12. Lord Biographical File.
13. Combat Report, 21 August 1918.
14. "History of No. 79 Squadron," 1–2.
15. Francis W. Gillet, an American from Baltimore, Maryland, was credited with some seventeen victories and was one of the top American fighter pilots who flew with the RAF.
16. Royal Air Force Communiqué Number 23. The Fokker D-7 with a BMW 185 horsepower engine and capable of 125 miles per hour was one of the top fighter planes of the 1914–1918 war.
17. Combat Report, 17 September 1918.
18. Combat Report, 28 September 1918.
19. Wayne R. Braby, "Nothing Can Stop Us," 174.
20. Lord Biographical File. Also see Braby, "Nothing Can Stop Us," 174.
21. "History of No. 79 Squadron," 2.
22. Braby, "Nothing Can Stop Us," 175.
23. Lord Biographical File. This battle area was in the far north of Russia. The Pinega River runs into the Arctic Ocean near Archangel.
24. Lord Biographical File. For this Pinega River action Lord was awarded a bar to his British Distinguished Flying Cross.
25, Cy Caldwell, "Personairlites," *Aero Digest,* August 1937, 82–83.
26. Lord Biographical File.
27. Caldwell, "Personairlites," 47.
28. Lord Biographical File.
29. Caldwell, "Personairlites," 47.
30. See his U.S. Army Air Corps Service Record in Lord Biographical File.
31. Caldwell, "Personairlites," 47. Apparently Lord went to Spain as a paid mercenary at the salary of $1500 per month.
32. "Fred Lord Writes of His War in Spain," manuscript, Directorate of History.
33. See *Literary Digest,* 21 August 1937; *Daily Worker,* 9 September 1937; and *Life,* 28 March 1938. Articles in *Life* and *Literary Digest* credit him with twenty-two air victories in World War I. Actually he had only nine official confirmed kills.
34. "Fred Lord Writes of His War in Spain."
35. Lord Biographical File.

TWELVE   Lt. Emile John Lussier

1. Emile John Lussier obituary, *Westminster Times,* Westminster, Md., 11 December 1974.
2. Interview, Russ Manning of the *Cross and Cockade Journal* with

Emile John Lussier, February 1973. Also see Emile John Lussier
Biographical File, Directorate of History.
3. "Record of No. 73 Squadron, RAF," Air 1, box 176, Public Records
   Office.
4. Ibid., 1–2.
5. Combat Report, 25 July 1918, Air 1, box 1226, Public Records
   Office. All other Lussier combat reports are to be found in the same
   box. See also Royal Air Force Communiqué No. 17.
6. Combat Report, 30 July 1918.
7. Royal Air Force Communiqué No. 18.
8. "Record of No. 73 Squadron, R.A.F."
9. Combat Report, 8 August 1918. See also RAF Communiqué as reported in Cole, *Royal Air Force 1918,* 157.
10. Combat Report, 19 August 1918.
11. Combat Report, 25 August 1918. See also Royal Air Force Commu-
    niqué No. 21.
12. Combat Report, 29 August 1918.
13. "Record of No. 73 Squadron, R.A.F.," Public Records Office.
14. Combat Report, 15 September 1918; Royal Air Force Communiqué
    No. 24.
15. Combat Report, 18 October 1918.
16. Royal Air Force Communiqué No. 24.
17. *London Gazette,* 2 November 1918.
18. Lussier Biographical File, Directorate of History.
19. Obituary, *Westminster Times,* 11 December 1974.

THIRTEEN   Capt. Francis Warrington Gillet

1. Combat Report, 3 August 1918, Air 1, box 2231, Public Records
   Office. Other combat reports cited are to be found in this collection.
   Also see Royal Air Force Communiqué No. 18, and "History of
   No. 79 Squadron," Air 1, box 176, Public Records Office.
2. *Maryland in the World War, 1917–1919: Military and Naval Service
   Records* (Baltimore: Maryland War Records Commission, 1933) Vol-
   ume I, 755. Also see *Cross and Cockade Journal* (Spring 1970), 94.
3. "History of No. 79 Squadron."
4. "History of No. 79 Squadron."
5. Combat Report, 18 August 1918. Also see Royal Air Force Communiqué No. 20.
6. Combat Report, 24 August 1918. Also see Royal Air Force Communiqué No. 21.
7. Combat Report, 1 September 1918. Also see Royal Air Force Communiqué No. 22.
8. Braby, "Nothing Can Stop Us," 168.
9. Bridgman, *The Clouds Remember,* 64–65.
10. Bridgman, *The Clouds Remember,* 65.
11. Braby, "Nothing Can Stop Us," 168.

12. Combat Report, 5 September 1918. This victory was also confirmed by Royal Air Force Communiqué No. 23.
13. Combat Report, 21 September 1918. The Royal Air Force Communiqué No. 25 also confirmed the second Fokker but did not mention the first.
14. Francis Warrington Gillet Biographical File, Directorate of History.
15. Combat Report, 28 September 1918, Air 1, box 2232, Public Records Office. All other Gillet combat records for the last weeks of the war are to be found in the same box.
16. Combat Report, 28 September 1918. Also see Royal Air Force Communiqué No. 26.
17. Braby, "Nothing Can Stop Us," 174.
18. Combat Report, 29 September 1918. This kill was also reported in the Royal Air Force Communiqué No. 26.
19. Royal Air Force Communiqué No. 25.
20. Royal Air Force Communiqué No. 27.
21. Combat Report, 2 October 1918. The destruction of the hostile kite balloon was confirmed by Royal Air Force Communiqué No. 27.
22. Combat Report, 5 October 1918. Also see Royal Air Force Communiqué No. 27.
23. Combat Report, October 1918. These two air victories were confirmed by the Royal Air Force Communiqué No. 28. See also Braby, "Nothing Can Stop Us," 174.
24. Combat Report, 14 October 1918. This is the first of two reports written by Captain Gillet that day.
25. Combat Report, 14 October 1918. This is the second combat report written by Captain Gillet on 14 October. See also Royal Air Force Communiqué No. 29.
26. See Royal Air Force Communiqué Nos. 29, 30, and 31.
27. "History of No. 79 Squadron," 2.
28. Combat Report, 4 November 1918. This victory was also confirmed by Royal Air Force Communiqué No. 32.
29. "List of Enemy Aircraft Driven Down or Destroyed, 22 March– 9 November 1918," Air 1, box 1904, Public Records Office.
30. *Cross and Cockade Journal* (Spring 1970), 94.
31. "History of No. 79 Squadron," 2.
32. *Cross and Cockade Journal* (Spring 1970), 94.

FOURTEEN   Capts. Paul T. Iaccaci and August T. Iaccaci

1. A. T. Iaccaci Biographical Card, Directorate of History. Also see Information Form produced by Iver Penttinen.
2. A. T. Iaccaci Biographical Card.
3. "Data for the History of No. 20 Squadron, R.F.C. and R.A.F.," Air 1, box 689, Public Records Office.
4. "Data for the History of No. 20 Squadron, RFC and RAF."
5. Combat Report, 19 May 1918, Air 1, box 2231, Public Records

Office. The victory was also described in Royal Air Force Communiqué No. 7.

6. Combat Report, 19 May 1918. This victim was recorded in Royal Air Force Communiqué No. 7.
7. Combat Report, 27 May 1918; Royal Air Force Communiqué No. 9.
8. Lt. P. T. Iaccaci's Combat Report, 31 May 1918. The observer's two victories were also mentioned in Royal Air Force Communiqué No. 9 and in "Decisive Combats—Pilots of No. 20 Squadron," Air 1, box 168, Public Records Office.
9. Lt. A. T. Iaccaci's Combat Report, 31 May 1918. This kill was listed in "Decisive Combats—Pilots of No. 20 Squadron."
10. "Data for the History of No. 20 Squadron, RFC and RAF."
11. Combat Report, 1 June 1918.
12. Combat Report, 8 June 1918. This incident was also recorded in Royal Air Force Communiqué No. 10 and in "Decisive Combats—Pilots of No. 20 Squadron."
13. Combat Report, 13 June 1918. See also "Decisive Combats—Pilots of No. 20 Squadron."
14. Lt. A. T. Iaccaci's Combat Report, 17 June 1918; Royal Air Force Communiqué No. 12.
15. Lt. P. T. Iaccaci's Combat Report, 17 June 1918. This victory was also recorded in Royal Air Force Communiqué No. 12.
16. Combat Report, 26 June 1918. Also see "Decisive Combats—Pilots of No. 20 Squadron."
17. Royal Air Force Communiqué No. 13. According to "Decisive Combats—Pilots of No. 20 Squadron," both A. T. Iaccaci and Newland fired bursts into the enemy machine destroyed.
18. Combat Report, 4 July 1918. This battle is also recorded in Royal Air Force Communiqué No. 14 and in "Decisive Combats—Pilots of No. 20 Squadron."
19. Combat Report, 10 July 1918. See also Royal Air Force Communiqué No. 15 and Bailey and Franks, "Combat Log No. 20 Squadron," 50.
20. Bailey and Franks, "Combat Log No. 20 Squadron," 50.
21. "Data for the History of No. 20 Squadron, R.F.C. and R.A.F."
22. "Decisive Combats—Pilots of No. 20 Squadron."
23. Lt. A. T. Iaccaci's award appears in Royal Air Force Communiqué No. 16, while Paul T. Iaccaci's DFC is recorded in Royal Air Force Communiqué No. 19.
24. "Data for the History of No. 20 Squadron."
25. "Decisive Combats—Pilots of No. 20 Squadron." This "kill" was listed in the Royal Air Force Communiqué No. 29.
26. Combat Report, 6 September 1918, Air 1, box 2224, Public Records Office. This combat was recorded in Royal Air Force Communiqué No. 23 and in "Decisive Combats—Pilots of No. 20 Squadron."
27. Biographical Note Card, Directorate of History.
28. "Information on Americans Who Served with Bristol Fighter Squadrons," provided by J. H. Hume.
29. Combat Report, 15 September 1918. Much of this action was men-

tioned in Royal Air Force Communiqué No. 24 and in "Decisive Combats—Pilots of No. 20 Squadron."

30. Combat Report, 16 September 1918; Royal Air Force Communiqué No. 25.
31. "20 Squadron, R.A.F.," Air 1, box 1595, Public Records Office.
32. Combat Report, 27 September 1918, "Decisive Combats—Pilots of No. 20 Squadron" and Royal Air Force Communiqué No. 26.
33. Bailey and Franks, "Combat Log No. 20 Squadron," 25.
34. Robertson, *Air Aces of the 1914–1918 War*, 43–44. Toliver and Constable, *Fighter Aces*, 293, has Paul Iaccaci with eighteen victories and August Iaccaci with eleven kills.

FIFTEEN   Capt. James William Pearson

1. Combat Report, 3 June 1918. This document is located in Air 1, box 2223, Public Records Office. Also see Royal Air Force Communiqué No. 10.
2. "No. 23 Squadron, RAF," Air 1, box 1595, Public Records Office.
3. Royal Air Force Communiqué No. 1.
4. Combat Report, 27 May 1918.
5. Combat Report, 30 May 1918.
6. Cole, *Royal Air Force, 1918,* 107–125.
7. Combat Report, 1 July 1918; Royal Air Force Communiqué No. 14.
8. Cole, *Royal Air Force, 1918,* 145.
9. Royal Air Force Communiqué No. 18.
10. Combat Report, 22 August 1918.
11. Combat Report, 23 August 1918.
12. Cole, *Royal Air Force, 1918,* 181–205.
13. Combat Report, 14 September 1918.
14. Combat Report, 18 September 1918.
15. Combat Report, 28 October 1918. Also see Royal Air Force Communiqué No. 31.
16. Royal Air Force Communiqué No. 31; Combat Report, 1 November 1918.
17. "No. 23 Squadron, RAF." Also see Pearson DFC award cited in *London Gazette,* 8 February 1919.
18. James W. Pearson Biographical File, Directorate of History.

SIXTEEN   Lt. Bogert Rogers

1. Combat Report, 22 July 1918, Air 1, box 122, Public Records Office. The victory was also recorded in "No. 32 Squadron, RFC/RAF Record of Enemy Aircraft Brought Down by Individual Officers and Record of Officer's Service, April 1917–November 1918," Air 1, box 1495, Public Records Office.
2. Glasebrook, *American Aviators in the Great War, 1914–1918,* 99; Callender and Callender, *War in an Open Cockpit,* 72–77.

3. Callender and Callender, *War In An Open Cockpit*, 71–75; Wise, *Canadian Airmen and the First World War*, 531–540.
4. Royal Air Force Communiqué No. 23.
5. Combat Report, 6 September 1918.
6. Combat Report, 6 September 1918. This report was the second one written by Lieutenant Rogers on that day.
7. Royal Air Force Communiqué No. 24.
8. Royal Air Force Communiqué No. 25.
9. Combat Report, 16 September 1918.
10. Combat Report, 27 September 1918. Also see Royal Air Force Communiqué No. 26.
11. For weather conditions and air activity see Royal Air Force Communiqué Nos. 28 and 29.
12. Combat Report, 1 November 1918.
13. Glasebrook, *American Aviators in the Great War, 1914–1918*, 99.
14. Braby, "Project."
15. Hudson, "Lieutenant John O. Donaldson."
16. Glasebrook, *American Aviators in the Great War, 1914–1918*, 99. Also see certificate on Bogert Rogers in RAF Museum, Hendon, England.

SEVENTEEN   Lt. Harold A. Kullberg

1. Harold A. Kullberg Biographical File, Directorate of History; *New England Aviators, 1914–1918: Their Portraits and Their Records* (Boston: Houghton Mifflin, 1920) Vol. 2, 94.
2. *New England Aviators*, Vol. 2, 94. After the United States entered the war in April 1917, an arrangement was made with Canada whereby aviators from both countries would train in Canada during the summer months then move to the Fort Worth, Texas, area for further training during the fierce Canadian winters. For a study of this program, see H. A. Jones, *War in the Air* (7 volumes, Oxford: Clarenden Press, 1922–1937) Vol. 5, 458–468.
3. *New England Aviators*, Vol. 2, 94.
4. Memorandum, Maj. W. E. Young to Headquarters, Fifty-first Wing, 4 September 1918, Air 1, box 1339, Public Records Office.
5. Shaw, *Twice Vertical*.
6. Richthofen was shot down and killed by Capt. Roy Brown of 209 Squadron, RAF, on 21 April 1918. (See discussion in chapter 4.)
7. Shaw, *Twice Vertical*, 58–60.
8. When the Royal Flying Corps and the Royal Naval Air Service combined to become the Royal Air Force on 1 April 1918, No. 1 Squadron had the honor of becoming the "senior squadron" in the new organization.
9. Captain P. J. Clayson, et al, Combat Report, 27 May 1918, Air 1, box 2231, Public Records Office.
10. Capt. P. J. Clayson, et al, Combat Report, 28 May 1918. Also see

"Machines and Balloons Brought Down by No. 1 Squadron," Air 1, box 1339, Public Records Office.

11. Capt. P. J. Clayson ended the war with twenty-one victories.
12. Shaw, *Twice Vertical*, 60.
13. "Machines and Balloons Brought Down by No. 1 Squadron," 1.
14. Ibid. This engagement occurred on 9 June 1918.
15. Ibid.
16. Capt. P. J. Clayson, Combat Report, 27 June 1918. Also see "Machines and Balloons Brought Down by No. 1 Squadron," 1.
17. See Lt. J. C. Bateman, Combat Report, 1 July 1918 and "Machines and Balloons Brought Down by No. 1 Squadron." In the latter document, Kullberg is given credit for the victory.
18. Kullberg, Combat Report, 9 July 1918.
19. "Machines and Balloons Brought Down by No. 1 Squadron." This kill is listed under Kullberg's name.
20. Kullberg, Combat Report, 19 July 1918. This victory was confirmed in Royal Air Force Communiqué No. 18. "Machines and Balloons Brought Down by No. 1 Squadron" indicated that this crash occurred north of Steenwerck.
21. Kullberg, Combat Report, 31, July 1918.
22. By the end of the war, the 148th Aero Squadron had destroyed sixty-four enemy planes, and Capts. Field E. Kindley and Elliot W. Springs had scored twelve victories each. The 17th Aero Squadron was credited with thirty-nine victories, and its top ace, Capt. George A. Vaughn, had scored thirteen kills.
23. Capts. Reed Landis with ten and J. O. Donaldson with eight kills scored all of their victories while flying with British squadrons.
24. E. Ernest Dupuy and Trevor N. Dupuy, *The Encyclopedia of Military History from 3500 B.C. to the Present* (New York: Harper and Row, 1970), 981–982.
25. Ibid.
26. Shaw, *Twice Vertical*, 61.
27. Esposito, *The West Point Atlas of American Wars,* Map 67.
28. Ibid. Also see Jones, *The War in the Air,* Vol. 4, 456.
29. Kullberg, Combat Report, 9 August 1918.
30. Jones, *The War in the Air,* Vol. 4, 469–497.
31. Kullberg, Combat Report, 30 August 1918. See also "Machines and Balloons Brought Down by No. 1 Squadron."
32. Kullberg, Combat Report, 3 September 1918.
33. Memorandum, Maj. W. E. Young to Headquarters, Fifty-first Wing, 4 September 1918. The Distinguished Flying Cross for Harold A. Kullberg was confirmed in Royal Air Force Communiqué Number 22.
34. Letter, Maj. W. E. Young to Headquarters, Fifty-first Wing, 5 September 1918. This document is located in "Correspondence Regarding Officers and Other Ranks of No. 1 Squadron," Air 1, box 1339, Public Records Office. Other letters in this case are in the same file.
35. Letter, Lt. Col. R. B. Blomfert to Maj. W. E. Young, 6 September 1918.

36. Letter, Kullberg to commanding officer of No. 1 Squadron, 7 September 1918.
37. Shaw, *Twice Vertical*, 62.
38. Combat Report, 16 September 1918. Because of Kullberg's wounds, Maj. W. E. Young wrote this report. Also see Casualty Card on Kullberg, Royal Air Force Museum.
39. Letter, Maj. W. E. Young to provost marshal of Third Army, 20 September 1918.
40. *New England Aviators,* Vol. 2, 94.
41. Kullberg Biographical File.

EIGHTEEN   Capt. Alvin Andrew Callender

1. Callender and Callender, *War In An Open Cockpit,* 15.
2. Callender and Callender, *War In An Open Cockpit,* 41.
3. Callender Biographical File housed in the Directorate of History. See also "No. 32 Squadron, 1916–1949," Imperial War Mission, London.
4. Callender and Callender, *War In An Open Cockpit,* 47.
5. Combat Report, 28 May 1918, Air 1, box 122, Public Records Office. Other Callender combat reports are to be found in the same box. Also see Capt. A. A. Callender record, Imperial War Museum. Callender and Callender, *War In An Open Cockpit,* 104, lists this victory as a Pfalz D-3, but Lt. A. A. Callender's combat report identifies the victim as an Albatros.
6. "No. 32 Squadron, 1916–1949," 1.
7. Ibid.
8. "No. 32 Squadron, 1916–1949," 1.
9. Combat Report, 6 June 1918.
10. Callender and Callender, *War In An Open Cockpit,* 59–60.
11. Ibid., 51.
12. Bridgman, *The Clouds Remember,* 90–91.
13. Callender and Callender, *War In An Open Cockpit,* 103.
14. Combat Report, 8 July 1918. Also see Callender and Callender, *War in an Open Cockpit,* 103.
15. Combat Report, 25 July 1918. This victory was confirmed by the Royal Air Force Communiqué No. 17.
16. Callender and Callender, *War in an Open Cockpit,* 71.
17. Wise, *Canadian Airmen and the First World War,* 531. See also Jones, *The War in the Air,* Vol. 6, 463–467.
18. Combat Report, 9 August 1918.
19. Combat Report, 10 August 1918. See also Callender and Callender, *War in an Open Cockpit,* 104.
20. Callender and Callender, *War in an Open Cockpit,* 73–87.
21. Combat Report 6 September 1918 (written by Lieutenant Lawson). This victory was confirmed by Royal Air Force Communiqué No. 23.
22. Combat Report, 16 September 1918.
23. Combat Report, 24 September 1918.
24. "No. 32 Squadron, 1916–1949," 1–2.

25. Callender and Callender, *War in an Open Cockpit*, 97–98. See also "Captain A. A. Callender: 32 Squadron, R.A.F.," Imperial War Museum, London.
26. *Cross and Cockade Journal* (Great Britain), Vol. 10, No. 3, 136–137.

NINETEEN   Capt. Oren J. Rose

1. Combat Report, 30 July 1918, Air 1, box 1855, Public Records Office. Other Rose combat reports cited are located in the same source.
2. Russell, "History of No. 92 Squadron, RAF," 3.
3. O. J. Rose Biographical File, Directorate of History. Also see "No. 92 Squadron History," Air 1, box 176, Public Records Office, and Russell, "History of No. 92 Squadron," 1–2.
4. Russell, "History of No. 92 Squadron," 2.
5. Combat Report, 31 July 1918.
6. Russell, "History of No. 92 Squadron," 3. The SE-5 was more effective above twelve thousand feet than was the highly maneuverable Sopwith Camel.
7. Combat Report, 11 August 1918. According to one source the Germans were apparently moving to another airdrome at the time of the attack. It is believed the German pilots involved were from *Jadgeschwader II* (*Jastas* 12, 13, 15, and 19). See Russell, "History of No. 92 Squadron," 4.
8. Combat Report, 14 August 1918.
9. Russell, "History of No. 92 Squadron," 6.
10. Combat Report, 25 August 1918.
11. Combat Report, 4 September 1918. The Halberstadt C-V reconnaissance plane was powered by a two hundred horsepower Benz engine and was capable of an air speed of one hundred miles per hour.
12. Combat Report, 15 September 1918.
13. Combat Report, 29 September 1918. This report concerned only the combat with the Fokker.
14. Combat Report, 29 September 1918. The narrative in this report covered the fight with the Halberstadt.
15. Rose Biographical File.
16. Although both of these air battles occurred on the same flight, Lieutenant Rose wrote two combat reports. See Combat Report, 3 October 1918 (8:15 A.M.) and Combat Report, 3 October 1918 (8:45 A.M.).
17. Russell, "History of No. 92 Squadron," 8.
18. Combat Report, 8 October 1918.
19. Combat Report, 9 October 1918.
20. "No. 92 Squadron History."
21. Ibid.
22. Combat Report, 29 October 1918.
23. Combat Report, 30 October 1918.
24. The RE-8, built by the Royal Aircraft Factory, was one of the more effective RAF observation planes.

25. Russell, "History of No. 92 Squadron," 13.
26. Combat Report, 4 November 1918.
27. "History of 92 Squadron."
28. See Headquarters, Air Reserve Records Center, United States Air Force, Memorandum housed in Rose Biographical File.
29. Ibid.

TWENTY   Lt. Cleo Francis Pineau

1. "Register of Officers in 210 Squadron," Air 1, box 1695, Public Records Office.
2. Leonard Bridgman, *The Clouds Remember*, 53–58.
3. Combat Report, 6 September 1918, Air 1, box 1696, Public Records Office. Other Pineau combat reports are located in the same source.
4. Pineau Biographical File, Directorate of History. Also see "Register of Officers in 210 Squadron." His next of kin was listed as T. L. Pineau, whose address was 119 S. Seventh Street, Albuquerque, New Mexico.
5. "History of No. 210 Squadron," Air 1, box 184, Public Records Office.
6. "History of No. 210 Squadron," 2.
7. Combat Report, 18 September 1918. This "kill" was witnessed by Lt. P. Boulton.
8. Combat Report, 24 September 1918. This combat took place at 2:40 P.M.
9. Combat Report, 24 September 1918. This action occurred at 2:45 P.M. No less than seven enemy planes were destroyed by members of No. 210 Squadron in this air battle.
10. Letter, Lt. C. F. Pineau to Mrs. T. L. Pineau, 30 September 1918.
11. Combat Report, 1 October 1918. This victory was confirmed by a Lieutenant Hopper from the same squadron.
12. Combat Report, 8 October 1918.
13. "Pineau Comes Back an Ace," *Motorcycling and Bicycling* (11 January 1919), 9. Also see "Register of Officers in 210 Squadron," Air 1, box 1695, Public Records Office.
14. "Pineau Comes Back an Ace," 9–10.
15. This is located in the Pineau Biographical File, Directorate of History.
16. "History of No. 210 Squadron," 3.
17. "Pineau Comes Back An Ace," 10. Pineau had been involved with the Miami Cycle and Manufacturing Co. and as a motorcycle race driver before the U.S. entered the First World War.

TWENTY-ONE   Lt. Kenneth R. Unger

1. Combat Report, 27 September 1918, Air 1, box 1696, Public Records Office. Other combat reports for Lt. Unger are to be found in this box.

2. Robinson, *Flying the World's Great Aircraft*, 52.
3. Combat Report, 27 September 1918.
4. Kenneth Russell Unger, Biographical Note Card, Directorate of History.
5. Unger Biographical File; also see "Register of Officers in 210 Squadron," Air 1, box 1695, Public Records Office.
6. "History of No. 210 Squadron," Air 1, box 184, Public Records Office.
7. O. A. Sater, Jamaica, New York. See Combat Reports for 26 June, 20 July, and 31 July 1918.
8. Combat Report, 24 September 1918.
9. Combat Report, 28 September 1918.
10. Combat Report, 1 October 1918.
11. Combat Report, 14 October 1918.
12. Royal Air Force Communiqué No. 30.
13. Combat Report, 27 October 1918; Royal Air Force Communiqué No. 30.
14. Royal Air Force Communiqué No. 31.
15. Ibid; also see Combat Report, 30 October 1918.
16. Combat Report, 1 November 1918. This victory also appeared in Royal Air Force Communiqué No. 31.
17. Royal Air Force Communiqué No. 32.
18. Kenneth Russell Unger Biographical Note states that the information on the Air Mail Service was taken from *Who's Who in American Aeronautics*, 1922. See also *Cross and Cockade Journal* (Spring 1979), 91.

TWENTY-TWO   Lt. Norman Cooper

1. Braby, "Project," 172.
2. Norman Cooper Biographical Card, Directorate of History.
3. "Record of No. 73 Squadron, RAF," Air 1, box 176, Public Records Office.
4. "Record of No. 73 Squadron, RAF."
5. Ibid.
6. Combat Report, 25 July 1918, Air 1, box 1226, Public Records Office. This victory was also recorded in Royal Air Force Communiqué No. 17. See also "War Diary Intelligence Summary for IX Brigade," Air 1, box 2249, Public Records Office.
7. Combat Report, 30 July 1918; Royal Air Force Communiqué No. 18, "War Diary Intelligence Summary for IX Brigade."
8. "Record of No. 73 Squadron, RAF."
9. Combat Report, 19 August 1918; Royal Air Force Communiqué No. 21.
10. Franks, *Aircraft Versus Aircraft*, 38.
11. Combat Report, 25 August 1918. Both of these victories were listed in the Royal Air Force Communiqué No. 21.
12. Combat Report, 15 September 1918. This victory, along with planes

destroyed by Capt. W. H. Hubbard and Lt. E. J. Lussier, was listed in Royal Air Force Communiqué No. 24.

13. Combat Report, 15 September 1918; Royal Air Force Communiqué No. 24.
14. "Record of No. 73 Squadron, RAF."
15. Letter, commanding officer of No. 73 Squadron to commander of Fifteenth Wing, Royal Air Force, Air 1, box 176, Public Records Office.
16. Royal Air Force Communiqué No. 29. Also see *London Gazette*, 8 February 1919.
17. Letter, C. R. Gamage, Ministry of Defence, to Wing Commander F. F. Lambert, 11 June 1985.
18. "Record of No. 73 Squadron, RAF." Also see Combat Reports for Norman Cooper.
19. Norman Cooper, Certification Card, Royal Air Force Museum.
20. Norman Cooper Biographical Card, Directorate of History.
21. Letter, C. R. Gamage to Wing Commander F. F. Lambert, 11 June 1985.

TWENTY-THREE   Lt. Louis Bennett

1. Williams, "Louis Bennett," 332. See also Louis Bennett Biographical File, Directorate of History.
2. Williams, "Louis Bennett," 332–333. Young Bennett withdrew from Yale University prior to graduation in the spring of 1917. He was, nontheless, granted his degree on 20 June 1917.
3. Williams, "Louis Bennett," 333.
4. Hudson, "Frederick K. Weyerhaeuser's Air War in Italy, 1918," 290–294.
5. Williams, "Louis Bennett," 334–335. According to records in the Directorate of History, there were at least six Americans in No. 90 Squadron during the time Bennett was assigned there. Bennett's Biographical File indicates that he was posted to No. 90 Squadron on 31 May.
6. Bennett Biographical File; Williams, "Louis Bennett," 335. Captain McElroy was credited with forty-six aerial victories before his death on 31 July 1918.
7. Hudson, "Reed G. Landis," 197. After Major Dallas's death, Maj. A. W. Keen took over as No. 40 Squadron commander.
8. "Histories of R.A.F. Service Squadrons," Air 1, box 173, Public Records Office.
9. Williams, "Louis Bennett," 336–337; Hudson, "Reed G. Landis," 197.
10. During the first two weeks of August, Maj. A. W. Keen, No. 40 Squadron commander, destroyed a Pfalz, and Lt. Reed Landis, an American in the outfit, shot down three enemy aircraft and one balloon.
11. Williams, "Louis Bennett," 338.

12. War Diary or Intelligence Summary, 1st Brigade, R.A.F. This document is to be found in Air 1/1446/204/36/45, Public Records Office.

13. Combat Report, 15 August 1918, Air 1/122/15/40/137, Public Records Office. Other Bennett combat reports are to be found in the same source.

14. Williams, "Louis Bennett," 339.

15. War Diary, 1st Brigade, R.A.F., 18 August 1918. Also see Bennett's Combat Report, 17 August 1918 and Royal Air Force Communiqué No. 20.

16. Bennett Combat Report, 17 August 1918. This was his second report of the day, and the balloon destruction was confirmed by Lt. L H. Sutton.

17. Williams, "Louis Bennett," 339.

18. Winter, *The First of the Few,* 174.

19. Combat Report, 19 August 1918. The destruction of the two balloons was confirmed in Royal Air Force Communiqué No. 21 and in War Diary, 1st Brigade, RAF, 19 August 1918.

20. Combat Report, 19 August 1918. This was the second combat report that he had written on that day. Also see Royal Air Force Communiqué No. 21.

21. Williams, "Louis Bennett," 341.

22. Ibid.

23. Combat Report, 22 August 1918; Royal Air Force Communiqué No. 21.

24. Combat Report, 23 August 1918. This "kill" was confirmed by Captain Dixon in War Diary, 1st Brigade, R.A.F. Also see Royal Air Force Communiqué No. 21.

25. Hudson, *Hostile Skies,* 293.

26. 1st Brigade Summaries, Air 1/977/204/5/1135, Public Records Office.

27. Williams, "Louis Bennett," 344–345; Bennett Biographical File.

28. Williams, "Louis Bennett," 445.

TWENTY-FOUR   Lt. Frank Lucien Hale

1. Coughlin and Obrecht, "Frank Lucien Hale," 329.

2. Ibid.

3. Coughlin and Obrecht, "Frank Lucien Hale," 229–230. See also Frank Lucien Hale Biographical File, Directorate of History.

4. Hale Biographical File; Coughlin and Obrecht, "Frank Lucien Hale," 330.

5. Coughlin and Obrecht, "Frank Lucien Hale," 330. See also biographical sketch entitled "Frank Lucien Hale," Air 1, box 1492, Public Records Office.

6. Callender and Callender, *War in an Open Cockpit,* 71.

7. Wise, *Canadian Airmen and the First World War,* 531. Göring was away at the time, leaving the *Jagdgeschwader* in the command of Lothar Von Richthofen, the younger brother of Manfred.

8. Coughlin and Obrecht, "Frank Lucien Hale," 330.

9. Lt. F. L. Hale, Combat Report, 25 August 1918, Air 1, box 122, Public Records Office. Other combat records dealing with Lieutenant Hale are to be found in the same source.

10. Hale, Combat Report, 4 September 1918.

11. Hale, Combat Report, 6 September 1918.

12. Hale, Combat Report, 16 September 1918.

13. Hale, Combat Report, 27 September 1918.

14. Royal Air Force Communiqué No. 29. The official date of the DFC Award was listed as 20 October 1918. The award citation was published in the *London Gazette* on 8 February 1919.

15. Callender and Callender, *War in an Open Cockpit,* 90.

16. Robertson, *Air Aces of the 1914–1918 War* lists Frank L. Hale as having eighteen victories. No. 32 Squadron combat reports show only eight kills for Hale.

17. Coughlin and Obrecht, "Frank Lucien Hale," 331; also see Frank Lucien Hale Biographical File, Directorate of History.

18. Coughlin and Obrecht, "Frank Lucien Hale," 331.

19. Ibid.

20. Coughlin and Obrecht, "Frank Lucien Hale," 331.

21. Ibid. Among the victims of this borrowing scheme were the Waco, Stinson, Howard, and Beech companies.

22. Coughlin and Obrecht, "Frank Lucien Hale," 332.

23. Ibid.

TWENTY-FIVE   American Air Aces Who Flew with Number 29 Squadron

1. "No. 29 Squadron, Royal Air Force," Air 1, box 172, Public Records Office.

2. Letter, Ola Sater to James J. Hudson, 14 December 1986.

3. Robertson, *Air Aces of the 1914–1918 War,* lists Sydney M. Brown, F. A. Robertson, and D. F. Hilton, while Bowyer and Franks, "No. 29 Squadron RFC/RAF, 1915–1919," labels Murray, Brown, and Hilton as aces.

4. S. M. Brown Biographical Card, Directorate of History.

5. D. M. Murray Biographical Card, Directorate of History.

6. Letter, William L. Dougan to his mother, 16 January 1918.

7. "No. 29 Squadron, Royal Air Force."

8. Bowyer and Franks, "No. 29 Squadron," 112.

9. Bowyer and Franks, "No. 29 Squadron," 104.

10. Ibid.

11. Lt. W. L. Dougan's Combat Logbook. Also see Bowyer and Franks, "No. 29 Squadron," 104.

12. Bowyer and Franks, "No. 29 Squadron," 104.

13. Combat Report, 12 August 1918, Public Records Office, Air 1, box 1863. Also see Dougan's Combat Logbook, and Bowyer and Franks, "No. 29 Squadron," 104.

14. S. M. Brown's Biographical Card; Bowyer and Franks, "No. 29 Squadron," 104.
15. Combat Report, 19 August 1918. See also Royal Air Force Communiqué No. 21. Capt. C. J. Venter, the South African, was shot down and taken prisoner on the same day.
16. Combat Report, 24 August 1918; Royal Air Force Communiqué No. 21.
17. Letter, Lt. W. L. Dougan to Kathleen Dougan, 25 August 1918. In this letter Dougan mentioned that his new roommate was Sydney Brown, who wrote poetry and lived in New York.
18. Bowyer and Franks, "No. 29 Squadron," 104.
19. "No. 29 Squadron, Royal Air Force."
20. Bowyer and Franks, "No. 29 Squadron," 105.
21. Combat Report, 16 September 1918. This "kill" was also reported in Royal Air Force Communiqué No. 25.
22. Bowyer and Franks, "No. 29 Squadron," 105.
23. Ibid., 106.
24. Bowyer and Franks, "No. 29 Squadron," 106.
25. Letter, Lt. W. L. Dougan to Mrs. Ida Dougan, 1 December 1918.
26. Ibid.
27. Combat Report, 28 September 1918. This victory also appeared in Royal Air Force Communiqué No. 26.
28. Bowyer and Franks, "No. 29 Squadron," 107.
29. Combat Report, 5 October 1918. This "kill" was also listed in Royal Air Force Communiqué No. 27.
30. Combat Report, 5 October 1918.
31. Combat Report, 8 October 1918; Royal Air Force Communiqué No. 28.
32. Combat Report, 27 October 1918; Royal Air Force Communiqué No. 30.
33. Combat Report, 28 Ocotber 1918; Royal Air Force Communiqué No. 31.
34. Lt. S. M. Brown Biographical Card, Directorate of History.
35. Letter, Stewart K. Taylor to James J. Hudson, 24 July 1985.
36. Bowyer and Franks, "No. 29 Squadron," 109.
37. Combat Report, 9 November 1918.
38. Bowyer and Franks in "No. 29 Squadron," list Hilton, Brown, and Murray with five victories. Bruce Robertson's *Air Aces of the 1914–1918 War* credits D. F. Hilton with six kills.
39. Letter, Maj. C. H. Droan to Mrs. Ida Dougan, 29 September 1918.
40. Interview with Mrs. William Dougan, 10 March 1987.

TWENTY-SIX   Summary and Conclusion

1. Dupuy and Dupuy, *Military Heritage of America,* 352.
2. William R. Dunn, *Frederick Libby, The First American Ace,* Air Force Museum, Dayton, Ohio.

3. Robertson, *Air Aces of the 1914–1918 War,* 44.
4. Douglas, *Years of Combat,* 253–258.
5. "History of No. 60 Squadron," 3.
6. Lambert oral history interviews by Robert J. Smith.
7. LeBoutillier interview, 43–46.
8. Dupuy and Dupuy, *Military Heritage of America,* 374–375.
9. Callender and Callender, *War in an Open Cockpit,* 59.
10. "Record of No. 73 Squadron, RAF."
11. Dupuy and Dupuy, *Military Heritage of America,* 377.
12. Ibid, 380.

Bibliography

The unpublished documents researched during the preparation of this book are to be found in archival sources. Most of the actual combat records and the histories of the various squadrons are located in the "Air 1 Collection" in the Public Records Office in London. In addition, many valuable sources dealing with World War I air combat are to be found in the Imperial War Museum in London and in the Royal Air Force Museum in Hendon, located in the northern part of London.

Another important research collection is to be found in the Directorate of History located in the National Defence Department, Ottawa, Canada. In fact, much of the biographical detail on individual American pilots is to be found in this source. Also the Public Archives in Ottawa, Canada, has considerable information on the First Great Air War.

The United States Air Force Academy Library in Colorado Springs, Colorado, and the World War I Aviation Museum and Historical Foundation in Parker, Colorado, also house some worthwhile information on those American pilots who served with the British during the 1914–1918 period. The J. J. Smith Collection is now housed in the World War I Aviation Museum. The United States Air Force Museum at Wright-Patterson Air Force Base in Ohio was able to supply me with material on some American aces, such as William C. Lambert and Frederick Libby, who flew with the British squadrons. World War I flyers have on several occasions loaned me letters and diaries dealing with the first great air war. In addition, I have studied a great many books and articles covering the World War I period.

Books

Bacon, W. Stevenson, ed. *Sky Fighters of World War I*. New York: Fawcett Publications, 1961.

Baldwin, Hanson W. *World War I: An Outline History*. New York: Harper and Row, 1962.

Barrett, William E. *The First War Planes*. Greenwich, Conn: Fawcett Publications, 1960.

Bishop, William A. *Winged Warfare*. New York: George H. Doran Company, 1918.

Bowyer, R. C. *Albert Ball V.C.* London: William Kimber, 1977.

Boyle, Andrew. *Trenchard*. London: Collins, 1962.

Brewer, Leighton. *Riders of the Sky*. Boston: Houghton Mifflin Co., 1934.

Bridgman, Leonard. *The Clouds Remember: The Aeroplanes of World War I*. London: Arms and Armour Press, 1972.

Buchan, John. *A History of the Great War*, 4 vols. New York: Houghton Mifflin Co., 1922.

Callender, Gordon W., Jr., and Callender, Gordon W., Sr., eds. *War in an Open Cockpit: The Wartime Letters of Captain Alvin Andrew Callender*. West Roxbury: World War I Aero Publishers, 1978.

Cheesman, E. F., ed. *Fighter Aircraft of the 1914–1918 War*. Letchworth, Herts: Harleyford Publications, 1960.

―――. *Reconnaissance and Bomber Aircraft of the 1914–1918 War*. Los Angeles: Aero Publications, 1962.

Clark, Don. *Wild Blue Yonder: An Air Epic*. Seattle: Superior Publishing Co., 1972.

Coffman, Edward M. *The War to End All Wars: The American Military Experience in World War I*. New York: Oxford University Press, 1969.

Cole, Christopher. *McCudden V. C.* London: William Kimber, 1967.

―――. *Royal Air Force, 1918*. London: William Kimber, 1968. Now controlled by Thorsons Publishing Co.

Cruttwell, C. R. M. F. *A History of the Great War, 1914–1918*. Oxford: Clarendon Press, 1936.

Cuneo, John R. *Winged Mars*, Vol. 1, *The German Air Weapon, 1870–1914*, and Vol. 2, *The Air Weapon, 1914–1916*. Harrisburg, Pa.: Military Service Publishing Co., 1942–1945.

Douglas, Sholto. *Years of Combat*, Vol. 1. London: Collins, 1963.

Douhet, Gen. Giulio. *The Command of the Air*. New York: Coward-McCann, 1942.

Driggs, Lawrence L. *Heroes of Aviation*. Boston: Little, Brown and Co., 1918.

Dupuy, R. Ernest, and Dupuy, Trevor N. *Military Heritage of America*. New York: McGraw-Hill Book Co., 1956.

―――. *The Encyclopedia of Military History from 3500 B.C. to the Present*. New York: Harper and Row, 1970.

Edmonds, J. E. *A Short History of World War I*. London: Oxford University Press, 1951.

Elliot, Stuart E. *Wooden Crates & Gallant Pilots*. Philadelphia: Dorrance and Co., 1974.

Emme, Eugene. *The Impact of Air Power*. Princeton, N.J.: Van Nostrand Co., 1959.

Esposito, Vincent J., ed. *The West Point Atlas of American Wars*, Vol. 2. New York: Frederick A. Praeger, 1959. Now handled by Henry Holt Co.

Falls, Cyril B. *The Great War*. New York: G. P. Putnam's Sons, 1961.

Flammer, Philip M. *The Vivid Air: The Lafayette Escadrille*. Athens, Georgia: University of Georgia Press, 1981.

Franks, Norman. *Aircraft Versus Aircraft: The Illustrated Story of Fighter Pilot Combat Since 1914*. New York: Macmillan, 1986.

Fredette, R. H. *The First Battle of Britain, 1917–1918*. London: Cassell, 1966.

Fuller, Gen. J. F. C. *Armament and History*. New York: Charles Scribner's Sons, 1945.

Gibbons, Floyd. *The Red Knight of Germany*. New York: Doubleday, Page and Co., 1927.

Glasebrook, Millie. *American Aviators in the Great War 1914–1918*. Carson City, Nevada: Glazebrook Foundation, 1984.

Goldberg, Alfred, ed. *A History of the United States Air Force, 1907–1957*. Princeton, N.J.: D. Van Nostrand Company, 1957.

Gribble, Leonard R. *Heroes of the Fighting R.A.F.* London: George G. Harrap and Co., 1941.

Grider, John MacGavock. *War Birds: Diary of an Unknown Aviator*. New York: George H. Doran Co., 1926.

Gurney, Gene. *The War in the Air*. New York: Crown Publishers, 1962.

———. *Flying Aces of World War I*. New York: Random House, 1965.

Hart, Liddell. *The Real War*. Boston: Little, Brown and Co., 1930.

Hart, B. H. Liddell. *Strategy*. New York: Frederick A. Praeger, 1954.

Higham, Robin. *Air Power: A Concise History*. New York: St. Martin's Press, 1972.

———. *The British Rigid Airship 1908–1931*. London: Foulis, 1963.

Holley, I. B. *Ideas and Weapons*. New Haven: Yale University Press, 1953.

Hudson, James J. *Hostile Skies: A Combat History of the American Air Service in World War I*. Syracuse, New York: Syracuse University Press, 1968.

Jackson, Robert. *Fighter Pilots of World War I*. London: Arthur Barker, 1977.

Jones, Ira. *King of Air Fighters: Biography of Major "Mick" Mannock*. London: Nicholson and Watson, 1934.

Knappen, Theodore M. *Wings of War*. New York: G. P. Putnam's Sons, 1920.

Lambert, William C. *Combat Report*. London: William Kimber, 1973.

Lee, Arthur Gould. *No Parachute: A Fighter Pilot in World War I*. New York: Harper and Row, 1968.

Levine, Isaac Don. *Mitchell: Pioneer of Air Power*. Cleveland: World, 1942.

Lewis, Cecil. *Sagittarius Rising*. London: Peter Davies, 1936.

Lewis, Peter M. *Squadron Histories: R.F.C., R.N.A.S., and R.A.F., 1912–1959*. London: Putnam, 1959.

Longstreet, Stephen. *The Canvas Falcons: The Story of the Men and the Planes of World War I.* New York: The World Publishing Company, 1970.

Marshall, S. L. A., narrator. *American Heritage History of World War I.* American Heritage Publishing Co., 1964.

Maurer, Maurer. *The U.S. Air Service in World War I.* 4 vols. Washington, D.C.: Government Printing Office, 1978–1979.

McCudden, James. *Flying Fury.* London: John Hamilton, 1930.

Mitchell, William. *Memoirs of World War I.* New York: Random House, 1960.

Mitchell, William A. *Outlines of the World's Military History.* Harrisburg, Pa.: Military Service Publishing Co., 1931.

Morrow, John H., Jr. *German Air Power in World War I.* Lincoln, Nebraska: University of Nebraska Press, 1982.

Musciano, Walter A. *Eagles of the Black Cross.* New York: Obolensky, 1965.

Neumann, Georg Paul. *The German Air Force in the Great War.* Portway Bath: Cedric Chivers, 1969.

New England Aviators, 1914–1918: Their Portraits and their Records, Vol. 2. Boston: Houghton Mifflin Co.,1920.

Norman, Aaron. *The Great Air War: The Men, the Planes, the Saga of Military Aviation, 1914–1918.* New York: Macmillan Co., 1968.

Norwarra, H. J., and Brown, Kimbrough. *Von Richthofen and the "Flying Circus".* Letchworth, Herts, England: Harleyford Publications, 1958.

Oughton, Frederick. *The Aces.* New York: G. P. Putnam's Sons, 1960.

Platt, Frank, ed. *Great Battles of World War I: In the Air.* New York: New American Library, 1966.

Poolman, Kenneth. *Zeppelins against London.* New York: John Day, 1961.

Preston, Richard A., and Wise, Sydney F. *Men in Arms: A History of Warfare and Its Interrelationships with Western Society.* New York: Praeger Publishers, 1970.

Raleigh, Walter, and Jones, H. A. *The War in the Air,* 6 Vols. Oxford: Clarendon Press, 1922–1937.

Rawlings, John. *Fighter Squadrons of the RAF and Their Aircraft.* London: MacDonald and Janes, 1976.

Reynolds, Quentin. *They Fought for the Sky.* New York: Rinehart & Co., 1957.

Rickenbacker, Edward V. *Fighting the Flying Circus.* New York: Stokes, 1919.

Roberts, E. M. *A Flying Fighter: An American Above the Lines in France.* New York: Harpers, 1918.

Robertson, Bruce, ed. *Air Aces of the 1914–1918 War.* Letchworth, Herts, England: Harleyford Publications, 1959.

———. *Von Richthofen and the Flying Circus.* Letchworth, Herts, England: Harleyford Publications, 1959.

Robinson, Anthony, ed. *Flying the World's Great Aircraft.* New York: Crescent Books, 1979.

Ropp, Theodore. *War in the Modern World*. Durham: Duke University Press, 1959.

Saunders, Hilary St. George. *Per Ardua: The Rise of British Air Power, 1911–1939*. London: Oxford University Press, 1944.

Shaw, Michael. *Twice Vertical: The History of No. I Squadron, Royal Air Force*. London: MacDonald, 1971.

Simkins, Peter. *Air Fighting 1914–18: The Struggle for Air Superiority over the Western Front*. London: Imperial War Museum, 1978.

Sims, Edward H. *Fighter Tactics and Strategy, 1914–1970*. New York: Harper and Row, 1967.

Slessor, J. C. *Air Power and Armies*. London: Oxford University Press, 1936.

Stringer, Henry R. *Heroes All!*. Washington, D.C.: Fassett Publishing Co., 1919.

Taylor, John W. R. *C.F.S. Birthplace of Air Power*. London: Putnam, 1958.

Tolliver, Raymond F., and Constable, Trevor J. *Fighter Aces*. New York: Macmillan Co., 1965.

Toulmin, H. A. *The Air Service, American Expeditionary Force*. New York: D. Van Nostrand Co., 1927.

Tuchman, Barbara. *The Guns of August*. New York: Macmillan Co., 1962.

Valencia, Gene. *Fred Libby: The Flying Buckaroo*. Chula Vista, Ca.: Valor Productions, 1970.

Whetton, Douglass. *Mannock, Patrol Leader Supreme*. Falls Church, Va.: Ajay Enterprises, 1977.

Whitehouse, Arch. *Years of the War Birds*. Garden City, New York: Doubleday and Co., 1960.

———. *Decisive Air Battles of the First World War*. New York: Duell, Sloan and Pearce, 1963.

———. *Heroes of the Sunlit Sky*. Garden City, New York: Doubleday and Co., 1967.

Winter, Denis. *The First of the Few: Fighter Pilots of the First World War*. Athens, Georgia: University of Georgia Press, 1982.

Wise, S. F. *Canadian Airmen and the First World War: The Official History of the Royal Canadian Air Force*. Toronto, Canada: University of Toronto Press, 1980.

Articles

Bailey, Frank W., and Franks, Norman. "Combat Log : No. 20 Squadron, RFC/RAF," *Cross and Cockade Journal* (Spring 1985): 24–54.

Bowyer, Charles, and Franks, Norman. "No. 29 Squadron RFC/RAF, 1915–1919," *Cross and Cockade Journal* (Winter 1970): 93–122.

Braby, Wayne R. "Nothing Can Stop Us: A Short History of No. 79 Squadron, RFC/RAF," *Cross and Cockade Journal* (Summer 1964): 168–175.

———. "Sketches of 28 Squadron, RAF," *Cross and Cockade Journal* (Autumn 1967): 273–303.

———. "Project: American Air Aces of the 1914–1918 War," *Cross and Cockade Journal* (Summer 1981): 171–174.

Chamberlain, Paul. "A Short History of No. 32 Squadron, 1916–1918," *Cross and Cockade Journal* (Spring 1981): 39–71.

Connell, Dennis. "The Richthofen Controversy; 1918–1962, Part II," *Cross and Cockade Journal* (Summer 1967): 189–194.

———. "The Richthofen Controversy; 1963–1965 Part III," *Cross and Cockade Journal* (Summer 1968): 170–187.

Cook, Fulton. "Lieut. Lloyd A. Hamilton of the 17th Aero Squadrons," *Cross and Cockade Journal* (Spring 1979): 66–84.

Cooper, Malcolm. "British Flying Operations on the Western Front, July 1917," *Cross and Cockade Journal* (Winter 1982): 354–370.

———. "The British Experience of Strategic Bombing," *Cross and Cockade* (Summer 1986): 48–61.

Coughlin, P. R., and Obrecht, D. H. "Frank Lucian Hale," *Cross and Cockade Journal* (Winter 1962): 329–332.

Earle, Edward Mead. "The Influence of Air Power," *Yale Review* (Summer 1946): 577–593.

Franks, Norman. "Dallas," *Cross and Cockade* (Winter 1972): 147–154.

Franks, Norman, and Bailey, F. W. "Top Scorers - Record of 20 Squadron, RFC/RAF," *Cross and Cockade* (Spring 1973): 1–20.

Franks, Norman, and Bailey, Frank. "65 Squadron, RFC/RAF," *Cross and Cockade* (Summer 1979): 49–59.

Frey, Royal D. "Forgotten Ace of World War I," *The Airman* (April 1968): 20–23.

———. "Setting the Record Straight: The First of Many American Air-to-Air Victories." *Aerospace Historian* (Fall 1974): 156–159.

Harvey, W. F. J. "The Bristol Fighter," *Cross and Cockade* (Spring 1970): 3–6.

Hauprich, N. H. "German Jagdstaffeln and *Jagdgeschwader* Commanding Officers, 1916–1918," *Cross and Cockade Journal* (Autumn 1961): 150–161.

Hudson, James J. "Air Knight of the Ozarks: Captain Field E. Kindley," *Journal of the American Aviation Historical Society* (Winter 1959): 233–260.

———. "Military History and the Great Air War," *Air University Review* (Winter 1970): 109–113.

———. "Reed G. Landis: America's SE-5 Ace," *Aerospace Historian* (December 1971): 195–199.

———. "Harold E. Hartney: Pursuit Group Commander and Author," *Air University Review* (January 1972): 81–88.

———. "Captain Reed Landis and America's 'Last Good War,'" *Arkansas Historical Quarterly* (Summer 1976): 127–141.

———. "Ambush Over No-Mans Land," *Cross and Cockade Journal* (Winter 1981): 344–348.

———. "Frederick K. Weyerhoeuser's Air War in Italy, 1918," *Cross and Cockade Journal* (Winter 1982): 289–317.

————. "Lieutenant John O. Donaldson: World War I Air Ace and Escape Artist," *Air University Review* (January 1986): 88–92.

Hylands, Denis. "Ace of Storks: Rene Fonck," *Cross and Cockade* (Winter 1978): 145–154.

Lambert, William C. "A Very Strange Story," *Aerospace Historian* (Spring 1983): 39–49.

May, Wilfred. "Lieut. Wilfrid 'WOP' May's Account," *Cross and Cockade Journal* (Summer 1982): 110–115.

McGuire, Frank R. "The Richthofen Controversy 1918–1963; Part I," *Cross and Cockade Journal* (Spring 1967), 43–52.

Miller, Thomas G. "USAS Flyers with the RFC/RAF, 1917–1918," *Cross and Cockade Journal* (Spring 1966): 29–44.

Parks, James J. "The Final Reunion of the Lafayette Flying Corps," *Cross and Cockade Journal* (Winter 1983): 371–378.

Peyton, David A. "The Forgotten Ace of W. W. I," *Pathway Magazine* (August 1970): 26–31.

Powell, Walter V. "The Final Dogfight of the Red Baron," *Over the Front* (Winter 1986): 340–341.

Puglisi, William R., ed. "German Army Air Aces," *Cross and Cockade Journal* (Autumn 1962): 216–227.

Puglisi, W. R. "German Aircraft Down in British Lines," *Cross and Cockade Journal* (Summer 1969): 153–187.

Rabe, Hanns-Gerd. "Fierce Days and Nights in Flanders," *Over the Front* (Spring, 1986): 3–7.

Reynolds, Jack. "A Yank in the RFC: The Wartime Experiences of Lt. George W. Schermerhorn," *Cross and Cockade Journal* (Autumn 1984): 231–241.

Russell, H. H. "History of No. 92 Squadron, RAF," *Cross and Cockade Journal* (Spring 1966): 1–15.

Sater, O. A. "The First and Second American Oxford Detachment," *Cross and Cockade* (Autumn 1974): 130–133.

Skelton, Marvin. "Captain Vernon Castle, RFC," *Cross and Cockade* (Summer 1977): 62–71.

Skelton, Marvin L. "John McGavock Grider—War Bird," *Cross and Cockade* (Spring 1980): 8–20.

Vann, R., and Bowyer, R. C. "XV Squadron, RFC/RAF, 1915–1919," *Cross and Cockade* (Summer 1973): 53–74.

Warne, Joe. "60 Squadron, A Detailed History—Part I," *Cross and Cockade* (Spring 1980): 29–34.

————. "60 Squadron, A Detailed History—Part II," *Cross and Cockade* (Summer 1980): 49–65.

————. "60 Squadron, A Detailed History—Part III," *Cross and Cockade* (Autumn 1980): 120–131.

————. "60 Squadron, A Detailed History—Part IV," *Cross and Cockade* (Winter 1980): 171–186.

————. "60 Squadron, A Detailed History—Part V," *Cross and Cockade* (Spring 1981): 30–43.

Waugh, Colin. "A Short History of No. I Squadron Australia Flying Corps," *Cross and Cockade Journal* (Autumn 1975): 244–253.

Whitten, Douglas. "Flying With Forty," *Cross and Cockade* (Winter 1970): 78–80.

———. "Roderic Stanley Dallas Forgotten Ace," *Cross and Cockade* (Spring 1971): 1–11.

———. "Give Me Yesterday: Recollection of Capt. R. L. Chidlow-Roberts" *Cross and Cockade Journal* (Winter 1979): 344–380.

Williams, George. "Men and Aircraft No. 45 Squadron, RFC/RAF: 1916–1918," *Cross and Cockade Journal* (Winter 1976): 348–380.

Williams, George H. "Louis Bennett, Jr.: No. 40 Squadron, RFC/RAF," *Cross and Cockade Journal* (Winter 1980): 331–350.

Wright, Peter. "Of Camels & Two-O-Eight: Lt. Harold Goodwin, RAF," *Cross and Cockade* (Winter 1986): 165–170.

Index

Aberle (airdrome): No. 29 Sq., 205
Ace: definition and origin of term, 3, 5, 10
Adams, H., Maj. (No. 1 Sq. commander), 50, 143
Aero Club of America, 13
Aircraft, British. See *individual entries* (*e.g.*, Sopwith Camel)
Aircraft, German. See *individual entries* (*e.g.*, Fokker D-7 Biplane)
Air Force Cross (British): awarded to Hilton, 30
Airplane, potential as weapon, 3–5
Aisne campaign (27 May–6 June 1918): Americans in, 7, 217; No. 32 Sq., 217
Aisne-Marne campaign (18 July–6 August 1918), 155; Americans in, 7; No. 32 Sq., 138, 198
Albatros (German airplane), 4, 5, 11, 12, 20, 21, 36, 49, 50, 54, 59, 62, 64, 80, 208, 215
Albatros D-3 (German airplane), 123
Albatros D-5 (German airplane), 63, 82, 83, 84, 86, 87, 152; characteristics, 252 n.7
Albatros Scout (German airplane), 18, 19, 25, 26, 30, 34, 35, 48, 60, 61, 62, 96, 121, 122, 131
Albatros two-seater (German airplane), 113, 130
American Air Service, 7, 13, 216; Champagne-Marne campaign, 218; top aces, 5; victory total, 259 n.22
American Ambulance Field Service, 47
American citizenship, fear of losing, among Americans in RAF, 6, 141, 189

American Fighter Aces Association, 14
Americans in RAF: casualties, 218; total number, 7, 218; victory totals, 218
Amiens campaign (August 1918), 145–47, 218; Allied air superiority, early in, 155, 198; Allied planning for, 145–46; Americans in, 7; casualties, 156; effect on air war, 71; German unpreparedness for, 146
—individual squadrons in: No. 1 Sq., 146; No. 20 Sq., 124; No. 24 Sq., 88; No. 32 Sq., 155–56, 198; No. 73 Sq., 104, 182; No. 92 Sq., 163; No. 210 Sq., 176
Amm, E. O., Lt., 208, 211
Arnold, A. R., Maj. (No. 79 Sq. commander), 97, 110
Arnold, Henry H. "Hap", Gen., 65
Arras, Battle of (1917): No. 32 Sq., 153
Atkinson, J. D. Capt., 244 n.5
Auchel (airdrome): No. 11 Sq., 69; No. 1 Sq., 152
Australian fighter squadrons, 163
Austrian air forces, 5
Aviatik (German airplane), 4, 10, 18, 21, 28–29, 49
Avro 504B (British airplane), 4, 25, 39, 78, 138, 170

Bailleul (airdrome): No. 1 Sq., 48; No. 32 Sq., 153; No. 60 Sq., 59
Bair, H. L., Lt., 87–88
Baldwin, Capt. (No. 73 Sq.), 106, 183
Baldwin, Lt., 182
Balloons, observation, difficulty in attacking, 190–91
Bannerman, R. B., Capt., 98, 114

Callender, Alvin Andrew, Capt., 6,
138; prewar life, 151; joins
RFC, training, 151; rest leave in
Scotland, 156; promoted to captain, flight commander, 157;
death, 140, 158; New Orleans
municipal airport and U.S.
Naval Air Station named for,
158; in Aisne campaign, 217;
among No. 32 Sq. American
aces, 140
—letters to family, 152, 153–54
—victories: first, 152; second, 153;
fifth, 155; sixth and seventh,
156; ninth and tenth, 157–58
Cambrai campaign (November 1917):
Americans in, 7, 216–17; No.
11 Sq., 70
Cambrai campaign (March 1918): No.
73 Sq., 103
Canadian Air Force, 21
"Canuck" (Canadian version of Curtiss JN-4 "Jenny"), 78, 137–38.
See also Curtiss JN-4 "Jenny"
Catterick, Yorkshire, 47
Caudron (French airplane), 4, 33
Central Flying School, Upavon, Wilt-
shire, 17, 18, 151, 188
Champagne-Marne campaign (15
July–17 July 1918): American
Air Service, 218; Americans in,
7; No. 23 Sq., 218
Champien (airdrome): No. 79 Sq., 110
Chandler, R. N., Lt., 105
Chapman, C. M. B., Capt., 26, 27, 28,
244 n.5
Child, J. M., Capt., 39
Christie, Lt., 59
citizenship, American, fear of losing,
among Americans in RAF, 6,
141, 189
Clairmarais (airdrome): No. 1 Sq.,
143, 146; No. 20 Sq., 119
Claydon, A., Capt., 152, 153, 154
Clayson, P. J., Capt., 144, 145
Clear, A. E., Lt., 41–42
Coler, Eugene Seeley, Capt., 6, 68
(photo); enlists in RFC, training, commissioned, posted to
No. 11 Sq., 69; Somme campaign (March–April 1918), 217;
awarded DFC, promoted to captain, flight leader, crashes, injured, 73; WWII service, 74

—personal accounts by, 70, 71, 72,
72–73, 73
—victories: first and second, 70;
third, fourth, and fifth, 71–72;
seventh, 72; eighth, 72–73;
ninth, 73; total, 74
Colin, A. J. B., Lt., 29
Collishaw, Raymond, Lt. Col. (British
ace), 5, 170, 174, 176
Compston, Robert J. O., Maj. (No. 40
Sq. commander), 194
Compton, H. N., Lt., 133–34
Coningham, A., Maj., 161, 162
Conteville-sur-Somme (airdrome):
No. 20 Sq., 79
Conyngham, D. P., Lt. (Coler's ob-
server), 72
Cooper, Norman, Capt., 104, 180
(photo); joins RFC in Canada,
posted to No. 73 Sq., 181; in
Noyon-Montdidier campaign
(June 1918), 217; awarded
DFC, 183; promoted to captain,
184; listed nationality as Brit-
ish, 184; real name E. S.
Tooker, 181
—victories: first, 181; second,
third, and fourth, 182; fifth and
sixth, 183
Copeland, Capt., 60
Coppens, Willie (Belgian ace), 5
Corbett, E. J., 2nd Lt. (Coler's ob-
server), 73
Corbin, Frank C., Lt., 205
Courtrai (airdrome): No. 29 Sq., 212
Croix de Guerre: awarded to Gillet,
116
Cromwell, Lancashire, 39
Crossen, Lt., 84
Crowe, C. M., Maj., 61
Curtiss JN-4 "Jenny" (American air-
plane), 78, 170, 187, 197;
Canadian version known as
"Canuck", 78, 137
Curtiss P-1 (American airplane), 65

Daley, J. A. E. R., Lt., 63, 82, 83,
84, 87
Dallas, R. S., Maj. (No. 40 Sq. com-
mander), 189
Davey, W. E., Maj. (No. 11 Sq. com-
mander), 70
Davidson, Charles, Lt., 205
Dawe, Lt. (No. 24 Sq.), 84

279

Fleming, P. G. A., Lt., 209
Flynn, H. L. W., Capt., 157
Foch, Ferdinand, Marshal, 146, 164
Fokker (German airplane), 132, 133,
    149, 208, 215; in Spanish Civil
    War, 99
Fokker D-7 Biplane (German air-
    plane), 5, 63, 64, 71, 72, 73, 84,
    85, 86, 87, 88, 97, 104, 105,
    106, 110, 112, 113, 114, 115, 116,
    123, 124, 125, 137, 138, 139,
    140, 145, 146, 147, 153, 154,
    156, 157, 158, 161, 162, 163,
    164, 165, 166, 170, 171, 172,
    176, 177, 178, 182, 183, 189,
    198, 208, 209, 211, 212, 213;
    136 (photo); characteristics,
    253 n.16; effect on air war, 71
Fokker D-8 (German airplane), 5
Fokker single-seater (German air-
    plane), 5
Fokker Dr-1 Triplane (German air-
    plane), 5, 42, 81, 85, 86, 96,
    120, 120–21, 144, 177–78,
    209, 211
—characteristics, 48, 252 n.9;
    compared to Sopwith Camel,
    169; compared to Nieuport 17,
    48
—*Jagdgeschwaders I & II*, 48;
    flown by Richthofen (Red
    Baron), 36
Fokker Eindekker (German air-
    plane), 4
Fokker, Anthony, 4
Fonck, Paul-René (French ace), 5, 143
Forrestal, James, trained by Callen-
    der, 151
Foster, R. M., Lt., 37
Foucaucourt (airdrome): No. 73
    Sq., 183
Fouquerolles (airdrome): No. 32
    Sq., 153
French Air Service, 3, 4, 5
Fry, William, 188

Garros, Roland, 4
Gascoyne, J. V., Lt., 165, 166
George V, King of England, 213
German Air Force, 3, 4, 5
Gillet, Francis Warrington, Capt., 108
    (photo), 219; called "Razors",
    112, 113; decorations, 113, 116;
    service in U.S. Army, joins
    RFC in Canada, posted to No.

79 Sq., 109; Somme campaign
    (March–April 1918), 217;
    awarded DFC, 113; promoted to
    captain, flight leader, 114–15;
    awarded bar to DFC, 115; post-
    war business career, death,
    116
—personal accounts by, 109, 110,
    112, 113, 114, 115
—victories: first, 109; second and
    third, 110; fourth and fifth, 111;
    sixth and seventh, 112; eighth
    and ninth, 112–13; tenth, 113;
    eleventh, twelfth, thirteenth,
    and fourteenth, 114; fifteenth,
    sixteenth, and seventeenth,
    115; eighteenth, nineteenth,
    and twentieth, 115–16; total, 6,
    98, 116, 253 n.15
Gladman, G. W., Lt. (Coler's ob-
    server), 70, 71
Godfrey, F., Capt., 122
Göring, Hermann, Oberleutenant
    (*Jagdgeschwader I* com-
    mander), 150 (photo), 155, 198,
    265 n.7
Graham, G. L., Lt., 105
Graham, S. W., Lt., 152
Griffith, John Sharpe, Capt., 58
    (photo); joins No. 60 Sq., 59;
    patrol leader, 60; Somme cam-
    paign (March–April 1918), 217;
    promoted to captain, awarded
    DFC and Bar, service in
    Egypt, service in U.S. Army
    Air Corps, awarded American
    DFC, WWII career, 65; death,
    66
—service in Russian Civil War;
    awarded Order of Grand Duke
    Vladimir and Order of St.
    Stanislaus, shot down and
    wounded, 65
—personal accounts by, 61, 62–
    63, 63, 64
—victories: first, 59; third, 60;
    fourth, 61; fifth, 62; sixth,
    62–63; seventh and eighth, 63;
    ninth, 64; total, 65–66
Grosvenor, R. A., Capt., 41, 42
Guynemer, Georges-Marie (French
    ace), 5, 143

Haig, Sir Douglas, Field Marshal,
    146, 218

Halberstadt (German airplane), 113, 115, 144, 145, 164, 175, 177,
Halberstadt C-V (German airplane): characteristics, 261n.11
Hale, F. L. "Bud", Capt., 138, 196 (photo); among No. 32 Sq. American aces, 140; prewar life, rejection by American Air Service, joins RFC in Canada, service as flight instructor, 197; posted to No. 32 Sq.,198; awarded DFC, 200; posted to No. 22 Sq., No. 79 Sq., No. 70 Sq., 200–01; promoted to captain, 201; resigns from RAF, postwar business career, WWII service, 201; death, 202
—personal accounts by, 198
—victories: first, 198–99; second, third, and fourth, 199; fifth, sixth, and seventh, 199–200
Hanoveraner (German airplane), 97, 164, 165
Hardcastle, E., 2nd Lt., 123
Harvey, Lt. (pilot of Libby's plane), 10
Hawker, Lanoe, Maj. (No. 24 Sq. commander), 79
Hazell, Tom F., Capt., 48, 90
Hegarty, H. G., Lt., 62
Hellett, T. T. B., Lt., 82, 89
Hell's Angels (film), LeBoutillier and, 37
Henri Farman (French airplane), 4; No. 11 Sq., 69
Hicks Field, Ft. Worth, Texas, 13, 143, 151
Hills, O. H., 2nd Lt. (Libby's observer), 12, 13
Hilton, D'Arcy Fowles, Lt., 24 (photo), 205; prewar life, joins RFC in Canada, training, posted to No. 29 Sq., 25; deputy flight leader, 26; Cambrai campaign, 7, 216; awarded Military Cross and Air Force Cross, 30; postwar life, 30
—personal accounts by, 27, 28
—victories: first, second, and third, 26; fourth, 27; fifth and sixth, 28; seventh, eighth, and ninth, 29; total, 30, 213
Holt, Capt., 26
Hoog Huis (airdrome): No. 29 Sq., 207, 209, 211

Hoy, E. C., Capt., 208–09, 210, 211
Hughes, Howard, 37
Hunter, S. J., Lt. (Bulmer's observer), 53–54
Hythe School of Aerial Gunnery, 17–18

Iaccaci, August T., Capt., 6, 118, 122; joins RFC in Canada, posted to No. 20 Sq., 119; awarded DFC, 124; promoted to captain, flight leader, 125; illness, 126
—victories: by observer, 125, 126; by himself, 120, 121, 125, 125–26
Iaccaci, P. T., Capt., 6; joins RFC in Canada, posted to No. 20 Sq., 119; awarded DFC, 124; transferred to No. 48 Sq., promoted to captain, flight commander, 125
—victories: by observer, 124; by himself, first, 120; second and third, 122; fourth, fifth, and sixth, 123
Immelmann, Max (German ace), 79
Ironside, Edmund, Gen., 98
Italian air forces, 5
Izel le Hameau (airdrome): No. 29 Sq., 205

Jagdgeschwader I (Richthofen Circus, Richthofen Jagdgeschwader), 80, 144, 265n.7; in Amiens campaign, 155, 198; commanded by Hermann Göring, 155, 198; commanded by Richthofen against No. 209 Sq., 35; Fokker Dr-1 Triplane, 48
Jagdgeschwader II, 48, 261n.7
Johnson, G. O., Capt., 80, 81, 83, 84, 85
Johnston, E. H., Maj. (No. 20 Sq. commander), 120, 124
Jones-Williams, A. G., Capt., 29–30, 244n.5
Joseph, Capt. (No. 20 Sq.), 178

Kazakov, Alexander A. (Russian ace), 5
Kelly, E. A., Capt., 187
Kindley, Field E., Capt., 6, 259n.22
Knobel, F. H., Lt., 190
Kullberg, Harold A., Lt., 142 (photo), 214 (photo), 219; rejected by American Air Service because

282

of height, joins RFC in Canada, training, posted to No. 1 Sq., 143; recommended for decoration, 147; legal difficulty, 148–49; wounded, 149; released from RAF, 149
—personal accounts by, 145, 146–47
—victories: first, second, and third, 144; fourth, 144–45; fifth, sixth, seventh, and eighth, 145; ninth and tenth, 146–47; eleventh, twelfth, and thirteenth, 147; total, 6, 149

Lagesse, C. H. R., Capt., 206, 208, 209
La Gorgue (airdrome): No. 60 Sq., 59
Lale, H. P., Capt., 124, 125
La Lovie (airdrome): No. 23 Sq., 18; No. 29 Sq., 205, 209, 210
Lambert, William C., Capt., 76 (photo), 219; prewar life, 77; joins RFC, 77–78; training, service as flight instructor, posted to No. 24 Sq., 78; Somme campaign (March–April 1918), 217; awarded DFC, 87; shot down, 89; combat fatigue, 90; return to Ohio, release from RAF, postwar business career, WWII service, death, 91
—personal accounts by, 80, 86
—victories: first, 79–80; second, 80; third, 81; fourth, 82; fifth, 83; sixth, 84; seventh and eighth, 85; tenth, 85–86; eleventh, twelfth, and thirteenth, 86; fourteenth and fifteenth, 87; sixteenth and seventeenth, 88; eighteenth, 89; nineteenth and twentieth, 90; total, 6, 91
Landis, Reed G., Capt., 193, 259 n.23
Larson, Jens Frederick "Swede", Lt.: prewar life, service in Canadian ground units, flight training, posted to No. 84 Sq., 39; Cambrai campaign (1917), 216–17; granted leave but recalled, 41; Somme campaign (March––April 1918), 217; injured, becomes flight instructor, 43
—personal accounts by, 40, 41–42
—victories: first and second, 40; third, 41; fourth, 41–42; fifth

and sixth, 42; seventh and eighth, 43; total, 43–44
Latimer, D., Capt., 118 (photo), 122
Lauer, Willard, 205
Lawson, G. E. B., Lt., 157, 198
Layton, D. M., Lt., 211
Leach, J. M., Lt., 29–30
Lealvilliers (airdrome): No. 32 Sq., 152
Leaske, K. M., Capt., 39
LeBoutillier, Oliver Colin, Capt.: called "Boots", 33; prewar life, joins RNAS, training, 33; posted to No. 9 Sq. RNAS, 34; Cambrai campaign (1917), 7, 216; promoted to captain, 35; Lys campaign (April 1918), 217; and death of Richthofen (Red Baron), 35–36; wounded, leaves RAF, 37; as pilot in films, 37; Amelia Earhart, Howard Hughes, 37; death, 37
—victories: first and second, 34; third, 35; fourth, 36–37; fifth and sixth, 37
Le Hameau (airdrome): No. 11 Sq., 10; No. 23 Sq., 10
Lewis machine gun, 27, 41, 49, 63, 71, 86, 111, 115, 157, 164, 165, 190; on Bristol Fighter, 53; on DH-4, 11; on Nieuport 17, 26; on SE-5A, 48, 154
Libby, Frederick, Capt.: description, prewar life, service in Canadian Army, joins RFC, assigned to No. 23 Sq., 9; as observer, 10–11; transfer to No. 11 Sq., 10; pilot training, transfer to No. 25 Sq., No. 43 Sq., 11; promoted to captain, 11, 215; awarded Military Cross, 8 (photo), 10, 215; American flag episode, 13; leaves RAF, 13; joins American Air Service, assigned to No. 22 Sq.; illness, 13; death, 13–14
—first American ace, 10
—victories: as observer, 10–11; as pilot, first and second, 11; third, fourth, fifth, and sixth, 12; seventh, 12–13; total, 13, 215
Liettres (airdrome): No. 210 Sq., 170, 176
Lincoln, England, 25
Loewenhardt, Erich (German ace), 5

Lord, Frederick Ives, Capt., 94 (photo); called "Tex", 96, 97; service in Texas National Guard, 95; joins RFC in Canada, posted to No. 79 Sq., 96; awarded DFC, promoted to captain, flight commander, 97; shot down, wounded, 98; joins White Russian forces, forced to crash land, awarded DSO, Order of St. Stanislaus, White Army Medal, Russian Service Cross, 98; postwar business career, service in Spanish Civil War, WWII service, writing and lecturing career, 99
—personal accounts by, 95, 96, 97–98
—victories: first, 95; second, third, and fourth, 96; fifth, 97; sixth, 97, 112; seventh and eighth, 97; ninth, 97–98
Lowe, Capt., 84
Ludendorff, Erich von, Gen., 146, 147, 218
Lussier, Emile John, Lt., 102 (photo), 181, 182; joins RFC in Canada, posted to No. 73 Sq., 103; Somme campaign (March–April 1918) and Noyon-Montdidier campaign (June 1918), 217; awarded DFC, 106; promoted to captain, WWII service, death, 107
—personal accounts by, 104, 105, 105–06
—victories: first and second, 104; third, fourth, and sixth, 105; seventh, 105–06; eighth and ninth, 106
Luke, Frank (American ace), 5
Lufbery, Raoul (American ace), 5
LVG (German airplane), 4, 12, 34, 37, 43, 50, 60, 62, 83, 88, 145, 181, 182, 190, 192, 208
LVG two-seater (German airplane), 84, 104, 111
Lys campaign (9 April–29 April 1918), 51; Americans in, 7, 217; No. 1 Sq., 143

Magoun, Francis Peabody, Lt., 46 (photo); prewar life, service in American Ambulance Field Service, joins RFC, posted to

No. 1 Sq., 47; in Cambrai campaign (November 1917), 6–7, 216; awarded Military Cross, 47, 50; Somme campaign (March–April 1918), 51, 217; wounded, furloughed to U.S., demobilized, graduate study, academic career, death, 51
—victories: first, 48–49; second and third, 49; fifth, 50; sixth, 51
MacGregor, Capt. (No. 85 Sq.), 109
Machaffie, Lt., 28
Machine guns, early attempts to use on aircraft, 4. *See also* Lewis machine gun, Vickers machine gun
McClean, Roderick S. G., Lt., 205
McConnell-Wood, A., Lt., 104, 181
McCudden, James T. B., Maj. (British ace), 5, 61, 206, 217
McDonald, H. O., Lt., 43
McDonald, I. D. R., Capt., 81, 84
McDonald, J. M. (Bulmer's observer), 56
McElroy, G. E. H., Capt., 78, 79, 87, 188, 189, 217
McKeever, A. E., Lt., 69
McNeaney, J. H., Capt., 98, 114
Madon, George Felix (French ace), 5
Malcolm, G. J., Maj. (No. 20 Sq. commander), 119
Malincourt (airdrome): No. 73 Sq., 183
Malpas, D. A., Sgt. (A. T. Iaccaci's observer), 121
Mannock, Edward "Mick", Maj. (British ace), 5, 87, 143, 189
Mansfield, W. H. C., Maj. (No. 20 Sq. commander), 119
Marks, R. T., Lt., 83
Marne, Second Battle of the. *See* Champagne-Marne campaign
Matigny (airdrome): No. 24 Sq., 79
Maurice Farman (French airplane), 4, 33
Mawbey, L. W., 2nd Lt., 49
May, Wilfred "Wop", Lt., 36
Merckelbach, Emil, (witness to Bennett's death), 194
Meuse-Argonne campaign (September–November 1918): Allied plans for, 164–65; Americans in, 7; No. 29 Sq., 211
Middleton, T. P., Capt., 118 (photo),122

Putnam, David (American ace), 6

RAF. *See* Royal Air Force

Ralph, F. J., 2nd Lt. (P. T. Iaccaci's observer), 122

Rathbone, England, 78

Rawlinson, Sir Henry, General, 146

Racken (airdrome): No. 79 Sq., 115

Red Baron. *See* Richthofen, Baron Manfred von

Redcar, Yorkshire, 33

Redgate, Capt. (No. 209 Sq.), 35–36

RE-8 (British airplane), 25, 105, 166; characteristics, 261n.24; in White Russian forces, 98

Rees, L. W. B., Maj. (No. 32 Sq. commander), 153

Reid, Lt. (No. 73 Sq.), 106

RFC. *See* Royal Flying Corps

Richthofen, Lothar von, 265n.7

Richthofen, Baron Manfred von, 35, 143, 144, 155; death of, 35–36, 80–81, 218; victory total, 5

Richthofen Circus, Richthofen *Jagdgeschwader. See Jagdgeschwader I*

Rickenbacker, Edward V. (American ace), 5, 91

RNAS. *See* Royal Naval Air Service

Robb, J. M., Capt., 162, 163

Robertson, F. A., Lt., 205

Robertson, R. G., Lt., 205

Rogers, Bogert, Capt., 199; nationality, 140–41; prewar life, joins RFC in Canada, 137; training, 137–38; Aisne campaign (27 May–6 June 1918), 217; awarded DFC, promoted to captain, leaves RAF, 140; death, 140

—victories: first, 137; second, 138; third and fourth, 139; fifth, 139–40; sixth, 140

Rolfe, B. R., Lt., 210, 211

Rose, Oren J., Capt., 160 (photo), 219; prewar life, joins RFC, training, posted to No. 92 Sq., 162; plane damaged, 165–66; granted rest leave, 166; promoted to captain, service in Russia, postwar business career, WWII service, 167

—personal accounts by, 162, 163, 165, 166

—victories: first, 161; second, 163; third and fourth, 163; fifth, 163–64; sixth, seventh, eighth, and ninth, 164; tenth, eleventh, twelfth, and thirteenth, 165; fourteenth, fifteenth, and sixteenth, 166; total, 6, 167

Rouen (airdrome): No. 29 Sq., 205

Royal Aircraft Factory, 48

Royal Air Force. *See also* Royal Flying Corps, Royal Naval Service

—Americans in, 6, 218; casualties, 7; fear of losing American citizenship, 6, 141, 189; motivation, 6, 215

—formation of, from RFC to RNAS, 3, 35, 42, 51, 60, 79, 258n.8

—top aces, 5

Royal Flying Corps. *See also* Royal Air Force, Royal Naval Service

—aircraft, 5

—Americans in, 6

—combined with RNAS to form RAF, 3, 35, 42, 51, 60, 79, 258n.8

—recruiting in trenches, 9–10

—against Somme campaign (March–April 1918), 49

—strength at beginning of war, 3

Royal Naval Air Service. *See also* Royal Air Force, Royal Flying Corps

—Americans in, 6

—combined with RFC to form RAF, 3, 35, 42, 51, 60, 79, 258n.8

—strength at beginning of war, 3

Royal Naval Air Service School, 47

Ruisseauville (airdrome): No. 32 Sq., 153

Rumpler (German airplane), 19, 132, 138

Rushforth, H. P., Capt., 112

Russell, J. C., Maj. (No. 32 Sq. commander), 137, 139, 140, 153, 198

Russian air forces, 5

Russian Civil War, 65, 98

St. Marie Cappell (airdrome): No. 1 Sq., 50, 120, 143–44; No. 20 Sq., 120; No. 79 Sq., 95, 110, 115; No. 210 Sq., 170, 176

St. Omer (airdrome): No. 32 Sq., 152;
No. 210 Sq., 170, 176
Sansome, W. Sgt. (P. T. Iaccaci's ob-
server), 120
Saunders, H. W., Lt., 43
Savy (airdrome): No. 11 Sq., 69
School of Aerial Gunnery, Turnberry,
Scotland, 18, 47, 78
School of Military Aeronautics, Ox-
ford, 17, 39, 47
School of Military Aeronautics, Read-
ing, 11, 25
School of Military Aeronautics, No. 4,
University of Toronto, 137, 162
Scott, N. B., Lt., 70
SE-5A (British airplane), 5, 37, 38
(photo), 39, 40, 43, 60, 63, 64,
65, 81–82, 83, 84, 85, 89, 139,
147, 148, 153, 155, 156, 158,
165, 189, 190, 191, 199, 208,
211, 217, 218, 246n.4
—characteristics, 48, 154; stability,
39, 138
—opinions about, 79; Maj. Sholto
Douglas, 39; Lambert, 78;
Rogers, 138
—No. 1 Sq., 48, 49, 144; No. 24
Sq., 78, 79; No. 32 Sq., 138,
151, 153, 198; No. 40 Sq., 188;
No. 84 Sq., 40; No. 92 Sq.,
161, 162
Selwyn, W., Capt., 84, 85, 86, 87
Senlis (airdrome), 51
Serny (airdrome): No. 92 Sq., 162
Shepherd, Col., 10
Shepherd, A. S., Capt., 206
Siemens-Shuckert (German air-
craft), 5
Somme campaign (late 1916), 6; No.
20 Sq., 119
Somme, Battle of (1917), 153
Somme campaign (21 March–4 April
1918), 35, 49, 51, 54, 79, 81
—Americans in, 7, 215, 217
—No. 1 Sq., 49; No. 20 Sq., 120;
No. 24 Sq., 80–81; No. 60
Sq., 59
Sopwith Camel (British airplane), 5,
32 (photo), 36, 43, 38, 105, 106,
111, 123, 137, 151, 157, 171, 177,
183, 199, 217, 218
—characteristics, 34, 169, 175,
182, 217
—compared with SE-5A, 154

—name, origin of, 169
—opinions of, 176
—No. 9 Sq., RNAS, 34; No. 54
Sq., 40; No. 73 Sq., 103, 181,
217; No. 210 Sq., 169
—victory total highest among Allied planes, 169, 175
Sopwith Dolphin (British airplane), 5,
109, 112, 115, 128, 130, 132,
133, 217, 218
—characteristics, 97, 110, 111–12,
252n.1
—effectiveness, 131
—opinions about, 111
—No. 19 Sq., 112; No. 23 Sq., 112,
129; No. 79 Sq., 95, 109, 112;
No. 87 Sq., 112; No. 90 Sq.,
188
Sopwith 1½ Strutter (British airplane),
98, 241n.15
Sopwith Pup (British airplane), 25,
34, 39, 78, 111, 151, 170
—compared with Sopwith Camel,
175
Sopwith Snipe (British airplane), 5,
98, 111, 178
Sopwith Triplane, characteristics, 34;
compared to Sopwith Camel,
175; No. 9 Sq., RNAS, 34
Spad (French airplane), 21, 78,
154, 177
Spad-7 (French and British airplane),
20; No. 23 Sq., 216
Spad-13 (French airplane), 5
Spanish Civil War, 99
Springs, Elliott W., Capt. (American
ace), 6, 259n.22
Squadrons, RAF, RFC, RNAS
—No. 1 Sq. RAF, 47, 49, 214
(photo)
—airplanes: Nieuport 17, 48,
246n.4; SE- 5A, 48, 144,
246n.4
—airdromes: Bailleul, 48; Clairmarais, 143, 146; Fienvilliers,
146; Senlis, 51; St. Marie Cappel, 50, 143
—history: 48, 51, 147, 246n.4;
Amiens campaign (August
1918), 146; Somme campaign
(March–April 1918), 49, 51
—No. 9 Sq., RNAS: Sopwith Triplane and Sopwith Camel, 34;
becomes No. 209 Sq. RAF, 35

Venter, C. J., Capt., 206, 208
Vert Galand (airdrome): No. 11 Sq.,
    69; No. 32 Sq., 152
Vickers FB-5 (British airplane), 69
Vickers machine gun, 18, 41, 49, 55,
    64, 71, 111, 139, 154, 165, 190;
    Bristol Fighter, 53; DH-4, 11;
    SE-5A, 48
Victoria Cross, pilots awarded to: Maj.
    W. G. Barker, 178; Maj. J. B.
    McCudden, 61
Vignacourt (airdrome): No. 20
    Sq., 124
Villers Brétonneux (airdrome): No. 11
    Sq., 69; No. 79 Sq., 110
Voisin (French airplane), 4
Von Richthofen, Baron Manfred. *See*
    Richthofen, Baron Manfred von
Voss, Werner (German ace), 5
V-Strutter (German airplane), 41,
    42, 43

Wareing, C. W., Capt., 210, 211
Warman, Clive, W., Capt., 16 (photo),
    219; prewar life, joins British
    forces, 17; reasons for joining
    British forces, 13; fear of losing
    American citizenship, 17; ser-
    vice in ground forces, 17, 216;
    wounded, transfer to RAF, 17;
    flight training, 17, 216; three
    months leave, instructor at

Turnberry, 18; posted to No. 23
    Sq., 18, 216; awarded DSO, 17,
    20, 130; awarded Military
    Cross, 17, 130; promoted to
    captain, flight commander,
    wounded, postwar career, 21,
    death, 21–22
—personal accounts by, 19, 20, 21
—victories: first, 19; fourth, 19–
    20; sixth, seventh, eighth, and
    ninth, 20, eleventh, 21; total, 6,
    21, 216
Watson, Lt. (No. 70 Sq.), 112
Weston, D. J., Lt., 122
White, H. A., Lt., 133
Whitney, H. K., Lt., 61, 61–62, 63, 64
Wilkinson, Alan M., Maj. (No. 23 Sq.
    commander), 18
Williams, P. S., Lt. (Bulmer's ob-
    server), 54, 55, 55–56
Wilson, C. W., Maj. (No. 20 Sq. com-
    mander), 119
Wings (film), LeBoutillier in, 37
Winterbothan, Frederick W., Lt., 26
Wiseman, W. D., 205

Young, W. E., Maj. (No. 1 Sq. com-
    mander), 146, 148, 148–49
Ypres, Second Battle of, 17, 242n.3
Ypres, Third Battle of, 153

Zink, E. L., Lt., 199